The Comple Fryer Cookbook for Beginners

1800+ Days Super Easy, Delicious & Energy-saving Recipes Book with Tips & Tricks to Fry, Grill, Roast, and Bake - Ready in Less Than 30 Minutes

Jacquline L. Schultz

Table of Contents

INTRODUCTION

Welcome to the tantalizing world of air frying, where crispy delights and healthy cooking collide! As an air fryer cookbook author, I am thrilled to embark on this culinary journey with you, exploring the endless possibilities that this revolutionary appliance offers.

In recent years, air fryers have captured the hearts and kitchens of food enthusiasts around the globe. They have become a go-to appliance for those seeking a healthier alternative to traditional frying methods, without sacrificing the mouthwatering flavors and satisfying textures we all crave. Air fryers have truly transformed the way we approach cooking, and my aim is to guide you through this exciting culinary adventure.

In this cookbook, I invite you to unlock the full potential of your air fryer and unleash your creativity in the kitchen. Whether you're a seasoned home cook or a curious beginner, these pages are filled with inspiration, techniques, and recipes that will elevate your cooking game to new heights.

But why air frying, you might ask? Well, let me share with you the magic that happens inside the air fryer. By utilizing rapid hot air circulation, these appliances produce a crispy and golden exterior while sealing in the natural juices and flavors of the food. The result? A guilt-free indulgence that satisfies both your taste buds and your desire for healthier choices.

Throughout this cookbook, I'll guide you through a diverse array of recipes that showcase the versatility of the air fryer. From classic favorites like crispy chicken tenders and perfectly seasoned sweet potato fries to more adventurous creations like zesty lemon-herb salmon and delectable cinnamon sugar donuts, there's something to entice every palate.

But it doesn't stop there. Beyond the recipes, I'll empower you with tips, techniques, and culinary insights to help you become an air frying aficionado. From understanding optimal temperature and cooking times to mastering the art of breading and achieving that perfect crispy texture, you'll gain the confidence to experiment and create your own signature dishes.

Additionally, I understand that dietary preferences and restrictions vary, and I've taken that into account. Throughout the cookbook, you'll find a range of options to cater to different needs, including vegetarian, gluten-free, and dairy-free recipes. I believe that everyone should be able to experience the joy of air frying, regardless of their dietary choices.

So, let's embark on this flavorful journey together. Embrace the possibilities of air frying, savor the mouthwatering results, and let your culinary imagination run wild. With the recipes, techniques, and inspiration found within these pages, you'll discover that air frying is not just a cooking method but a gateway to a healthier, tastier, and more satisfying culinary experience.

Get ready to transform everyday ingredients into extraordinary dishes, and join me as we uncover the delicious magic of air frying. Let's dive in and create culinary masterpieces that will leave you and your loved ones craving more. Happy air frying!

Chapter 1

Breakfasts

Egg Muffins

Prep time: 10 minutes | Cook time: 11 to 13 minutes | Serves 4

4 eggs	1 cup shredded Colby Jack
Salt and pepper, to taste	cheese
Olive oil	4 slices ham or Canadian
4 English muffins, split	bacon

1. Preheat the air fryer to 390ºF (199ºC). 2. Beat together eggs and add salt and pepper to taste. Spray a baking pan lightly with oil and add eggs. Bake for 2 minutes, stir, and continue cooking for 3 or 4 minutes, stirring every minute, until eggs are scrambled to your preference. Remove pan from air fryer. 3. Place bottom halves of English muffins in air fryer basket. Take half of the shredded cheese and divide it among the muffins. Top each with a slice of ham and one-quarter of the eggs. Sprinkle remaining cheese on top of the eggs. Use a fork to press the cheese into the egg a little so it doesn't slip off before it melts. 4. Air fry at 360ºF (182ºC) for 1 minute. Add English muffin tops and cook for 2 to 4 minutes to heat through and toast the muffins.

Egg and Bacon Muffins

Prep time: 5 minutes | Cook time: 15 minutes | Serves 1

2 eggs	Cheddar cheese
Salt and ground black pepper,	5 ounces (142 g) cooked
to taste	bacon
1 tablespoon green pesto	1 scallion, chopped
3 ounces (85 g) shredded	

1. Preheat the air fryer to 350ºF (177ºC). Line a cupcake tin with parchment paper. 2. Beat the eggs with pepper, salt, and pesto in a bowl. Mix in the cheese. 3. Pour the eggs into the cupcake tin and top with the bacon and scallion. 4. Bake in the preheated air fryer for 15 minutes, or until the egg is set. 5. Serve immediately.

Strawberry Tarts

Prep time: 15 minutes | Cook time: 10 minutes | Serves 6

2 refrigerated piecrusts	at room temperature
½ cup strawberry preserves	3 tablespoons confectioners'
1 teaspoon cornstarch	sugar
Cooking oil spray	Rainbow sprinkles, for
½ cup low-fat vanilla yogurt	decorating
1 ounce (28 g) cream cheese,	

1. Place the piecrusts on a flat surface. Using a knife or pizza cutter, cut each piecrust into 3 rectangles, for 6 total. Discard any unused dough from the piecrust edges. 2. In a small bowl, stir together the preserves and cornstarch. Mix well, ensuring there are no lumps of cornstarch remaining. 3. Scoop 1 tablespoon of the strawberry mixture onto the top half of each piece of piecrust. 4. Fold the bottom of each piece up to enclose the filling. Using the back of a fork, press along the edges of each tart to seal. 5. Insert the crisper plate into the basket and the basket into the unit. Preheat the unit by selecting BAKE, setting the temperature to 375ºF (191ºC), and setting the time to 3 minutes. Select START/STOP to begin. 6. Once the unit is preheated, spray the crisper plate with cooking oil. Working in batches, spray the breakfast tarts with cooking oil and place them into the basket in a single layer. Do not stack the tarts. 7. Select BAKE, set the temperature to 375ºF (191ºC), and set the time to 10 minutes. Select START/STOP to begin. 8. When the cooking is complete, the tarts should be light golden brown. Let the breakfast tarts cool fully before removing them from the basket. 9. Repeat steps 5, 6, 7, and 8 for the remaining breakfast tarts. 10. In a small bowl, stir together the yogurt, cream cheese, and confectioners' sugar. Spread the breakfast tarts with the frosting and top with sprinkles.

Jalapeño and Bacon Breakfast Pizza

Prep time: 5 minutes | Cook time: 10 minutes | Serves 2

1 cup shredded Mozzarella	bacon, chopped
cheese	¼ cup chopped pickled
1 ounce (28 g) cream cheese,	jalapeños
broken into small pieces	1 large egg, whisked
4 slices cooked sugar-free	¼ teaspoon salt

1. Place Mozzarella in a single layer on the bottom of an ungreased round nonstick baking dish. Scatter cream cheese pieces, bacon, and jalapeños over Mozzarella, then pour egg evenly around baking dish. 2. Sprinkle with salt and place into air fryer basket. Adjust the temperature to 330ºF (166ºC) and bake for 10 minutes. When cheese is brown and egg is set, pizza will be done. 3. Let cool on a large plate 5 minutes before serving.

Easy Sausage Pizza

Prep time: 10 minutes | Cook time: 6 minutes | Serves 4

2 tablespoons ketchup	cheese
1 pita bread	1 teaspoon garlic powder
⅓ cup sausage	1 tablespoon olive oil
½ pound (227 g) Mozzarella	

1. Preheat the air fryer to 340ºF (171ºC). 2. Spread the ketchup over the pita bread. 3. Top with the sausage and cheese. Sprinkle with the garlic powder and olive oil. 4. Put the pizza in the air fryer basket and bake for 6 minutes. 5. Serve warm.

Egg White Cups

Prep time: 10 minutes | Cook time: 15 minutes | Serves 4

2 cups 100% liquid egg whites	½ medium Roma tomato,
3 tablespoons salted butter,	cored and diced
melted	½ cup chopped fresh spinach
¼ teaspoon salt	leaves
¼ teaspoon onion powder	

1. In a large bowl, whisk egg whites with butter, salt, and onion powder. Stir in tomato and spinach, then pour evenly into four ramekins greased with cooking spray. 2. Place ramekins into air fryer basket. Adjust the temperature to 300ºF (149ºC) and bake for 15 minutes. Eggs will be fully cooked and firm in the center when done. Serve warm.

Nutty Granola

Prep time: 5 minutes | Cook time: 1 hour | Serves 4

½ cup pecans, coarsely chopped	2 tablespoons sunflower seeds
½ cup walnuts or almonds, coarsely chopped	2 tablespoons melted butter
¼ cup unsweetened flaked coconut	¼ cup Swerve
¼ cup almond flour	½ teaspoon ground cinnamon
¼ cup ground flaxseed or chia seeds	½ teaspoon vanilla extract
	¼ teaspoon ground nutmeg
	¼ teaspoon salt
	2 tablespoons water

1. Preheat the air fryer to 250ºF (121ºC). Cut a piece of parchment paper to fit inside the air fryer basket. 2. In a large bowl, toss the nuts, coconut, almond flour, ground flaxseed or chia seeds, sunflower seeds, butter, Swerve, cinnamon, vanilla, nutmeg, salt, and water until thoroughly combined. 3. Spread the granola on the parchment paper and flatten to an even thickness. 4. Air fry for about an hour, or until golden throughout. Remove from the air fryer and allow to fully cool. Break the granola into bite-size pieces and store in a covered container for up to a week.

Classic British Breakfast

Prep time: 5 minutes | Cook time: 25 minutes | Serves 2

1 cup potatoes, sliced and diced	1 tablespoon olive oil
2 cups beans in tomato sauce	1 sausage
2 eggs	Salt, to taste

1. Preheat the air fryer to 390ºF (199ºC) and allow to warm. 2. Break the eggs onto a baking dish and sprinkle with salt. 3. Lay the beans on the dish, next to the eggs. 4. In a bowl, coat the potatoes with the olive oil. Sprinkle with salt. 5. Transfer the bowl of potato slices to the air fryer and bake for 10 minutes. 6. Swap out the bowl of potatoes for the dish containing the eggs and beans. Bake for another 10 minutes. Cover the potatoes with parchment paper. 7. Slice up the sausage and throw the slices on top of the beans and eggs. Bake for another 5 minutes. 8. Serve with the potatoes.

Whole Wheat Banana-Walnut Bread

Prep time: 10 minutes | Cook time: 23 minutes | Serves 6

Olive oil cooking spray	2 tablespoons raw honey
2 ripe medium bananas	1 cup whole wheat flour
1 large egg	¼ teaspoon salt
¼ cup nonfat plain Greek yogurt	¼ teaspoon baking soda
¼ cup olive oil	½ teaspoon ground cinnamon
½ teaspoon vanilla extract	¼ cup chopped walnuts

1. Preheat the air fryer to 360ºF(182ºC). Lightly coat the inside of a 8-by-4-inch loaf pan with olive oil cooking spray. (Or use two 5 ½-by-3-inch loaf pans.) 2. In a large bowl, mash the bananas with a fork. Add the egg, yogurt, olive oil, vanilla, and honey. Mix until well combined and mostly smooth. 3. Sift the whole wheat flour, salt, baking soda, and cinnamon into the wet mixture, then stir until just combined. Do not overmix. 4. Gently fold in the walnuts. 5. Pour into the prepared loaf pan and spread to distribute evenly. 6. Place the loaf pan in the air fryer basket and bake for 20 to 23 minutes, or until golden brown on top and a toothpick inserted into the center comes out clean. 7. Allow to cool for 5 minutes before serving.

Sausage and Egg Breakfast Burrito

Prep time: 5 minutes | Cook time: 30 minutes | Serves 6

6 eggs	8 ounces (227 g) ground chicken sausage
Salt and pepper, to taste	½ cup salsa
Cooking oil	6 medium (8-inch) flour tortillas
½ cup chopped red bell pepper	½ cup shredded Cheddar cheese
½ cup chopped green bell pepper	

1. In a medium bowl, whisk the eggs. Add salt and pepper to taste. 2. Place a skillet on medium-high heat. Spray with cooking oil. Add the eggs. Scramble for 2 to 3 minutes, until the eggs are fluffy. Remove the eggs from the skillet and set aside. 3. If needed, spray the skillet with more oil. Add the chopped red and green bell peppers. Cook for 2 to 3 minutes, until the peppers are soft. 4. Add the ground sausage to the skillet. Break the sausage into smaller pieces using a spatula or spoon. Cook for 3 to 4 minutes, until the sausage is brown. 5. Add the salsa and scrambled eggs. Stir to combine. Remove the skillet from heat. 6. Spoon the mixture evenly onto the tortillas. 7. To form the burritos, fold the sides of each tortilla in toward the middle and then roll up from the bottom. You can secure each burrito with a toothpick. Or you can moisten the outside edge of the tortilla with a small amount of water. I prefer to use a cooking brush, but you can also dab with your fingers. 8. Spray the burritos with cooking oil and place them in the air fryer. Do not stack. Cook the burritos in batches if they do not all fit in the basket. Air fry at 400ºF (204ºC) for 8 minutes. 9. Open the air fryer and flip the burritos. Cook for an additional 2 minutes or until crisp. 10. If necessary, repeat steps 8 and 9 for the remaining burritos. 11. Sprinkle the Cheddar cheese over the burritos. Cool before serving.

Green Eggs and Ham

Prep time: 5 minutes | Cook time: 10 minutes | Serves 2

1 large Hass avocado, halved and pitted	½ teaspoon fine sea salt
2 thin slices ham	¼ teaspoon ground black pepper
2 large eggs	¼ cup shredded Cheddar cheese (omit for dairy-free)
2 tablespoons chopped green onions, plus more for garnish	

1. Preheat the air fryer to 400ºF (204ºC). 2. Place a slice of ham into the cavity of each avocado half. Crack an egg on top of the ham, then sprinkle on the green onions, salt, and pepper. 3. Place the avocado halves in the air fryer cut side up and air fry for 10 minutes, or until the egg is cooked to your desired doneness. Top with the cheese (if using) and air fry for 30 seconds more, or until the cheese is melted. Garnish with chopped green onions. 4. Best served fresh. Store extras in an airtight container in the fridge for up to 4 days. Reheat in a preheated 350ºF (177ºC) air fryer for a few minutes, until warmed through.

Parmesan Ranch Risotto

Prep time: 10 minutes | Cook time: 30 minutes | Serves 2

1 tablespoon olive oil	¾ cup Arborio rice
1 clove garlic, minced	2 cups chicken stock, boiling
1 tablespoon unsalted butter	½ cup Parmesan cheese,
1 onion, diced	grated

1. Preheat the air fryer to 390ºF (199ºC). 2. Grease a round baking tin with olive oil and stir in the garlic, butter, and onion. 3. Transfer the tin to the air fryer and bake for 4 minutes. Add the rice and bake for 4 more minutes. 4. Turn the air fryer to 320ºF (160ºC) and pour in the chicken stock. Cover and bake for 22 minutes. 5. Scatter with cheese and serve.

Bacon Cheese Egg with Avocado

Prep time: 15 minutes | Cook time: 20 minutes | Serves 4

6 large eggs	and pitted
¼ cup heavy whipping cream	8 tablespoons full-fat sour
1½ cups chopped cauliflower	cream
1 cup shredded medium	2 scallions, sliced on the bias
Cheddar cheese	12 slices sugar-free bacon,
1 medium avocado, peeled	cooked and crumbled

1. In a medium bowl, whisk eggs and cream together. Pour into a round baking dish. 2. Add cauliflower and mix, then top with Cheddar. Place dish into the air fryer basket. 3. Adjust the temperature to 320ºF (160ºC) and set the timer for 20 minutes. 4. When completely cooked, eggs will be firm and cheese will be browned. Slice into four pieces. 5. Slice avocado and divide evenly among pieces. Top each piece with 2 tablespoons sour cream, sliced scallions, and crumbled bacon.

Breakfast Calzone

Prep time: 15 minutes | Cook time: 15 minutes | Serves 4

1½ cups shredded Mozzarella cheese	1 large whole egg
½ cup blanched finely ground almond flour	4 large eggs, scrambled
	½ pound (227 g) cooked breakfast sausage, crumbled
1 ounce (28 g) full-fat cream cheese	8 tablespoons shredded mild Cheddar cheese

1. In a large microwave-safe bowl, add Mozzarella, almond flour, and cream cheese. Microwave for 1 minute. Stir until the mixture is smooth and forms a ball. Add the egg and stir until dough forms. 2. Place dough between two sheets of parchment and roll out to ¼-inch thickness. Cut the dough into four rectangles. 3. Mix scrambled eggs and cooked sausage together in a large bowl. Divide the mixture evenly among each piece of dough, placing it on the lower half of the rectangle. Sprinkle each with 2 tablespoons Cheddar. 4. Fold over the rectangle to cover the egg and meat mixture. Pinch, roll, or use a wet fork to close the edges completely. 5. Cut a piece of parchment to fit your air fryer basket and place the calzones onto the parchment. Place parchment into the air fryer basket. 6. Adjust the temperature to 380ºF (193ºC) and air fry for 15 minutes. 7. Flip the calzones halfway through the cooking time. When done, calzones should be golden in

color. Serve immediately.

Gluten-Free Granola Cereal

Prep time: 7 minutes | Cook time: 30 minutes | Makes 3 cups

Oil, for spraying	¼ cup maple syrup or honey
1½ cups gluten-free rolled oats	1 tablespoon toasted sesame oil or vegetable oil
½ cup chopped walnuts	1 teaspoon ground cinnamon
½ cup chopped almonds	½ teaspoon salt
½ cup pumpkin seeds	½ cup dried cranberries

1. Preheat the air fryer to 250ºF (121ºC). Line the air fryer basket with parchment and spray lightly with oil. (Do not skip the step of lining the basket; the parchment will keep the granola from falling through the holes.) 2. In a large bowl, mix together the oats, walnuts, almonds, pumpkin seeds, maple syrup, sesame oil, cinnamon, and salt. 3. Spread the mixture in an even layer in the prepared basket. 4. Cook for 30 minutes, stirring every 10 minutes. 5. Transfer the granola to a bowl, add the dried cranberries, and toss to combine. 6. Let cool to room temperature before storing in an airtight container.

Cajun Breakfast Sausage

Prep time: 10 minutes | Cook time: 15 to 20 minutes | Serves 8

1½ pounds (680 g) 85% lean ground turkey	1 teaspoon Creole seasoning
3 cloves garlic, finely chopped	1 teaspoon dried thyme
¼ onion, grated	½ teaspoon paprika
1 teaspoon Tabasco sauce	½ teaspoon cayenne

1. Preheat the air fryer to 370ºF (188ºC). 2. In a large bowl, combine the turkey, garlic, onion, Tabasco, Creole seasoning, thyme, paprika, and cayenne. Mix with clean hands until thoroughly combined. Shape into 16 patties, about ½ inch thick. (Wet your hands slightly if you find the sausage too sticky to handle.) 3. Working in batches if necessary, arrange the patties in a single layer in the air fryer basket. Pausing halfway through the cooking time to flip the patties, air fry for 15 to 20 minutes until a thermometer inserted into the thickest portion registers 165ºF (74ºC).

Onion Omelet

Prep time: 10 minutes | Cook time: 12 minutes | Serves 2

3 eggs	1 large onion, chopped
Salt and ground black pepper, to taste	2 tablespoons grated Cheddar cheese
½ teaspoons soy sauce	Cooking spray

1. Preheat the air fryer to 355ºF (179ºC). 2. In a bowl, whisk together the eggs, salt, pepper, and soy sauce. 3. Spritz a small pan with cooking spray. Spread the chopped onion across the bottom of the pan, then transfer the pan to the air fryer. 4. Bake in the preheated air fryer for 6 minutes or until the onion is translucent. 5. Add the egg mixture on top of the onions to coat well. Add the cheese on top, then continue baking for another 6 minutes. 6. Allow to cool before serving.

Bacon Hot Dogs

Prep time: 5 minutes | Cook time: 15 minutes | Serves 4

3 brazilian sausages, cut into 3 equal pieces	1 tablespoon Italian herbs
9 slices bacon	Salt and ground black pepper, to taste

1. Preheat the air fryer to 355ºF (179ºC). 2. Take each slice of bacon and wrap around each piece of sausage. Sprinkle with Italian herbs, salt and pepper. 3. Air fry the sausages in the preheated air fryer for 15 minutes. 4. Serve warm.

White Bean–Oat Waffles

Prep time: 10 minutes | Cook time: 20 minutes | Serves 2

1 large egg white	drained and rinsed
2 tablespoons finely ground flaxseed	1 teaspoon coconut oil
½ cup water	1 teaspoon liquid stevia
¼ teaspoon salt	½ cup old-fashioned rolled oats
1 teaspoon vanilla extract	Extra-virgin olive oil cooking spray
½ cup cannellini beans,	

1. In a blender, combine the egg white, flaxseed, water, salt, vanilla, cannellini beans, coconut oil, and stevia. Blend on high for 90 seconds. 2. Add the oats. Blend for 1 minute more. 3. Preheat the waffle iron. The batter will thicken to the correct consistency while the waffle iron preheats. 4. Spray the heated waffle iron with cooking spray. 5. Add ¾ cup of batter. Close the waffle iron. Cook for 6 to 8 minutes, or until done. Repeated with the remaining batter. 6. Serve hot, with your favorite sugar-free topping.

Keto Quiche

Prep time: 10 minutes | Cook time: 1 hour | Makes 1 (6-inch) quiche

Crust:	(about 4 ounces / 113 g)
1¼ cups blanched almond flour	4 ounces (113 g) cream cheese (½ cup)
1¼ cups grated Parmesan or Gouda cheese	1 tablespoon unsalted butter, melted
¼ teaspoon fine sea salt	4 large eggs, beaten
1 large egg, beaten	⅓ cup minced leeks or sliced green onions
Filling:	
½ cup chicken or beef broth (or vegetable broth for vegetarian)	¾ teaspoon fine sea salt
	⅛ teaspoon cayenne pepper
1 cup shredded Swiss cheese	Chopped green onions, for garnish

1. Preheat the air fryer to 325ºF (163ºC). Grease a pie pan. Spray two large pieces of parchment paper with avocado oil and set them on the countertop. 2. Make the crust: In a medium-sized bowl, combine the flour, cheese, and salt and mix well. Add the egg and mix until the dough is well combined and stiff. 3. Place the dough in the center of one of the greased pieces of parchment. Top with the other piece of parchment. Using a rolling pin, roll out the dough into a circle about 1/16 inch thick. 4. Press the pie crust into the prepared pie pan. Place it in the air fryer and bake for 12 minutes, or until it starts to lightly brown. 5. While the crust bakes, make the filling: In a large bowl, combine the broth, Swiss cheese, cream cheese, and butter. Stir in the eggs, leeks, salt, and cayenne pepper. When the crust is ready, pour the mixture into the crust. 6. Place the quiche in the air fryer and bake for 15 minutes. Turn the heat down to 300ºF (149ºC) and bake for an additional 30 minutes, or until a knife inserted 1 inch from the edge comes out clean. You may have to cover the edges of the crust with foil to prevent burning. 7. Allow the quiche to cool for 10 minutes before garnishing it with chopped green onions and cutting it into wedges. 8. Store leftovers in an airtight container in the refrigerator for up to 4 days or in the freezer for up to a month. Reheat in a preheated 350ºF (177ºC) air fryer for a few minutes, until warmed through.

Chimichanga Breakfast Burrito

Prep time: 10 minutes | Cook time: 10 minutes | Serves 2

2 large (10- to 12-inch) flour tortillas	4 corn tortilla chips, crushed
½ cup canned refried beans (pinto or black work equally well)	½ cup grated Pepper Jack cheese
	12 pickled jalapeño slices
4 large eggs, cooked scrambled	1 tablespoon vegetable oil
	Guacamole, salsa, and sour cream, for serving (optional)

1. Place the tortillas on a work surface and divide the refried beans between them, spreading them in a rough rectangle in the center of the tortillas. Top the beans with the scrambled eggs, crushed chips, pepper jack, and jalapeños. Fold one side over the fillings, then fold in each short side and roll up the rest of the way like a burrito. 2. Brush the outside of the burritos with the oil, then transfer to the air fryer, seam-side down. Air fry at 350ºF (177ºC) until the tortillas are browned and crisp and the filling is warm throughout, about 10 minutes. 3. Transfer the chimichangas to plates and serve warm with guacamole, salsa, and sour cream, if you like.

Mississippi Spice Muffins

Prep time: 15 minutes | Cook time: 13 minutes | Makes 12 muffins

4 cups all-purpose flour	temperature
1 tablespoon ground cinnamon	2 cups sugar
2 teaspoons baking soda	2 large eggs, lightly beaten
2 teaspoons allspice	2 cups unsweetened applesauce
1 teaspoon ground cloves	¼ cup chopped pecans
1 teaspoon salt	1 to 2 tablespoons oil
1 cup (2 sticks) butter, room	

1. In a large bowl, whisk the flour, cinnamon, baking soda, allspice, cloves, and salt until blended. 2. In another large bowl, combine the butter and sugar. Using an electric mixer, beat the mixture for 2 to 3 minutes until light and fluffy. Add the beaten eggs and stir until blended. 3. Add the flour mixture and applesauce, alternating between the two and blending after each addition. Stir in the pecans. 4. Preheat the air fryer to 325ºF (163ºC). Spritz 12 silicone muffin cups with oil. 5. Pour the batter into the prepared muffin cups, filling each halfway. Place the muffins in the air fryer basket. 6. Air fry for 6 minutes. Shake the basket and air fry for 7 minutes more. The muffins are done when a toothpick inserted into the middle comes out clean.

Mozzarella Bacon Calzones

Prep time: 15 minutes | Cook time: 12 minutes | Serves 4

2 large eggs	2 ounces (57 g) cream cheese,
1 cup blanched finely ground	softened and broken into
almond flour	small pieces
2 cups shredded Mozzarella	4 slices cooked sugar-free
cheese	bacon, crumbled

1. Beat eggs in a small bowl. Pour into a medium nonstick skillet over medium heat and scramble. Set aside. 2. In a large microwave-safe bowl, mix flour and Mozzarella. Add cream cheese to the bowl. 3. Place bowl in microwave and cook 45 seconds on high to melt cheese, then stir with a fork until a soft dough ball forms. 4. Cut a piece of parchment to fit air fryer basket. Separate dough into two sections and press each out into an 8-inch round. 5. On half of each dough round, place half of the scrambled eggs and crumbled bacon. Fold the other side of the dough over and press to seal the edges. 6. Place calzones on ungreased parchment and into air fryer basket. Adjust the temperature to 350ºF (177ºC) and set the timer for 12 minutes, turning calzones halfway through cooking. Crust will be golden and firm when done. 7. Let calzones cool on a cooking rack 5 minutes before serving.

Quesadillas

Prep time: 10 minutes | Cook time: 15 minutes | Serves 4

4 eggs	4 tablespoons salsa
2 tablespoons skim milk	2 ounces (57 g) Cheddar
Salt and pepper, to taste	cheese, grated
Oil for misting or cooking	½ small avocado, peeled and
spray	thinly sliced
4 flour tortillas	

1. Preheat the air fryer to 270ºF (132ºC). 2. Beat together eggs, milk, salt, and pepper. 3. Spray a baking pan lightly with cooking spray and add egg mixture. 4. Bake for 8 to 9 minutes, stirring every 1 to 2 minutes, until eggs are scrambled to your liking. Remove and set aside. 5. Spray one side of each tortilla with oil or cooking spray. Flip over. 6. Divide eggs, salsa, cheese, and avocado among the tortillas, covering only half of each tortilla. 7. Fold each tortilla in half and press down lightly. 8. Place 2 tortillas in air fryer basket and air fry at 390ºF (199ºC) for 3 minutes or until cheese melts and outside feels slightly crispy. Repeat with remaining two tortillas. 9. Cut each cooked tortilla into halves or thirds.

Spaghetti Squash Fritters

Prep time: 15 minutes | Cook time: 8 minutes | Serves 4

2 cups cooked spaghetti	¼ cup blanched finely ground
squash	almond flour
2 tablespoons unsalted butter,	2 stalks green onion, sliced
softened	½ teaspoon garlic powder
1 large egg	1 teaspoon dried parsley

1. Remove excess moisture from the squash using a cheesecloth or kitchen towel. 2. Mix all ingredients in a large bowl. Form into four patties. 3. Cut a piece of parchment to fit your air fryer basket.

Place each patty on the parchment and place into the air fryer basket. 4. Adjust the temperature to 400ºF (204ºC) and set the timer for 8 minutes. 5. Flip the patties halfway through the cooking time. Serve warm.

Spinach and Mushroom Mini Quiche

Prep time: 10 minutes | Cook time: 15 minutes | Serves 4

1 teaspoon olive oil, plus	½ cup shredded Cheddar
more for spraying	cheese
1 cup coarsely chopped	½ cup shredded Mozzarella
mushrooms	cheese
1 cup fresh baby spinach,	¼ teaspoon salt
shredded	¼ teaspoon black pepper
4 eggs, beaten	

1. Spray 4 silicone baking cups with olive oil and set aside. 2. In a medium sauté pan over medium heat, warm 1 teaspoon of olive oil. Add the mushrooms and sauté until soft, 3 to 4 minutes. 3. Add the spinach and cook until wilted, 1 to 2 minutes. Set aside. 4. In a medium bowl, whisk together the eggs, Cheddar cheese, Mozzarella cheese, salt, and pepper. 5. Gently fold the mushrooms and spinach into the egg mixture. 6. Pour ¼ of the mixture into each silicone baking cup. 7. Place the baking cups into the air fryer basket and air fry at 350ºF (177ºC) for 5 minutes. Stir the mixture in each ramekin slightly and air fry until the egg has set, an additional 3 to 5 minutes.

Cheddar Eggs

Prep time: 5 minutes | Cook time: 15 minutes | Serves 2

4 large eggs	½ cup shredded sharp
2 tablespoons unsalted butter,	Cheddar cheese
melted	

1. Crack eggs into a round baking dish and whisk. Place dish into the air fryer basket. 2. Adjust the temperature to 400ºF (204ºC) and set the timer for 10 minutes. 3. After 5 minutes, stir the eggs and add the butter and cheese. Let cook 3 more minutes and stir again. 4. Allow eggs to finish cooking an additional 2 minutes or remove if they are to your desired liking. 5. Use a fork to fluff. Serve warm.

Ham and Cheese Crescents

Prep time: 5 minutes | Cook time: 7 minutes | Makes 8 rolls

Oil, for spraying	8 slices American cheese
1 (8-ounce / 227-g) can	2 tablespoons unsalted butter,
refrigerated crescent rolls	melted
4 slices deli ham	

1. Line the air fryer basket with parchment and spray lightly with oil. 2. Separate the dough into 8 pieces. 3. Tear the ham slices in half and place 1 piece on each piece of dough. Top each with 1 slice of cheese. 4. Roll up each piece of dough, starting on the wider side. 5. Place the rolls in the prepared basket. Brush with the melted butter. 6. Air fry at 320ºF (160ºC) for 6 to 7 minutes, or until puffed and golden brown and the cheese is melted.

Greek Bagels

Prep time: 10 minutes | Cook time: 10 minutes | Makes 2 bagels

½ cup self-rising flour, plus more for dusting	4 teaspoons everything bagel spice mix
½ cup plain Greek yogurt	Cooking oil spray
1 egg	1 tablespoon butter, melted
1 tablespoon water	

1. In a large bowl, using a wooden spoon, stir together the flour and yogurt until a tacky dough forms. Transfer the dough to a lightly floured work surface and roll the dough into a ball. 2. Cut the dough into 2 pieces and roll each piece into a log. Form each log into a bagel shape, pinching the ends together. 3. In a small bowl, whisk the egg and water. Brush the egg wash on the bagels. 4. Sprinkle 2 teaspoons of the spice mix on each bagel and gently press it into the dough. 5. Insert the crisper plate into the basket and the basket into the unit. Preheat the unit by selecting BAKE, setting the temperature to 330ºF (166ºC), and setting the time to 3 minutes. Select START/STOP to begin. 6. Once the unit is preheated, spray the crisper plate with cooking spray. Drizzle the bagels with the butter and place them into the basket. 7. Select BAKE, set the temperature to 330ºF (166ºC), and set the time to 10 minutes. Select START/STOP to begin. 8. When the cooking is complete, the bagels should be lightly golden on the outside. Serve warm.

Scotch Eggs

Prep time: 10 minutes | Cook time: 20 to 25 minutes | Serves 4

2 tablespoons flour, plus extra for coating	1 tablespoon water
1 pound (454 g) ground breakfast sausage	Oil for misting or cooking spray
4 hard-boiled eggs, peeled	Crumb Coating:
1 raw egg	¾ cup panko bread crumbs
	¾ cup flour

1. Combine flour with ground sausage and mix thoroughly. 2. Divide into 4 equal portions and mold each around a hard-boiled egg so the sausage completely covers the egg. 3. In a small bowl, beat together the raw egg and water. 4. Dip sausage-covered eggs in the remaining flour, then the egg mixture, then roll in the crumb coating. 5. Air fry at 360ºF (182ºC) for 10 minutes. Spray eggs, turn, and spray other side. 6. Continue cooking for another 10 to 15 minutes or until sausage is well done.

Spinach Omelet

Prep time: 5 minutes | Cook time: 12 minutes | Serves 2

4 large eggs	2 tablespoons salted butter, melted
1½ cups chopped fresh spinach leaves	½ cup shredded mild Cheddar cheese
2 tablespoons peeled and chopped yellow onion	¼ teaspoon salt

1. In an ungreased round nonstick baking dish, whisk eggs. Stir in spinach, onion, butter, Cheddar, and salt. 2. Place dish into air fryer basket. Adjust the temperature to 320ºF (160ºC) and bake for 12 minutes. Omelet will be done when browned on the top and firm in the middle. 3. Slice in half and serve warm on two medium plates.

Mexican Breakfast Pepper Rings

Prep time: 5 minutes | Cook time: 10 minutes | Serves 4

Olive oil	4 eggs
1 large red, yellow, or orange bell pepper, cut into four ¾-inch rings	Salt and freshly ground black pepper, to taste
	2 teaspoons salsa

1. Preheat the air fryer to 350ºF (177ºC). Lightly spray a baking pan with olive oil. 2. Place 2 bell pepper rings on the pan. Crack one egg into each bell pepper ring. Season with salt and black pepper. 3. Spoon ½ teaspoon of salsa on top of each egg. 4. Place the pan in the air fryer basket. Air fry until the yolk is slightly runny, 5 to 6 minutes or until the yolk is fully cooked, 8 to 10 minutes. 5. Repeat with the remaining 2 pepper rings. Serve hot.

Smoky Sausage Patties

Prep time: 30 minutes | Cook time: 9 minutes | Serves 8

1 pound (454 g) ground pork	½ teaspoon fennel seeds
1 tablespoon coconut aminos	½ teaspoon dried thyme
2 teaspoons liquid smoke	½ teaspoon freshly ground black pepper
1 teaspoon dried sage	¼ teaspoon cayenne pepper
1 teaspoon sea salt	

1. In a large bowl, combine the pork, coconut aminos, liquid smoke, sage, salt, fennel seeds, thyme, black pepper, and cayenne pepper. Work the meat with your hands until the seasonings are fully incorporated. 2. Shape the mixture into 8 equal-size patties. Using your thumb, make a dent in the center of each patty. Place the patties on a plate and cover with plastic wrap. Refrigerate the patties for at least 30 minutes. 3. Working in batches if necessary, place the patties in a single layer in the air fryer, being careful not to overcrowd them. 4. Set the air fryer to 400ºF (204ºC) and air fry for 5 minutes. Flip and cook for about 4 minutes more.

Fried Cheese Grits

Prep time: 10 minutes | Cook time: 10 to 12 minutes | Serves 4

⅔ cup instant grits	at room temperature
1 teaspoon salt	1 large egg, beaten
1 teaspoon freshly ground black pepper	1 tablespoon butter, melted
¾ cup whole or 2% milk	1 cup shredded mild Cheddar cheese
3 ounces (85 g) cream cheese,	Cooking spray

1. Mix the grits, salt, and black pepper in a large bowl. Add the milk, cream cheese, beaten egg, and melted butter and whisk to combine. Fold in the Cheddar cheese and stir well. 2. Preheat the air fryer to 400ºF (204ºC). Spray a baking pan with cooking spray. 3. Spread the grits mixture into the baking pan and place in the air fryer basket. 4. Air fry for 1o to 12 minutes, or until the grits are cooked and a knife inserted in the center comes out clean. Stir the mixture once halfway through the cooking time. 5. Rest for 5 minutes and serve warm.

Berry Muffins

Prep time: 15 minutes | Cook time: 12 to 17 minutes | Makes 8 muffins

1⅓ cups plus 1 tablespoon all-purpose flour, divided	2 teaspoons baking powder
¼ cup granulated sugar	2 eggs
2 tablespoons light brown sugar	⅔ cup whole milk
	⅓ cup safflower oil
	1 cup mixed fresh berries

1. In a medium bowl, stir together 1⅓ cups of flour, the granulated sugar, brown sugar, and baking powder until mixed well. 2. In a small bowl, whisk the eggs, milk, and oil until combined. Stir the egg mixture into the dry ingredients just until combined. 3. In another small bowl, toss the mixed berries with the remaining 1 tablespoon of flour until coated. Gently stir the berries into the batter. 4. Double up 16 foil muffin cups to make 8 cups. 5. Insert the crisper plate into the basket and the basket into the unit. Preheat the unit by selecting BAKE, setting the temperature to 315ºF (157ºC), and setting the time to 3 minutes. Select START/STOP to begin. 6. Once the unit is preheated, place 4 cups into the basket and fill each three-quarters full with the batter. 7. Select BAKE, set the temperature to 315ºF (157ºC), and set the time for 17 minutes. Select START/STOP to begin. 8. After about 12 minutes, check the muffins. If they spring back when lightly touched with your finger, they are done. If not, resume cooking. 9. When the cooking is done, transfer the muffins to a wire rack to cool. 10. Repeat steps 6, 7, and 8 with the remaining muffin cups and batter. 11. Let the muffins cool for 10 minutes before serving.

Gyro Breakfast Patties with Tzatziki

Prep time: 10 minutes | Cook time: 20 minutes per batch | Makes 16 patties

Patties:	1 small cucumber, chopped
2 pounds (907 g) ground lamb or beef	½ teaspoon fine sea salt
½ cup diced red onions	½ teaspoon garlic powder, or 1 clove garlic, minced
¼ cup sliced black olives	¼ teaspoon dried dill weed, or 1 teaspoon finely chopped fresh dill
2 tablespoons tomato sauce	
1 teaspoon dried oregano leaves	For Garnish/Serving:
1 teaspoon Greek seasoning	½ cup crumbled feta cheese (about 2 ounces / 57 g)
2 cloves garlic, minced	Diced red onions
1 teaspoon fine sea salt	Sliced black olives
Tzatziki:	Sliced cucumbers
1 cup full-fat sour cream	

1. Preheat the air fryer to 350ºF (177ºC). 2. Place the ground lamb, onions, olives, tomato sauce, oregano, Greek seasoning, garlic, and salt in a large bowl. Mix well to combine the ingredients. 3. Using your hands, form the mixture into sixteen 3-inch patties. Place about 5 of the patties in the air fryer and air fry for 20 minutes, flipping halfway through. Remove the patties and place them on a serving platter. Repeat with the remaining patties. 4. While the patties cook, make the tzatziki: Place all the ingredients in a small bowl and stir well. Cover and store in the fridge until ready to serve. Garnish with ground black pepper before serving. 5. Serve the patties with a dollop of tzatziki, a sprinkle of crumbled feta cheese, diced red onions, sliced black olives, and sliced cucumbers. 6. Store leftovers in an airtight container in the refrigerator for up to 5 days or in the freezer for up to a month. Reheat the patties in a preheated 390ºF (199ºC) air fryer for a few minutes, until warmed through.

Simple Cinnamon Toasts

Prep time: 5 minutes | Cook time: 4 minutes | Serves 4

1 tablespoon salted butter	½ teaspoon vanilla extract
2 teaspoons ground cinnamon	10 bread slices
4 tablespoons sugar	

1. Preheat the air fryer to 380ºF (193ºC). 2. In a bowl, combine the butter, cinnamon, sugar, and vanilla extract. Spread onto the slices of bread. 3. Put the bread inside the air fryer and bake for 4 minutes or until golden brown. 4. Serve warm.

Bunless Breakfast Turkey Burgers

Prep time: 5 minutes | Cook time: 15 minutes | Serves 4

1 pound (454 g) ground turkey breakfast sausage	¼ cup seeded and chopped green bell pepper
½ teaspoon salt	2 tablespoons mayonnaise
¼ teaspoon ground black pepper	1 medium avocado, peeled, pitted, and sliced

1. In a large bowl, mix sausage with salt, black pepper, bell pepper, and mayonnaise. Form meat into four patties. 2. Place patties into ungreased air fryer basket. Adjust the temperature to 370ºF (188ºC) and air fry for 15 minutes, turning patties halfway through cooking. Burgers will be done when dark brown and they have an internal temperature of at least 165ºF (74ºC). 3. Serve burgers topped with avocado slices on four medium plates.

Whole Wheat Blueberry Muffins

Prep time: 10 minutes | Cook time: 15 minutes | Serves 6

Olive oil cooking spray	1½ cups plus 1 tablespoon whole wheat flour, divided
½ cup unsweetened applesauce	½ teaspoon baking soda
¼ cup raw honey	½ teaspoon baking powder
½ cup nonfat plain Greek yogurt	½ teaspoon salt
1 teaspoon vanilla extract	½ cup blueberries, fresh or frozen
1 large egg	

1. Preheat the air fryer to 360ºF(182ºC). Lightly coat the inside of six silicone muffin cups or a six-cup muffin tin with olive oil cooking spray. 2. In a large bowl, combine the applesauce, honey, yogurt, vanilla, and egg and mix until smooth. 3. Sift in 1½ cups of the flour, the baking soda, baking powder, and salt into the wet mixture, then stir until just combined. 4. In a small bowl, toss the blueberries with the remaining 1 tablespoon flour, then fold the mixture into the muffin batter. 5. Divide the mixture evenly among the prepared muffin cups and place into the basket of the air fryer. Bake for 12 to 15 minutes, or until golden brown on top and a toothpick inserted into the middle of one of the muffins comes out clean. 6. Allow to cool for 5 minutes before serving.

Oat and Chia Porridge

Prep time: 10 minutes | Cook time: 5 minutes | Serves 4

2 tablespoons peanut butter	4 cups milk
4 tablespoons honey	2 cups oats
1 tablespoon butter, melted	1 cup chia seeds

1. Preheat the air fryer to 390ºF (199ºC). 2. Put the peanut butter, honey, butter, and milk in a bowl and stir to mix. Add the oats and chia seeds and stir. 3. Transfer the mixture to a bowl and bake in the air fryer for 5 minutes. Give another stir before serving.

Broccoli-Mushroom Frittata

Prep time: 10 minutes | Cook time: 20 minutes | Serves 2

1 tablespoon olive oil	½ teaspoon salt
1½ cups broccoli florets, finely chopped	¼ teaspoon freshly ground black pepper
½ cup sliced brown mushrooms	6 eggs
¼ cup finely chopped onion	¼ cup Parmesan cheese

1. In a nonstick cake pan, combine the olive oil, broccoli, mushrooms, onion, salt, and pepper. Stir until the vegetables are thoroughly coated with oil. Place the cake pan in the air fryer basket and set the air fryer to 400ºF (204ºC). Air fry for 5 minutes until the vegetables soften. 2. Meanwhile, in a medium bowl, whisk the eggs and Parmesan until thoroughly combined. Pour the egg mixture into the pan and shake gently to distribute the vegetables. Air fry for another 15 minutes until the eggs are set. 3. Remove from the air fryer and let sit for 5 minutes to cool slightly. Use a silicone spatula to gently lift the frittata onto a plate before serving.

Homemade Cherry Breakfast Tarts

Prep time: 15 minutes | Cook time: 20 minutes | Serves 6

Tarts:	Frosting:
2 refrigerated piecrusts	½ cup vanilla yogurt
⅓ cup cherry preserves	1 ounce (28 g) cream cheese
1 teaspoon cornstarch	1 teaspoon stevia
Cooking oil	Rainbow sprinkles

Make the Tarts 1. Place the piecrusts on a flat surface. Using a knife or pizza cutter, cut each piecrust into 3 rectangles, for 6 total. (I discard the unused dough left from slicing the edges.) 2. In a small bowl, combine the preserves and cornstarch. Mix well. 3. Scoop 1 tablespoon of the preserves mixture onto the top half of each piece of piecrust. 4. Fold the bottom of each piece up to close the tart. Using the back of a fork, press along the edges of each tart to seal. 5. Spray the breakfast tarts with cooking oil and place them in the air fryer. I do not recommend stacking the breakfast tarts. They will stick together if stacked. You may need to prepare them in two batches. Bake at 375ºF for 10 minutes. 6. Allow the breakfast tarts to cool fully before removing from the air fryer. 7. If necessary, repeat steps 5 and 6 for the remaining breakfast tarts. Make the Frosting 8. In a small bowl, combine the yogurt, cream cheese, and stevia. Mix well. 9. Spread the breakfast tarts with frosting and top with sprinkles, and serve.

Bacon and Cheese Quiche

Prep time: 5 minutes | Cook time: 12 minutes | Serves 2

3 large eggs	4 slices cooked sugar-free bacon, crumbled
2 tablespoons heavy whipping cream	½ cup shredded mild Cheddar cheese
¼ teaspoon salt	

1. In a large bowl, whisk eggs, cream, and salt together until combined. Mix in bacon and Cheddar. 2. Pour mixture evenly into two ungreased ramekins. Place into air fryer basket. Adjust the temperature to 320ºF (160ºC) and bake for 12 minutes. Quiche will be fluffy and set in the middle when done. 3. Let quiche cool in ramekins 5 minutes. Serve warm.

Blueberry Cobbler

Prep time: 5 minutes | Cook time: 15 minutes | Serves 4

⅓ cup whole-wheat pastry flour	syrup
¾ teaspoon baking powder	½ teaspoon vanilla extract
Dash sea salt	Cooking oil spray
½ cup 2% milk	½ cup fresh blueberries
2 tablespoons pure maple	¼ cup granola

1. In a medium bowl, whisk the flour, baking powder, and salt. Add the milk, maple syrup, and vanilla and gently whisk, just until thoroughly combined. 2. Preheat the unit by selecting BAKE, setting the temperature to 350ºF (177ºC), and setting the time to 3 minutes. Select START/STOP to begin. 3. Spray a 6-by-2-inch round baking pan with cooking oil and pour the batter into the pan. Top evenly with the blueberries and granola. 4. Once the unit is preheated, place the pan into the basket. 5. Select BAKE, set the temperature to 350ºF (177ºC), and set the time to 15 minutes. Select START/STOP to begin. 6. When the cooking is complete, the cobbler should be nicely browned and a knife inserted into the middle should come out clean. Enjoy plain or topped with a little vanilla yogurt.

All-in-One Toast

Prep time: 10 minutes | Cook time: 10 minutes | Serves 1

1 strip bacon, diced	Salt and freshly ground black pepper, to taste
1 slice 1-inch thick bread	
1 egg	¼ cup grated Colby cheese

1. Preheat the air fryer to 400ºF (204ºC). 2. Air fry the bacon for 3 minutes, shaking the basket once or twice while it cooks. Remove the bacon to a paper towel lined plate and set aside. 3. Use a sharp paring knife to score a large circle in the middle of the slice of bread, cutting halfway through, but not all the way through to the cutting board. Press down on the circle in the center of the bread slice to create an indentation. 4. Transfer the slice of bread, hole side up, to the air fryer basket. Crack the egg into the center of the bread, and season with salt and pepper. 5. Adjust the air fryer temperature to 380ºF (193ºC) and air fry for 5 minutes. Sprinkle the grated cheese around the edges of the bread, leaving the center of the yolk uncovered, and top with the cooked bacon. Press the cheese and bacon into the bread lightly to

help anchor it to the bread and prevent it from blowing around in the air fryer. 6. Air fry for one or two more minutes, just to melt the cheese and finish cooking the egg. Serve immediately.

Pizza Eggs

Prep time: 5 minutes | Cook time: 10 minutes | Serves 2

1 cup shredded Mozzarella cheese
7 slices pepperoni, chopped
1 large egg, whisked
¼ teaspoon dried oregano

¼ teaspoon dried parsley
¼ teaspoon garlic powder
¼ teaspoon salt

1. Place Mozzarella in a single layer on the bottom of an ungreased round nonstick baking dish. Scatter pepperoni over cheese, then pour egg evenly around baking dish. 2. Sprinkle with remaining ingredients and place into air fryer basket. Adjust the temperature to 330ºF (166ºC) and bake for 10 minutes. When cheese is brown and egg is set, dish will be done. 3. Let cool in dish 5 minutes before serving.

Denver Omelet

Prep time: 5 minutes | Cook time: 8 minutes | Serves 1

2 large eggs
¼ cup unsweetened, unflavored almond milk
¼ teaspoon fine sea salt
⅛ teaspoon ground black pepper
¼ cup diced ham (omit for vegetarian)

¼ cup diced green and red bell peppers
2 tablespoons diced green onions, plus more for garnish
¼ cup shredded Cheddar cheese (about 1 ounce / 28 g) (omit for dairy-free)
Quartered cherry tomatoes, for serving (optional)

1. Preheat the air fryer to 350ºF (177ºC). Grease a cake pan and set aside. 2. In a small bowl, use a fork to whisk together the eggs, almond milk, salt, and pepper. Add the ham, bell peppers, and green onions. Pour the mixture into the greased pan. Add the cheese on top (if using). 3. Place the pan in the basket of the air fryer. Bake for 8 minutes, or until the eggs are cooked to your liking. 4. Loosen the omelet from the sides of the pan with a spatula and place it on a serving plate. Garnish with green onions and serve with cherry tomatoes, if desired. Best served fresh.

Mini Shrimp Frittata

Prep time: 15 minutes | Cook time: 20 minutes | Serves 4

1 teaspoon olive oil, plus more for spraying
½ small red bell pepper, finely diced
1 teaspoon minced garlic
1 (4-ounce / 113-g) can of tiny shrimp, drained

Salt and freshly ground black pepper, to taste
4 eggs, beaten
4 teaspoons ricotta cheese

1. Spray four ramekins with olive oil. 2. In a medium skillet over medium-low heat, heat 1 teaspoon of olive oil. Add the bell pepper and garlic and sauté until the pepper is soft, about 5 minutes 3. Add the shrimp, season with salt and pepper, and cook until warm, 1 to 2 minutes. Remove from the heat. 4. Add the eggs and stir to combine. 5. Pour one quarter of the mixture into each ramekin. 6. Place 2 ramekins in the air fryer basket and bake at 350ºF (177ºC) for 6 minutes. 7. Remove the air fryer basket from the air fryer and stir the mixture in each ramekin. Top each fritatta with 1 teaspoon of ricotta cheese. Return the air fryer basket to the air fryer and cook until eggs are set and the top is lightly browned, 4 to 5 minutes. 8. Repeat with the remaining two ramekins.

Chapter 2

Fast and Easy Everyday Favorites

Traditional Queso Fundido

Prep time: 10 minutes | Cook time: 25 minutes | Serves 4

4 ounces (113 g) fresh Mexican chorizo, casings removed
1 medium onion, chopped
3 cloves garlic, minced
1 cup chopped tomato
2 jalapeños, deseeded and diced
2 teaspoons ground cumin
2 cups shredded Oaxaca or Mozzarella cheese
½ cup half-and-half
Celery sticks or tortilla chips, for serving

1. Preheat the air fryer to 400ºF (204ºC). 2. In a baking pan, combine the chorizo, onion, garlic, tomato, jalapeños, and cumin. Stir to combine. 3. Place the pan in the air fryer basket. Air fry for 15 minutes, or until the sausage is cooked, stirring halfway through the cooking time to break up the sausage. 4. Add the cheese and half-and-half; stir to combine. Air fry for 10 minutes, or until the cheese has melted. 5. Serve with celery sticks or tortilla chips.

Air Fried Butternut Squash with Chopped Hazelnuts

Prep time: 10 minutes | Cook time: 20 minutes | Makes 3 cups

2 tablespoons whole hazelnuts
3 cups butternut squash, peeled, deseeded, and cubed
¼ teaspoon kosher salt
¼ teaspoon freshly ground black pepper
2 teaspoons olive oil
Cooking spray

1. Preheat the air fryer to 300ºF (149ºC). Spritz the air fryer basket with cooking spray. 2. Arrange the hazelnuts in the preheated air fryer. Air fry for 3 minutes or until soft. 3. Chopped the hazelnuts roughly and transfer to a small bowl. Set aside. 4. Set the air fryer temperature to 360ºF (182ºC). Spritz with cooking spray. 5. Put the butternut squash in a large bowl, then sprinkle with salt and pepper and drizzle with olive oil. Toss to coat well. 6. Transfer the squash in the air fryer. Air fry for 20 minutes or until the squash is soft. Shake the basket halfway through the frying time. 7. When the frying is complete, transfer the squash onto a plate and sprinkle with chopped hazelnuts before serving.

Spinach and Carrot Balls

Prep time: 10 minutes | Cook time: 10 minutes | Serves 4

2 slices toasted bread
1 carrot, peeled and grated
1 package fresh spinach, blanched and chopped
½ onion, chopped
1 egg, beaten
½ teaspoon garlic powder
1 teaspoon minced garlic
1 teaspoon salt
½ teaspoon black pepper
1 tablespoon nutritional yeast
1 tablespoon flour

1. Preheat the air fryer to 390ºF (199ºC). 2. In a food processor, pulse the toasted bread to form bread crumbs. Transfer into a shallow dish or bowl. 3. In a bowl, mix together all the other ingredients. 4. Use your hands to shape the mixture into small-sized balls. Roll the balls in the bread crumbs, ensuring to cover them well. 5. Put in the air fryer basket and air fry for 10 minutes. 6. Serve immediately.

Crispy Potato Chips with Lemony Cream Dip

Prep time: 20 minutes | Cook time: 15 minutes | Serves 2 to 4

2 large russet potatoes, sliced into ⅛-inch slices, rinsed
Sea salt and freshly ground black pepper, to taste
Cooking spray
Lemony Cream Dip:
½ cup sour cream
¼ teaspoon lemon juice
2 scallions, white part only, minced
1 tablespoon olive oil
¼ teaspoon salt
Freshly ground black pepper, to taste

1. Soak the potato slices in water for 10 minutes, then pat dry with paper towels. 2. Preheat the air fryer to 300ºF (149ºC). 3. Transfer the potato slices in the preheated air fryer. Spritz the slices with cooking spray. You may need to work in batches to avoid overcrowding. 4. Air fry for 15 minutes or until crispy and golden brown. Shake the basket periodically. Sprinkle with salt and ground black pepper in the last minute. 5. Meanwhile, combine the ingredients for the dip in a small bowl. Stir to mix well. 6. Serve the potato chips immediately with the dip.

Indian-Style Sweet Potato Fries

Prep time: 5 minutes | Cook time: 8 minutes | Makes 20 fries

Seasoning Mixture:
¾ teaspoon ground coriander
½ teaspoon garam masala
½ teaspoon garlic powder
½ teaspoon ground cumin
¼ teaspoon ground cayenne pepper
Fries:
2 large sweet potatoes, peeled
2 teaspoons olive oil

1. Preheat the air fryer to 400ºF (204ºC). 2. In a small bowl, combine the coriander, garam masala, garlic powder, cumin, and cayenne pepper. 3. Slice the sweet potatoes into ¼-inch-thick fries. 4. In a large bowl, toss the sliced sweet potatoes with the olive oil and the seasoning mixture. 5. Transfer the seasoned sweet potatoes to the air fryer basket and fry for 8 minutes, until crispy. 6. Serve warm.

Rosemary and Orange Roasted Chickpeas

Prep time: 5 minutes | Cook time: 10 to 12 minutes | Makes 4 cups

4 cups cooked chickpeas
2 tablespoons vegetable oil
1 teaspoon kosher salt
1 teaspoon cumin
1 teaspoon paprika
Zest of 1 orange
1 tablespoon chopped fresh rosemary

1. Preheat the air fryer to 400ºF (204ºC). 2. Make sure the chickpeas are completely dry prior to roasting. In a medium bowl, toss the chickpeas with oil, salt, cumin, and paprika. 3. Working in batches, spread the chickpeas in a single layer in the air fryer basket. Air fry for 10 to 12 minutes until crisp, shaking once halfway through. 4. Return the warm chickpeas to the bowl and toss with the orange zest and rosemary. Allow to cool completely. 5. Serve.

Golden Salmon and Carrot Croquettes

Prep time: 15 minutes | Cook time: 10 minutes | Serves 6

2 egg whites
1 cup almond flour
1 cup panko breadcrumbs
1 pound (454 g) chopped salmon fillet
⅔ cup grated carrots
2 tablespoons minced garlic cloves
½ cup chopped onion
2 tablespoons chopped chives
Cooking spray

1. Preheat the air fryer to 350ºF (177ºC). Spritz the air fryer basket with cooking spray. 2. Whisk the egg whites in a bowl. Put the flour in a second bowl. Pour the breadcrumbs in a third bowl. Set aside. 3. Combine the salmon, carrots, garlic, onion, and chives in a large bowl. Stir to mix well. 4. Form the mixture into balls with your hands. Dredge the balls into the flour, then egg, and then breadcrumbs to coat well. 5. Arrange the salmon balls in the preheated air fryer and spritz with cooking spray. 6. Air fry for 10 minutes or until crispy and browned. Shake the basket halfway through. 7. Serve immediately.

Easy Roasted Asparagus

Prep time: 5 minutes | Cook time: 6 minutes | Serves 4

1 pound (454 g) asparagus, trimmed and halved crosswise
1 teaspoon extra-virgin olive
oil
Salt and pepper, to taste
Lemon wedges, for serving

1. Preheat the air fryer to 400ºF (204ºC). 2. Toss the asparagus with the oil, ⅛ teaspoon salt, and ⅛ teaspoon pepper in bowl. Transfer to air fryer basket. 3. Place the basket in air fryer and roast for 6 to 8 minutes, or until tender and bright green, tossing halfway through cooking. 4. Season with salt and pepper and serve with lemon wedges.

Honey Bartlett Pears with Lemony Ricotta

Prep time: 10 minutes | Cook time: 8 minutes | Serves 4

2 large Bartlett pears, peeled, cut in half, cored
3 tablespoons melted butter
½ teaspoon ground ginger
¼ teaspoon ground cardamom
3 tablespoons brown sugar
½ cup whole-milk ricotta
cheese
1 teaspoon pure lemon extract
1 teaspoon pure almond extract
1 tablespoon honey, plus additional for drizzling

1. Preheat the air fryer to 375ºF (191ºC). 2. Toss the pears with butter, ginger, cardamom, and sugar in a large bowl. Toss to coat well. 3. Arrange the pears in the preheated air fryer, cut side down. Air fry for 5 minutes, then flip the pears and air fry for 3 more minutes or until the pears are soft and browned. 4. In the meantime, combine the remaining ingredients in a separate bowl. Whip for 1 minute with a hand mixer until the mixture is puffed. 5. Divide the mixture into four bowls, then put the pears over the mixture and drizzle with more honey to serve.

Air Fried Broccoli

Prep time: 5 minutes | Cook time: 6 minutes | Serves 1

4 egg yolks
¼ cup butter, melted
2 cups coconut flower
Salt and pepper, to taste
2 cups broccoli florets

1. Preheat the air fryer to 400ºF (204ºC). 2. In a bowl, whisk the egg yolks and melted butter together. Throw in the coconut flour, salt and pepper, then stir again to combine well. 3. Dip each broccoli floret into the mixture and place in the air fryer basket. Air fry for 6 minutes in batches if necessary. Take care when removing them from the air fryer and serve immediately.

Simple Baked Green Beans

Prep time: 5 minutes | Cook time: 10 minutes | Makes 2 cups

½ teaspoon lemon pepper
2 teaspoons granulated garlic
½ teaspoon salt
1 tablespoon olive oil
2 cups fresh green beans, trimmed and snapped in half

1. Preheat the air fryer to 370ºF (188ºC). 2. Combine the lemon pepper, garlic, salt, and olive oil in a bowl. Stir to mix well. 3. Add the green beans to the bowl of mixture and toss to coat well. 4. Arrange the green beans in the preheated air fryer. Bake for 10 minutes or until tender and crispy. Shake the basket halfway through to make sure the green beans are cooked evenly. 5. Serve immediately.

Air Fried Zucchini Sticks

Prep time: 5 minutes | Cook time: 20 minutes | Serves 4

1 medium zucchini, cut into 48 sticks
¼ cup seasoned breadcrumbs
1 tablespoon melted buttery spread
Cooking spray

1. Preheat the air fryer to 360ºF (182ºC). Spritz the air fryer basket with cooking spray and set aside. 2. In 2 different shallow bowls, add the seasoned breadcrumbs and the buttery spread. 3. One by one, dredge the zucchini sticks into the buttery spread, then roll in the breadcrumbs to coat evenly. Arrange the crusted sticks on a plate. 4. Place the zucchini sticks in the prepared air fryer basket. Work in two batches to avoid overcrowding. 5. Air fry for 10 minutes, or until golden brown and crispy. Shake the basket halfway through to cook evenly. 6. When the cooking time is over, transfer the fries to a wire rack. Rest for 5 minutes and serve warm.

Beef Bratwursts

Prep time: 5 minutes | Cook time: 15 minutes | Serves 4

4 (3-ounce / 85-g) beef bratwursts

1. Preheat the air fryer to 375ºF (191ºC). 2. Place the beef bratwursts in the air fryer basket and air fry for 15 minutes, turning once halfway through. 3. Serve hot.

Simple and Easy Croutons

Prep time: 5 minutes | Cook time: 8 minutes | Serves 4

2 slices friendly bread	Hot soup, for serving
1 tablespoon olive oil	

1. Preheat the air fryer to 390ºF (199ºC). 2. Cut the slices of bread into medium-size chunks. 3. Brush the air fryer basket with the oil. 4. Place the chunks inside and air fry for at least 8 minutes. 5. Serve with hot soup.

Air Fried Shishito Peppers

Prep time: 5 minutes | Cook time: 5 minutes | Serves 4

½ pound (227 g) shishito peppers (about 24)	Coarse sea salt, to taste
	Lemon wedges, for serving
1 tablespoon olive oil	Cooking spray

1. Preheat the air fryer to 400ºF (204ºC). Spritz the air fryer basket with cooking spray. 2. Toss the peppers with olive oil in a large bowl to coat well. 3. Arrange the peppers in the preheated air fryer. 4. Air fryer for 5 minutes or until blistered and lightly charred. Shake the basket and sprinkle the peppers with salt halfway through the cooking time. 5. Transfer the peppers onto a plate and squeeze the lemon wedges on top before serving.

Peppery Brown Rice Fritters

Prep time: 10 minutes | Cook time: 8 to 10 minutes | Serves 4

1 (10-ounce / 284-g) bag frozen cooked brown rice, thawed	⅓ cup minced red bell pepper
	2 tablespoons minced fresh basil
1 egg	3 tablespoons grated Parmesan cheese
3 tablespoons brown rice flour	
⅓ cup finely grated carrots	2 teaspoons olive oil

1. Preheat the air fryer to 380ºF (193ºC). 2. In a small bowl, combine the thawed rice, egg, and flour and mix to blend. 3. Stir in the carrots, bell pepper, basil, and Parmesan cheese. 4. Form the mixture into 8 fritters and drizzle with the olive oil. 5. Put the fritters carefully into the air fryer basket. Air fry for 8 to 10 minutes, or until the fritters are golden brown and cooked through. 6. Serve immediately.

Baked Chorizo Scotch Eggs

Prep time: 5 minutes | Cook time: 15 to 20 minutes | Makes 4 eggs

1 pound (454 g) Mexican chorizo or other seasoned sausage meat	1 tablespoon water
	½ cup all-purpose flour
4 soft-boiled eggs plus 1 raw egg	1 cup panko bread crumbs
	Cooking spray

1. Divide the chorizo into 4 equal portions. Flatten each portion into a disc. Place a soft-boiled egg in the center of each disc. Wrap the chorizo around the egg, encasing it completely. Place the encased eggs on a plate and chill for at least 30 minutes. 2. Preheat the air fryer to 360ºF (182ºC). 3. Beat the raw egg with 1 tablespoon of water. Place the flour on a small plate and the panko on a second plate. Working with 1 egg at a time, roll the encased egg in the flour, then dip it in the egg mixture. Dredge the egg in the panko and place on a plate. Repeat with the remaining eggs. 4. Spray the eggs with oil and place in the air fryer basket. Bake for 10 minutes. Turn and bake for an additional 5 to 10 minutes, or until browned and crisp on all sides. 5. Serve immediately.

Cheesy Jalapeño Cornbread

Prep time: 10 minutes | Cook time: 20 minutes | Serves 8

⅔ cup cornmeal	¾ cup whole milk
⅓ cup all-purpose flour	1 large egg, beaten
¾ teaspoon baking powder	1 jalapeño pepper, thinly sliced
2 tablespoons buttery spread, melted	⅓ cup shredded sharp Cheddar cheese
½ teaspoon kosher salt	
1 tablespoon granulated sugar	Cooking spray

1. Preheat the air fryer to 300ºF (149ºC). Spritz the air fryer basket with cooking spray. 2. Combine all the ingredients in a large bowl. Stir to mix well. Pour the mixture in a baking pan. 3. Arrange the pan in the preheated air fryer. Bake for 20 minutes or until a toothpick inserted in the center of the bread comes out clean. 4. When the cooking is complete, remove the baking pan from the air fryer and allow the bread to cool for a few minutes before slicing to serve.

Herb-Roasted Veggies

Prep time: 10 minutes | Cook time: 14 to 18 minutes | Serves 4

1 red bell pepper, sliced	⅓ cup diced red onion
1 (8-ounce / 227-g) package sliced mushrooms	3 garlic cloves, sliced
	1 teaspoon olive oil
1 cup green beans, cut into 2-inch pieces	½ teaspoon dried basil
	½ teaspoon dried tarragon

1. Preheat the air fryer to 350ºF (177ºC). 2. In a medium bowl, mix the red bell pepper, mushrooms, green beans, red onion, and garlic. Drizzle with the olive oil. Toss to coat. 3. Add the herbs and toss again. 4. Place the vegetables in the air fryer basket. Roast for 14 to 18 minutes, or until tender. Serve immediately.

Baked Cheese Sandwich

Prep time: 5 minutes | Cook time: 8 minutes | Serves 2

2 tablespoons mayonnaise	4 thick slices Brie cheese
4 thick slices sourdough bread	8 slices hot capicola

1. Preheat the air fryer to 350ºF (177ºC). 2. Spread the mayonnaise on one side of each slice of bread. Place 2 slices of bread in the air fryer basket, mayonnaise-side down. 3. Place the slices of Brie and capicola on the bread and cover with the remaining two slices of bread, mayonnaise-side up. 4. Bake for 8 minutes, or until the cheese has melted. 5. Serve immediately.

Spicy Air Fried Old Bay Shrimp

Prep time: 7 minutes | Cook time: 10 minutes | Makes 2 cups

½ teaspoon Old Bay Seasoning	1 tablespoon olive oil
1 teaspoon ground cayenne pepper	⅛ teaspoon salt
½ teaspoon paprika	½ pound (227 g) shrimps, peeled and deveined
	Juice of half a lemon

1. Preheat the air fryer to 390ºF (199ºC). 2. Combine the Old Bay Seasoning, cayenne pepper, paprika, olive oil, and salt in a large bowl, then add the shrimps and toss to coat well. 3. Put the shrimps in the preheated air fryer. Air fry for 10 minutes or until opaque. Flip the shrimps halfway through. 4. Serve the shrimps with lemon juice on top.

Southwest Corn and Bell Pepper Roast

Prep time: 10 minutes | Cook time: 10 minutes | Serves 4

For the Corn:	1 tablespoon fresh lemon juice
1½ cups thawed frozen corn kernels	1 teaspoon ground cumin
1 cup mixed diced bell peppers	½ teaspoon kosher salt
1 jalapeño, diced	Cooking spray
1 cup diced yellow onion	For Serving:
½ teaspoon ancho chile powder	¼ cup feta cheese
	¼ cup chopped fresh cilantro
	1 tablespoon fresh lemon juice

1. Preheat the air fryer to 375ºF (191ºC). Spritz the air fryer with cooking spray. 2. Combine the ingredients for the corn in a large bowl. Stir to mix well. 3. Pout the mixture into the air fryer. Air fry for 10 minutes or until the corn and bell peppers are soft. Shake the basket halfway through the cooking time. 4. Transfer them onto a large plate, then spread with feta cheese and cilantro. Drizzle with lemon juice and serve.

Lemony and Garlicky Asparagus

Prep time: 5 minutes | Cook time: 10 minutes | Makes 10 spears

10 spears asparagus (about ½ pound / 227 g in total), snap the ends off	½ teaspoon salt
1 tablespoon lemon juice	¼ teaspoon ground black pepper
2 teaspoons minced garlic	Cooking spray

1. Preheat the air fryer to 400ºF (204ºC). Line a parchment paper in the air fryer basket. 2. Put the asparagus spears in a large bowl. Drizzle with lemon juice and sprinkle with minced garlic, salt, and ground black pepper. Toss to coat well. 3. Transfer the asparagus in the preheated air fryer and spritz with cooking spray. Air fryer for 10 minutes or until wilted and soft. Flip the asparagus halfway through. 4. Serve immediately.

Crispy Green Tomatoes Slices

Prep time: 10 minutes | Cook time: 8 minutes | Makes 12 slices

½ cup all-purpose flour	¼-inch-thick slices, patted dry
1 egg	½ teaspoon salt
½ cup buttermilk	½ teaspoon ground black pepper
1 cup cornmeal	Cooking spray
1 cup panko	
2 green tomatoes, cut into	

1. Preheat the air fryer to 400ºF (204ºC). Line the air fryer basket with parchment paper. 2. Pour the flour in a bowl. Whisk the egg and buttermilk in a second bowl. Combine the cornmeal and panko in a third bowl. 3. Dredge the tomato slices in the bowl of flour first, then into the egg mixture, and then dunk the slices into the cornmeal mixture. Shake the excess off. 4. Transfer the well-coated tomato slices in the preheated air fryer and sprinkle with salt and ground black pepper. 5. Spritz the tomato slices with cooking spray. Air fry for 8 minutes or until crispy and lightly browned. Flip the slices halfway through the cooking time. 6. Serve immediately.

Corn Fritters

Prep time: 15 minutes | Cook time: 8 minutes | Serves 6

1 cup self-rising flour	¼ cup buttermilk
1 tablespoon sugar	¾ cup corn kernels
1 teaspoon salt	¼ cup minced onion
1 large egg, lightly beaten	Cooking spray

1. Preheat the air fryer to 350ºF (177ºC). Line the air fryer basket with parchment paper. 2. In a medium bowl, whisk the flour, sugar, and salt until blended. Stir in the egg and buttermilk. Add the corn and minced onion. Mix well. Shape the corn fritter batter into 12 balls. 3. Place the fritters on the parchment and spritz with oil. Bake for 4 minutes. Flip the fritters, spritz them with oil, and bake for 4 minutes more until firm and lightly browned. 4. Serve immediately.

Beet Salad with Lemon Vinaigrette

Prep time: 10 minutes | Cook time: 12 to 15 minutes | Serves 4

6 medium red and golden beets, peeled and sliced	Cooking spray
1 teaspoon olive oil	Vinaigrette:
¼ teaspoon kosher salt	2 teaspoons olive oil
½ cup crumbled feta cheese	2 tablespoons chopped fresh chives
8 cups mixed greens	Juice of 1 lemon

1. Preheat the air fryer to 360ºF (182ºC). 2. In a large bowl, toss the beets, olive oil, and kosher salt. 3. Spray the air fryer basket with cooking spray, then place the beets in the basket and air fry for 12 to 15 minutes or until tender. 4. While the beets cook, make the vinaigrette in a large bowl by whisking together the olive oil, lemon juice, and chives. 5. Remove the beets from the air fryer, toss in the vinaigrette, and allow to cool for 5 minutes. Add the feta and serve on top of the mixed greens.

Air Fried Tortilla Chips

Prep time: 5 minutes | Cook time: 10 minutes | Serves 4

4 six-inch corn tortillas, cut in half and slice into thirds	¼ teaspoon kosher salt
1 tablespoon canola oil	Cooking spray

1. Preheat the air fryer to 360ºF (182ºC). Spritz the air fryer basket with cooking spray. 2. On a clean work surface, brush the tortilla chips with canola oil, then transfer the chips in the preheated air fryer. 3. Air fry for 10 minutes or until crunchy and lightly browned. Shake the basket and sprinkle with salt halfway through the cooking time. 4. Transfer the chips onto a plate lined with paper towels. Serve immediately.

Parsnip Fries with Garlic-Yogurt Dip

Prep time: 10 minutes | Cook time: 10 minutes | Serves 4

3 medium parsnips, peeled, cut into sticks	¼ cup plain Greek yogurt
¼ teaspoon kosher salt	⅛ teaspoon garlic powder
1 teaspoon olive oil	1 tablespoon sour cream
1 garlic clove, unpeeled	¼ teaspoon kosher salt
Cooking spray	Freshly ground black pepper, to taste
Dip:	

1. Preheat the air fryer to 360ºF (182ºC). Spritz the air fryer basket with cooking spray. 2. Put the parsnip sticks in a large bowl, then sprinkle with salt and drizzle with olive oil. 3. Transfer the parsnip into the preheated air fryer and add the garlic. 4. Air fry for 5 minutes, then remove the garlic from the air fryer and shake the basket. Air fry for 5 more minutes or until the parsnip sticks are crisp. 5. Meanwhile, peel the garlic and crush it. Combine the crushed garlic with the ingredients for the dip. Stir to mix well. 6. When the frying is complete, remove the parsnip fries from the air fryer and serve with the dipping sauce.

Cheesy Baked Grits

Prep time: 10 minutes | Cook time: 12 minutes | Serves 6

¾ cup hot water	½ to 1 teaspoon red pepper flakes
2 (1-ounce / 28-g) packages instant grits	1 cup shredded Cheddar cheese or jalapeño Jack cheese
1 large egg, beaten	
1 tablespoon butter, melted	
2 cloves garlic, minced	

1. Preheat the air fryer to 400ºF (204ºC). 2. In a baking pan, combine the water, grits, egg, butter, garlic, and red pepper flakes. Stir until well combined. Stir in the shredded cheese. 3. Place the pan in the air fryer basket and air fry for 12 minutes, or until the grits have cooked through and a knife inserted near the center comes out clean. 4. Let stand for 5 minutes before serving.

Frico

Prep time: 5 minutes | Cook time: 5 minutes | Serves 2

1 cup shredded aged Manchego cheese	½ teaspoon cumin seeds
1 teaspoon all-purpose flour	¼ teaspoon cracked black pepper

1. Preheat the air fryer to 375ºF (191ºC). Line the air fryer basket with parchment paper. 2. Combine the cheese and flour in a bowl. Stir to mix well. Spread the mixture in the basket into a 4-inch round. 3. Combine the cumin and black pepper in a small bowl. Stir to mix well. Sprinkle the cumin mixture over the cheese round. 4. Air fry 5 minutes or until the cheese is lightly browned and frothy. 5. Use tongs to transfer the cheese wafer onto a plate and slice to serve.

Chapter 3
Family Favorites

Cheesy Roasted Sweet Potatoes

Prep time: 7 minutes | Cook time: 18 to 23 minutes | Serves 4

2 large sweet potatoes, peeled and sliced	vinegar
1 teaspoon olive oil	1 teaspoon dried thyme
1 tablespoon white balsamic	¼ cup grated Parmesan cheese

1. In a large bowl, drizzle the sweet potato slices with the olive oil and toss. 2. Sprinkle with the balsamic vinegar and thyme and toss again. 3. Sprinkle the potatoes with the Parmesan cheese and toss to coat. 4. Roast the slices, in batches, in the air fryer basket at 400ºF (204ºC) for 18 to 23 minutes, tossing the sweet potato slices in the basket once during cooking, until tender. 5. Repeat with the remaining sweet potato slices. Serve immediately.

Fish and Vegetable Tacos

Prep time: 15 minutes | Cook time: 9 to 12 minutes | Serves 4

1 pound (454 g) white fish fillets, such as sole or cod	1 large carrot, grated
2 teaspoons olive oil	½ cup low-sodium salsa
3 tablespoons freshly squeezed lemon juice, divided	⅓ cup low-fat Greek yogurt
1½ cups chopped red cabbage	4 soft low-sodium whole-wheat tortillas

1. Brush the fish with the olive oil and sprinkle with 1 tablespoon of lemon juice. Air fry in the air fryer basket at 390ºF (199ºC) for 9 to 12 minutes, or until the fish just flakes when tested with a fork. 2. Meanwhile, in a medium bowl, stir together the remaining 2 tablespoons of lemon juice, the red cabbage, carrot, salsa, and yogurt. 3. When the fish is cooked, remove it from the air fryer basket and break it up into large pieces. 4. Offer the fish, tortillas, and the cabbage mixture, and let each person assemble a taco.

Puffed Egg Tarts

Prep time: 10 minutes | Cook time: 42 minutes | Makes 4 tarts

Oil, for spraying	4 large eggs
All-purpose flour, for dusting	2 teaspoons chopped fresh parsley
1 (12-ounce / 340-g) sheet frozen puff pastry, thawed	Salt and freshly ground black pepper, to taste
¾ cup shredded Cheddar cheese, divided	

1. Preheat the air fryer to 390ºF (199ºC). Line the air fryer basket with parchment and spray lightly with oil. 2. Lightly dust your work surface with flour. Unfold the puff pastry and cut it into 4 equal squares. Place 2 squares in the prepared basket. 3. Cook for 10 minutes. 4. Remove the basket. Press the center of each tart shell with a spoon to make an indentation. 5. Sprinkle 3 tablespoons of cheese into each indentation and crack 1 egg into the center of each tart shell. 6. Cook for another 7 to 11 minutes, or until the eggs are cooked to your desired doneness. 7. Repeat with the remaining puff pastry squares, cheese, and eggs. 8. Sprinkle evenly with the parsley, and season with salt and black pepper. Serve immediately.

Churro Bites

Prep time: 5 minutes | Cook time: 6 minutes | Makes 36 bites

Oil, for spraying	1 tablespoon ground cinnamon
1 (17¼-ounce / 489-g) package frozen puffed pastry, thawed	½ cup confectioners' sugar
1 cup granulated sugar	1 tablespoon milk

1. Preheat the air fryer to 400ºF (204ºC). Line the air fryer basket with parchment and spray lightly with oil. 2. Unfold the puff pastry onto a clean work surface. Using a sharp knife, cut the dough into 36 bite-size pieces. 3. Place the dough pieces in one layer in the prepared basket, taking care not to let the pieces touch or overlap. 4. Cook for 3 minutes, flip, and cook for another 3 minutes, or until puffed and golden. 5. In a small bowl, mix together the granulated sugar and cinnamon. 6. In another small bowl, whisk together the confectioners' sugar and milk. 7. Dredge the bites in the cinnamon-sugar mixture until evenly coated. 8. Serve with the icing on the side for dipping.

Mixed Berry Crumble

Prep time: 10 minutes | Cook time: 11 to 16 minutes | Serves 4

½ cup chopped fresh strawberries	⅔ cup whole-wheat pastry flour
½ cup fresh blueberries	3 tablespoons packed brown sugar
⅓ cup frozen raspberries	2 tablespoons unsalted butter, melted
1 tablespoon freshly squeezed lemon juice	
1 tablespoon honey	

1. In a baking pan, combine the strawberries, blueberries, and raspberries. Drizzle with the lemon juice and honey. 2. In a small bowl, mix the pastry flour and brown sugar. 3. Stir in the butter and mix until crumbly. Sprinkle this mixture over the fruit. 4. Bake at 380ºF (193ºC) for 11 to 16 minutes, or until the fruit is tender and bubbly and the topping is golden brown. Serve warm.

Fried Green Tomatoes

Prep time: 15 minutes | Cook time: 6 to 8 minutes | Serves 4

4 medium green tomatoes	½ cup panko bread crumbs
⅓ cup all-purpose flour	2 teaspoons olive oil
2 egg whites	1 teaspoon paprika
¼ cup almond milk	1 clove garlic, minced
1 cup ground almonds	

1. Rinse the tomatoes and pat dry. Cut the tomatoes into ½-inch slices, discarding the thinner ends. 2. Put the flour on a plate. In a shallow bowl, beat the egg whites with the almond milk until frothy. And on another plate, combine the almonds, bread crumbs, olive oil, paprika, and garlic and mix well. 3. Dip the tomato slices into the flour, then into the egg white mixture, then into the almond mixture to coat. 4. Place four of the coated tomato slices in the air fryer basket. Air fry at 400ºF (204ºC) for 6 to 8 minutes or until the tomato coating is crisp and golden brown. Repeat with remaining tomato slices and serve immediately.

Apple Pie Egg Rolls

Prep time: 10 minutes | Cook time: 8 minutes | Makes 6 rolls

Oil, for spraying	½ teaspoon lemon juice
1 (21-ounce / 595-g) can apple pie filling	¼ teaspoon ground nutmeg
	¼ teaspoon ground cinnamon
1 tablespoon all-purpose flour	6 egg roll wrappers

1. Preheat the air fryer to 400ºF (204ºC). Line the air fryer basket with parchment and spray lightly with oil. 2. In a medium bowl, mix together the pie filling, flour, lemon juice, nutmeg, and cinnamon. 3. Lay out the egg roll wrappers on a work surface and spoon a dollop of pie filling in the center of each. 4. Fill a small bowl with water. Dip your finger in the water and, working one at a time, moisten the edges of the wrappers. Fold the wrapper like an envelope: First fold one corner into the center. Fold each side corner in, and then fold over the remaining corner, making sure each corner overlaps a bit and the moistened edges stay closed. Use additional water and your fingers to seal any open edges. 5. Place the rolls in the prepared basket and spray liberally with oil. You may need to work in batches, depending on the size of your air fryer. 6. Cook for 4 minutes, flip, spray with oil, and cook for another 4 minutes, or until crispy and golden brown. Serve immediately.

Berry Cheesecake

Prep time: 5 minutes | Cook time: 10 minutes | Serves 4

Oil, for spraying	1 large egg
8 ounces (227 g) cream cheese	½ teaspoon vanilla extract
6 tablespoons sugar	¼ teaspoon lemon juice
1 tablespoon sour cream	½ cup fresh mixed berries

1. Preheat the air fryer to 350ºF (177ºC). Line the air fryer basket with parchment and spray lightly with oil. 2. In a blender, combine the cream cheese, sugar, sour cream, egg, vanilla, and lemon juice and blend until smooth. Pour the mixture into a 4-inch springform pan. 3. Place the pan in the prepared basket. 4. Cook for 8 to 10 minutes, or until only the very center jiggles slightly when the pan is moved. 5. Refrigerate the cheesecake in the pan for at least 2 hours. 6. Release the sides from the springform pan, top the cheesecake with the mixed berries, and serve.

Phyllo Vegetable Triangles

Prep time: 15 minutes | Cook time: 6 to 11 minutes | Serves 6

3 tablespoons minced onion	2 tablespoons nonfat cream cheese, at room temperature
2 garlic cloves, minced	
2 tablespoons grated carrot	6 sheets frozen phyllo dough, thawed
1 teaspoon olive oil	
3 tablespoons frozen baby peas, thawed	Olive oil spray, for coating the dough

1. In a baking pan, combine the onion, garlic, carrot, and olive oil. Air fry at 390ºF (199ºC) for 2 to 4 minutes, or until the vegetables are crisp-tender. Transfer to a bowl. 2. Stir in the peas and cream cheese to the vegetable mixture. Let cool while you prepare the dough. 3. Lay one sheet of phyllo on a work surface and lightly spray with olive oil spray. Top with another sheet of phyllo. Repeat with the remaining 4 phyllo sheets; you'll have 3 stacks with 2 layers each. Cut each stack lengthwise into 4 strips (12 strips total). 4. Place a scant 2 teaspoons of the filling near the bottom of each strip. Bring one corner up over the filling to make a triangle; continue folding the triangles over, as you would fold a flag. Seal the edge with a bit of water. Repeat with the remaining strips and filling. 5. Air fry the triangles, in 2 batches, for 4 to 7 minutes, or until golden brown. Serve.

Old Bay Tilapia

Prep time: 15 minutes | Cook time: 6 minutes | Serves 4

Oil, for spraying	½ teaspoon salt
1 cup panko bread crumbs	¼ teaspoon freshly ground black pepper
2 tablespoons Old Bay seasoning	
	1 large egg
2 teaspoons granulated garlic	4 tilapia fillets
1 teaspoon onion powder	

1. Preheat the air fryer to 400ºF (204ºC). Line the air fryer basket with parchment and spray lightly with oil. 2. In a shallow bowl, mix together the bread crumbs, Old Bay, garlic, onion powder, salt, and black pepper. 3. In a small bowl, whisk the egg. 4. Coat the tilapia in the egg, then dredge in the bread crumb mixture until completely coated. 5. Place the tilapia in the prepared basket. You may need to work in batches, depending on the size of your air fryer. Spray lightly with oil. 6. Cook for 4 to 6 minutes, depending on the thickness of the fillets, until the internal temperature reaches 145ºF (63ºC). Serve immediately.

Beignets

Prep time: 30 minutes | Cook time: 6 minutes | Makes 9 beignets

Oil, for greasing and spraying	1 cup milk
3 cups all-purpose flour, plus more for dusting	2 tablespoons packed light brown sugar
1½ teaspoons salt	1 tablespoon unsalted butter
1 (2¼-teaspoon) envelope active dry yeast	1 large egg
	1 cup confectioners' sugar

1. Oil a large bowl. 2. In a small bowl, mix together the flour, salt, and yeast. Set aside. 3. Pour the milk into a glass measuring cup and microwave in 1-minute intervals until it boils. 4. In a large bowl, mix together the brown sugar and butter. Pour in the hot milk and whisk until the sugar has dissolved. Let cool to room temperature. 5. Whisk the egg into the cooled milk mixture and fold in the flour mixture until a dough forms. 6. On a lightly floured work surface, knead the dough for 3 to 5 minutes. 7. Place the dough in the oiled bowl and cover with a clean kitchen towel. Let rise in a warm place for about 1 hour, or until doubled in size. 8. Roll the dough out on a lightly floured work surface until it's about ¼ inch thick. Cut the dough into 3-inch squares and place them on a lightly floured baking sheet. Cover loosely with a kitchen towel and let rise again until doubled in size, about 30 minutes. 9. Line the air fryer basket with parchment and spray lightly with oil. 10. Place the dough squares in the prepared basket and spray lightly with oil. You may need to work in batches, depending on the size of your air fryer. 11. Air fry at 390ºF (199ºC) for 3 minutes, flip, spray with oil, and cook for another 3 minutes, until crispy. 12. Dust with the confectioners' sugar before serving.

Pork Stuffing Meatballs

Prep time: 10 minutes | Cook time: 12 minutes | Makes 35 meatballs

Oil, for spraying	1 tablespoon dried rosemary
1½ pounds (680 g) ground pork	1 tablespoon dried thyme
1 cup bread crumbs	1 teaspoon salt
½ cup milk	1 teaspoon freshly ground black pepper
¼ cup minced onion	1 teaspoon finely chopped fresh parsley
1 large egg	

1. Line the air fryer basket with parchment and spray lightly with oil. 2. In a large bowl, mix together the ground pork, bread crumbs, milk, onion, egg, rosemary, thyme, salt, black pepper, and parsley. 3. Roll about 2 tablespoons of the mixture into a ball. Repeat with the rest of the mixture. You should have 30 to 35 meatballs. 4. Place the meatballs in the prepared basket in a single layer, leaving space between each one. You may need to work in batches, depending on the size of your air fryer. 5. Air fry at 390ºF (199ºC) for 10 to 12 minutes, flipping after 5 minutes, or until golden brown and the internal temperature reaches 160ºF (71ºC).

Chinese-Inspired Spareribs

Prep time: 30 minutes | Cook time: 8 minutes | Serves 4

Oil, for spraying	½ cup beef or chicken stock
12 ounces (340 g) boneless pork spareribs, cut into 3-inch-long pieces	¼ cup honey
1 cup soy sauce	2 tablespoons minced garlic
¾ cup sugar	1 teaspoon ground ginger
	2 drops red food coloring (optional)

1. Line the air fryer basket with parchment and spray lightly with oil. 2. Combine the ribs, soy sauce, sugar, beef stock, honey, garlic, ginger, and food coloring (if using) in a large zip-top plastic bag, seal, and shake well until completely coated. Refrigerate for at least 30 minutes. 3. Place the ribs in the prepared basket. 4. Air fry at 375ºF (191ºC) for 8 minutes, or until the internal temperature reaches 165ºF (74ºC).

Bacon-Wrapped Hot Dogs

Prep time: 5 minutes | Cook time: 10 minutes | Serves 4

Oil, for spraying	4 hot dog buns
4 bacon slices	Toppings of choice
4 all-beef hot dogs	

1. Line the air fryer basket with parchment and spray lightly with oil. 2. Wrap a strip of bacon tightly around each hot dog, taking care to cover the tips so they don't get too crispy. Secure with a toothpick at each end to keep the bacon from shrinking. 3. Place the hot dogs in the prepared basket. 4. Air fry at 380ºF (193ºC) for 8 to 9 minutes, depending on how crispy you like the bacon. For extra-crispy, cook the hot dogs at 400ºF (204ºC) for 6 to 8 minutes. 5. Place the hot dogs in the buns, return them to the air fryer, and cook for another 1 to 2 minutes, or until the buns are warm. Add your desired toppings and serve.

Buffalo Cauliflower

Prep time: 15 minutes | Cook time: 5 minutes | Serves 6

1 large head cauliflower, separated into small florets	⅔ cup nonfat Greek yogurt
1 tablespoon olive oil	½ teaspoons Tabasco sauce
½ teaspoon garlic powder	1 celery stalk, chopped
⅓ cup low-sodium hot wing sauce	1 tablespoon crumbled blue cheese

1. In a large bowl, toss the cauliflower florets with the olive oil. Sprinkle with the garlic powder and toss again to coat. Put half of the cauliflower in the air fryer basket. Air fry at 380ºF (193ºC) for 5 to 7 minutes, until the cauliflower is browned, shaking the basket once during cooking. 2. Transfer to a serving bowl and toss with half of the wing sauce. Repeat with the remaining cauliflower and wing sauce. 3. In a small bowl, stir together the yogurt, Tabasco sauce, celery, and blue cheese. Serve with the cauliflower for dipping.

Steak and Vegetable Kebabs

Prep time: 15 minutes | Cook time: 5 to 7 minutes | Serves 4

2 tablespoons balsamic vinegar	¾ pound (340 g) round steak, cut into 1-inch pieces
2 teaspoons olive oil	1 red bell pepper, sliced
½ teaspoon dried marjoram	16 button mushrooms
⅛ teaspoon freshly ground black pepper	1 cup cherry tomatoes

1. In a medium bowl, stir together the balsamic vinegar, olive oil, marjoram, and black pepper. 2. Add the steak and stir to coat. Let stand for 10 minutes at room temperature. 3. Alternating items, thread the beef, red bell pepper, mushrooms, and tomatoes onto 8 bamboo or metal skewers that fit in the air fryer. 4. Air fry at 390ºF (199ºC) for 5 to 7 minutes, or until the beef is browned and reaches at least 145ºF (63ºC) on a meat thermometer. Serve immediately.

Meringue Cookies

Prep time: 15 minutes | Cook time: 1 hour 30 minutes | Makes 20 cookies

Oil, for spraying	1 cup sugar
4 large egg whites	Pinch cream of tartar

1. Preheat the air fryer to 140ºF (60ºC). Line the air fryer basket with parchment and spray lightly with oil. 2. In a small heatproof bowl, whisk together the egg whites and sugar. Fill a small saucepan halfway with water, place it over medium heat, and bring to a light simmer. Place the bowl with the egg whites on the saucepan, making sure the bottom of the bowl does not touch the water. Whisk the mixture until the sugar is dissolved. 3. Transfer the mixture to a large bowl and add the cream of tartar. Using an electric mixer, beat the mixture on high until it is glossy and stiff peaks form. Transfer the mixture to a piping bag or a zip-top plastic bag with a corner cut off. 4. Pipe rounds into the prepared basket. You may need to work in batches, depending on the size of your air fryer. 5. Cook for 1 hour 30 minutes. 6. Turn off the air fryer and let the meringues cool completely inside. The residual heat will continue to dry them out.

Veggie Tuna Melts

Prep time: 15 minutes | Cook time: 7 to 11 minutes | Serves 4

2 low-sodium whole-wheat English muffins, split
1 (6-ounce / 170-g) can chunk light low-sodium tuna, drained
1 cup shredded carrot
⅓ cup chopped mushrooms
2 scallions, white and green parts, sliced
⅓ cup nonfat Greek yogurt
2 tablespoons low-sodium stone-ground mustard
2 slices low-sodium low-fat Swiss cheese, halved

1. Place the English muffin halves in the air fryer basket. Air fry at 340ºF (171ºC) for 3 to 4 minutes, or until crisp. Remove from the basket and set aside. 2. In a medium bowl, thoroughly mix the tuna, carrot, mushrooms, scallions, yogurt, and mustard. Top each half of the muffins with one-fourth of the tuna mixture and a half slice of Swiss cheese. 3. Air fry for 4 to 7 minutes, or until the tuna mixture is hot and the cheese melts and starts to brown. Serve immediately.

Pecan Rolls

Prep time: 20 minutes | Cook time: 20 to 24 minutes | Makes 12 rolls

2 cups all-purpose flour, plus more for dusting
2 tablespoons granulated sugar, plus ¼ cup, divided
1 teaspoon salt
3 tablespoons butter, at room temperature
¾ cup milk, whole or 2%
¼ cup packed light brown sugar
½ cup chopped pecans, toasted
1 to 2 tablespoons oil
¼ cup confectioners' sugar (optional)

1. In a large bowl, whisk the flour, 2 tablespoons granulated sugar, and salt until blended. Stir in the butter and milk briefly until a sticky dough forms. 2. In a small bowl, stir together the brown sugar and remaining ¼ cup of granulated sugar. 3. Place a piece of parchment paper on a work surface and dust it with flour. Roll the dough on the prepared surface to ¼ inch thickness. 4. Spread the sugar mixture over the dough. Sprinkle the pecans on top. Roll up the dough jelly roll-style, pinching the ends to seal. Cut the dough into 12 rolls. 5. Preheat the air fryer to 320ºF (160ºC). 6. Line the air fryer basket with parchment paper and spritz the parchment with oil. Place 6 rolls on the prepared parchment. 7. Bake for 5 minutes. Flip the rolls and bake for 5 to 7 minutes more until lightly browned. Repeat with the remaining rolls. 8. Sprinkle with confectioners' sugar (if using).

Pork Burgers with Red Cabbage Salad

Prep time: 20 minutes | Cook time: 7 to 9 minutes | Serves 4

½ cup Greek yogurt
2 tablespoons low-sodium mustard, divided
1 tablespoon lemon juice
¼ cup sliced red cabbage
¼ cup grated carrots
1 pound (454 g) lean ground pork
½ teaspoon paprika
1 cup mixed baby lettuce greens
2 small tomatoes, sliced
8 small low-sodium whole-wheat sandwich buns, cut in half

1. In a small bowl, combine the yogurt, 1 tablespoon mustard, lemon juice, cabbage, and carrots; mix and refrigerate. 2. In a medium bowl, combine the pork, remaining 1 tablespoon mustard, and paprika. Form into 8 small patties. 3. Put the sliders into the air fryer basket. Air fry at 400ºF (204ºC) for 7 to 9 minutes, or until the sliders register 165ºF (74ºC) as tested with a meat thermometer. 4. Assemble the burgers by placing some of the lettuce greens on a bun bottom. Top with a tomato slice, the burgers, and the cabbage mixture. Add the bun top and serve immediately.

Cajun Shrimp

Prep time: 15 minutes | Cook time: 9 minutes | Serves 4

Oil, for spraying
1 pound (454 g) jumbo raw shrimp, peeled and deveined
1 tablespoon Cajun seasoning
6 ounces (170 g) cooked kielbasa, cut into thick slices
½ medium zucchini, cut into
¼-inch-thick slices
½ medium yellow squash, cut into ¼-inch-thick slices
1 green bell pepper, seeded and cut into 1-inch pieces
2 tablespoons olive oil
½ teaspoon salt

1. Preheat the air fryer to 400ºF (204ºC). Line the air fryer basket with parchment and spray lightly with oil. 2. In a large bowl, toss together the shrimp and Cajun seasoning. Add the kielbasa, zucchini, squash, bell pepper, olive oil, and salt and mix well. 3. Transfer the mixture to the prepared basket, taking care not to overcrowd. You may need to work in batches, depending on the size of your air fryer. 4. Cook for 9 minutes, shaking and stirring every 3 minutes. Serve immediately.

Chapter 4

Fish and Seafood

Fish Taco Bowl

Prep time: 10 minutes | Cook time: 12 minutes | Serves 4

½ teaspoon salt	⅓ cup mayonnaise
¼ teaspoon garlic powder	¼ teaspoon ground black
¼ teaspoon ground cumin	pepper
4 (4-ounce / 113-g) cod fillets	¼ cup chopped pickled
4 cups finely shredded green	jalapeños
cabbage	

1. Sprinkle salt, garlic powder, and cumin over cod and place into ungreased air fryer basket. Adjust the temperature to 350ºF (177ºC) and air fry for 12 minutes, turning fillets halfway through cooking. Cod will flake easily and have an internal temperature of at least 145ºF (63ºC) when done. 2. In a large bowl, toss cabbage with mayonnaise, pepper, and jalapeños until fully coated. Serve cod warm over cabbage slaw on four medium plates.

Crawfish Creole Casserole

Prep time: 20 minutes | Cook time: 25 minutes | Serves 4

1½ cups crawfish meat	1 tablespoon cornstarch
½ cup chopped celery	1 teaspoon Creole seasoning
½ cup chopped onion	¾ teaspoon salt
½ cup chopped green bell	½ teaspoon freshly ground
pepper	black pepper
2 large eggs, beaten	1 cup shredded Cheddar
1 cup half-and-half	cheese
1 tablespoon butter, melted	Cooking spray

1. In a medium bowl, stir together the crawfish, celery, onion, and green pepper. 2. In another medium bowl, whisk the eggs, half-and-half, butter, cornstarch, Creole seasoning, salt, and pepper until blended. Stir the egg mixture into the crawfish mixture. Add the cheese and stir to combine. 3. Preheat the air fryer to 300ºF (149ºC). Spritz a baking pan with oil. 4. Transfer the crawfish mixture to the prepared pan and place it in the air fryer basket. 5. Bake for 25 minutes, stirring every 10 minutes, until a knife inserted into the center comes out clean. 6. Serve immediately.

Tuna and Fruit Kebabs

Prep time: 15 minutes | Cook time: 8 to 12 minutes | Serves 4

1 pound (454 g) tuna steaks,	1 tablespoon honey
cut into 1-inch cubes	2 teaspoons grated fresh
½ cup canned pineapple	ginger
chunks, drained, juice	1 teaspoon olive oil
reserved	Pinch cayenne pepper
½ cup large red grapes	

1. Thread the tuna, pineapple, and grapes on 8 bamboo or 4 metal skewers that fit in the air fryer. 2. In a small bowl, whisk the honey, 1 tablespoon of reserved pineapple juice, the ginger, olive oil, and cayenne. Brush this mixture over the kebabs. Let them stand for 10 minutes. 3. Air fry the kebabs at 370ºF (188ºC) for 8 to 12 minutes, or until the tuna reaches an internal temperature of at least 145ºF (63ºC) on a meat thermometer, and the fruit is tender and glazed, brushing once with the remaining sauce. Discard any remaining marinade. Serve immediately.

Tuna Avocado Bites

Prep time: 10 minutes | Cook time: 7 minutes | Makes 12 bites

1 (10-ounce / 283-g) can tuna,	pitted, and mashed
drained	½ cup blanched finely ground
¼ cup full-fat mayonnaise	almond flour, divided
1 stalk celery, chopped	2 teaspoons coconut oil
1 medium avocado, peeled,	

1. In a large bowl, mix tuna, mayonnaise, celery, and mashed avocado. Form the mixture into balls. 2. Roll balls in almond flour and spritz with coconut oil. Place balls into the air fryer basket. 3. Adjust the temperature to 400ºF (204ºC) and set the timer for 7 minutes. 4. Gently turn tuna bites after 5 minutes. Serve warm.

Ahi Tuna Steaks

Prep time: 5 minutes | Cook time: 14 minutes | Serves 2

2 (6-ounce / 170-g) ahi tuna	3 tablespoons everything
steaks	bagel seasoning
2 tablespoons olive oil	

1. Drizzle both sides of each steak with olive oil. Place seasoning on a medium plate and press each side of tuna steaks into seasoning to form a thick layer. 2. Place steaks into ungreased air fryer basket. Adjust the temperature to 400ºF (204ºC) and air fry for 14 minutes, turning steaks halfway through cooking. Steaks will be done when internal temperature is at least 145ºF (63ºC) for well-done. Serve warm.

Lime Lobster Tails

Prep time: 10 minutes | Cook time: 6 minutes | Serves 4

4 lobster tails, peeled	½ teaspoon coconut oil,
2 tablespoons lime juice	melted
½ teaspoon dried basil	

1. Mix lobster tails with lime juice, dried basil, and coconut oil. 2. Put the lobster tails in the air fryer and cook at 380ºF (193ºC) for 6 minutes.

Coconut Cream Mackerel

Prep time: 10 minutes | Cook time: 6 minutes | Serves 4

2 pounds (907 g) mackerel	1 teaspoon cumin seeds
fillet	1 garlic clove, peeled,
1 cup coconut cream	chopped
1 teaspoon ground coriander	

1. Chop the mackerel roughly and sprinkle it with coconut cream, ground coriander, cumin seeds, and garlic. 2. Then put the fish in the air fryer and cook at 400ºF (204ºC) for 6 minutes.

Shrimp Kebabs

Prep time: 15 minutes | Cook time: 6 minutes | Serves 4

Oil, for spraying
1 pound (454 g) medium raw shrimp, peeled and deveined
4 tablespoons unsalted butter, melted
1 tablespoon Old Bay seasoning
1 tablespoon packed light brown sugar
1 teaspoon granulated garlic
1 teaspoon onion powder
½ teaspoon freshly ground black pepper

1. Line the air fryer basket with parchment and spray lightly with oil. 2. Thread the shrimp onto the skewers and place them in the prepared basket. 3. In a small bowl, mix together the butter, Old Bay, brown sugar, garlic, onion powder, and black pepper. Brush the sauce on the shrimp. 4. Air fry at 400ºF (204ºC) for 5 to 6 minutes, or until pink and firm. Serve immediately.

Parmesan Fish Fillets

Prep time: 8 minutes | Cook time: 17 minutes | Serves 4

⅓ cup grated Parmesan cheese
½ teaspoon fennel seed
½ teaspoon tarragon
⅓ teaspoon mixed peppercorns
2 eggs, beaten
4 (4-ounce / 113-g) fish fillets, halved
2 tablespoons dry white wine
1 teaspoon seasoned salt

1. Preheat the air fryer to 345ºF (174ºC). 2. Place the grated Parmesan cheese, fennel seed, tarragon, and mixed peppercorns in a food processor and pulse for about 20 seconds until well combined. Transfer the cheese mixture to a shallow dish. 3. Place the beaten eggs in another shallow dish. 4. Drizzle the dry white wine over the top of fish fillets. Dredge each fillet in the beaten eggs on both sides, shaking off any excess, then roll them in the cheese mixture until fully coated. Season with the salt. 5. Arrange the fillets in the air fryer basket and air fry for about 17 minutes, or until the fish is cooked through and no longer translucent. Flip the fillets once halfway through the cooking time. 6. Cool for 5 minutes before serving.

Cornmeal-Crusted Trout Fingers

Prep time: 15 minutes | Cook time: 6 minutes | Serves 2

½ cup yellow cornmeal, medium or finely ground (not coarse)
⅓ cup all-purpose flour
1½ teaspoons baking powder
1 teaspoon kosher salt, plus more as needed
½ teaspoon freshly ground black pepper, plus more as needed
⅛ teaspoon cayenne pepper
¾ pound (340 g) skinless trout
fillets, cut into strips 1 inch wide and 3 inches long
3 large eggs, lightly beaten
Cooking spray
½ cup mayonnaise
2 tablespoons capers, rinsed and finely chopped
1 tablespoon fresh tarragon
1 teaspoon fresh lemon juice, plus lemon wedges, for serving

1. Preheat the air fryer to 400ºF (204ºC). 2. In a large bowl, whisk together the cornmeal, flour, baking powder, salt, black pepper, and cayenne. Dip the trout strips in the egg, then toss them in the cornmeal mixture until fully coated. Transfer the trout to a rack set over a baking sheet and liberally spray all over with cooking spray. 3. Transfer half the fish to the air fryer and air fry until the fish is cooked through and golden brown, about 6 minutes. Transfer the fish sticks to a plate and repeat with the remaining fish. 4. Meanwhile, in a bowl, whisk together the mayonnaise, capers, tarragon, and lemon juice. Season the tartar sauce with salt and black pepper. 5. Serve the trout fingers hot along with the tartar sauce and lemon wedges.

Stuffed Flounder Florentine

Prep time: 10 minutes | Cook time: 25 minutes | Serves 4

¼ cup pine nuts
2 tablespoons olive oil
½ cup chopped tomatoes
1 (6-ounce / 170-g) bag spinach, coarsely chopped
2 cloves garlic, chopped
Salt and freshly ground black
pepper, to taste
2 tablespoons unsalted butter, divided
4 flounder fillets (about 1½ pounds / 680 g)
Dash of paprika
½ lemon, sliced into 4 wedges

1. Place the pine nuts in a baking dish that fits in your air fryer. Set the air fryer to 400ºF (204ºC) and air fry for 4 minutes until the nuts are lightly browned and fragrant. Remove the baking dish from the air fryer, tip the nuts onto a plate to cool, and continue preheating the air fryer. When the nuts are cool enough to handle, chop them into fine pieces. 2. In the baking dish, combine the oil, tomatoes, spinach, and garlic. Use tongs to toss until thoroughly combined. Air fry for 5 minutes until the tomatoes are softened and the spinach is wilted. 3. Transfer the vegetables to a bowl and stir in the toasted pine nuts. Season to taste with salt and freshly ground black pepper. 4. Place 1 tablespoon of the butter in the bottom of the baking dish. Lower the heat on the air fryer to 350ºF (177ºC). 5. Place the flounder on a clean work surface. Sprinkle both sides with salt and black pepper. Divide the vegetable mixture among the flounder fillets and carefully roll up, securing with toothpicks. 6. Working in batches if necessary, arrange the fillets seam-side down in the baking dish along with 1 tablespoon of water. Top the fillets with remaining 1 tablespoon butter and sprinkle with a dash of paprika. 7.Cover loosely with foil and air fry for 10 to 15 minutes until the fish is opaque and flakes easily with a fork. Remove the toothpicks before serving with the lemon wedges.

Tuna-Stuffed Tomatoes

Prep time: 5 minutes | Cook time: 5 minutes | Serves 2

2 medium beefsteak tomatoes, tops removed, seeded, membranes removed
2 (2.6-ounce / 74-g) pouches tuna packed in water, drained
1 medium stalk celery, trimmed and chopped
2 tablespoons mayonnaise
¼ teaspoon salt
¼ teaspoon ground black pepper
2 teaspoons coconut oil
¼ cup shredded mild Cheddar cheese

1. Scoop pulp out of each tomato, leaving ½-inch shell. 2. In a medium bowl, mix tuna, celery, mayonnaise, salt, and pepper. Drizzle with coconut oil. Spoon ½ mixture into each tomato and top each with 2 tablespoons Cheddar. 3. Place tomatoes into ungreased air fryer basket. Adjust the temperature to 320ºF (160ºC) and air fry for 5 minutes. Cheese will be melted when done. Serve warm.

Catfish Bites

Prep time: 15 minutes | Cook time: 20 minutes | Serves 4

Oil, for spraying	½ cup cornmeal
1 pound (454 g) catfish fillets, cut into 2-inch pieces	¼ cup all-purpose flour
	2 teaspoons Creole seasoning
1 cup buttermilk	½ cup yellow mustard

1. Line the air fryer basket with parchment and spray lightly with oil. 2. Place the catfish pieces and buttermilk in a zip-top plastic bag, seal, and refrigerate for about 10 minutes. 3. In a shallow bowl, mix together the cornmeal, flour, and Creole seasoning. 4. Remove the catfish from the bag and pat dry with a paper towel. 5. Spread the mustard on all sides of the catfish, then dip them in the cornmeal mixture until evenly coated. 6. Place the catfish in the prepared basket. You may need to work in batches, depending on the size of your air fryer. Spray lightly with oil. 7. Air fry at 400°F (204°C) for 10 minutes, flip carefully, spray with oil, and cook for another 10 minutes. Serve immediately.

Salmon Croquettes

Prep time: 10 minutes | Cook time: 7 to 8 minutes | Serves 4

1 tablespoon oil	crackers (about 8 crackers)
½ cup bread crumbs	½ teaspoon Old Bay Seasoning
1 (14¾ -ounce / 418-g) can salmon, drained and all skin and fat removed	½ teaspoon onion powder
1 egg, beaten	½ teaspoon Worcestershire sauce
⅓ cup coarsely crushed saltine	

1. Preheat the air fryer to 390°F (199°C). 2. In a shallow dish, mix oil and bread crumbs until crumbly. 3. In a large bowl, combine the salmon, egg, cracker crumbs, Old Bay, onion powder, and Worcestershire. Mix well and shape into 8 small patties about ½-inch thick. 4. Gently dip each patty into bread crumb mixture and turn to coat well on all sides. 5. Cook for 7 to 8 minutes or until outside is crispy and browned.

Coconut Shrimp with Spicy Dipping Sauce

Prep time: 15 minutes | Cook time: 8 minutes | Serves 4

1 (2½-ounce / 71-g) bag pork rinds	shrimp, peeled and deveined
¾ cup unsweetened shredded coconut flakes	½ teaspoon salt
	¼ teaspoon freshly ground black pepper
¾ cup coconut flour	Spicy Dipping Sauce:
1 teaspoon onion powder	½ cup mayonnaise
1 teaspoon garlic powder	2 tablespoons Sriracha
2 eggs	Zest and juice of ½ lime
1½ pounds (680 g) large	1 clove garlic, minced

1. Preheat the air fryer to 390°F (199°C). 2. In a food processor fitted with a metal blade, combine the pork rinds and coconut flakes. Pulse until the mixture resembles coarse crumbs. Transfer to a shallow bowl. 3. In another shallow bowl, combine the coconut flour, onion powder, and garlic powder; mix until thoroughly combined. 4. In a third shallow bowl, whisk the eggs until slightly frothy. 5. In a large bowl, season the shrimp with the salt and pepper, tossing gently to coat. 6. Working a few pieces at a time, dredge the shrimp in the flour mixture, followed by the eggs, and finishing with the pork rind crumb mixture. Arrange the shrimp on a baking sheet until ready to air fry. 7. Working in batches if necessary, arrange the shrimp in a single layer in the air fryer basket. Pausing halfway through the cooking time to turn the shrimp, air fry for 8 minutes until cooked through. 8. To make the sauce: In a small bowl, combine the mayonnaise, Sriracha, lime zest and juice, and garlic. Whisk until thoroughly combined. Serve alongside the shrimp.

Shrimp Curry

Prep time: 30 minutes | Cook time: 10 minutes | Serves 4

¾ cup unsweetened full-fat coconut milk	1 teaspoon salt
¼ cup finely chopped yellow onion	¼ to ½ teaspoon cayenne pepper
2 teaspoons garam masala	1 pound (454 g) raw shrimp (21 to 25 count), peeled and deveined
1 tablespoon minced fresh ginger	
1 tablespoon minced garlic	2 teaspoons chopped fresh cilantro
1 teaspoon ground turmeric	

1. In a large bowl, stir together the coconut milk, onion, garam masala, ginger, garlic, turmeric, salt and cayenne, until well blended. 2. Add the shrimp and toss until coated with sauce on all sides. Marinate at room temperature for 30 minutes. 3. Transfer the shrimp and marinade to a baking pan. Place the pan in the air fryer basket. Set the air fryer to 375°F (191°C) for 10 minutes, stirring halfway through the cooking time. 4. Transfer the shrimp to a serving bowl or platter. Sprinkle with the cilantro and serve.

Blackened Salmon

Prep time: 10 minutes | Cook time: 8 minutes | Serves 2

10 ounces (283 g) salmon fillet	1 teaspoon ground cumin
	1 teaspoon dried basil
½ teaspoon ground coriander	1 tablespoon avocado oil

1. In the shallow bowl, mix ground coriander, ground cumin, and dried basil. 2. Then coat the salmon fillet in the spices and sprinkle with avocado oil. 3. Put the fish in the air fryer basket and cook at 395°F (202°C) for 4 minutes per side.

Calamari with Hot Sauce

Prep time: 10 minutes | Cook time: 6 minutes | Serves 2

10 ounces (283 g) calamari, trimmed	2 tablespoons keto hot sauce
	1 tablespoon avocado oil

1. Slice the calamari and sprinkle with avocado oil. 2. Put the calamari in the air fryer and cook at 400°F (204°C) for 3 minutes per side. 3. Then transfer the calamari in the serving plate and sprinkle with hot sauce.

Roasted Salmon Fillets

Prep time: 5 minutes | Cook time: 10 minutes | Serves 2

2 (8-ounce / 227 -g) skin-on salmon fillets, 1½ inches thick 1 teaspoon vegetable oil	Salt and pepper, to taste Vegetable oil spray

1. Preheat the air fryer to 400°F (204°C). 2. Make foil sling for air fryer basket by folding 1 long sheet of aluminum foil so it is 4 inches wide. Lay sheet of foil widthwise across basket, pressing foil into and up sides of basket. Fold excess foil as needed so that edges of foil are flush with top of basket. Lightly spray foil and basket with vegetable oil spray. 3. Pat salmon dry with paper towels, rub with oil, and season with salt and pepper. Arrange fillets skin side down on sling in prepared basket, spaced evenly apart. Air fry salmon until center is still translucent when checked with the tip of a paring knife and registers 125°F (52°C) (for medium-rare), 10 to 14 minutes, using sling to rotate fillets halfway through cooking. 4. Using the sling, carefully remove salmon from air fryer. Slide fish spatula along underside of fillets and transfer to individual serving plates, leaving skin behind. Serve.

Apple Cider Mussels

Prep time: 10 minutes | Cook time: 2 minutes | Serves 5

2 pounds (907 g) mussels, cleaned, peeled 1 teaspoon onion powder	1 teaspoon ground cumin 1 tablespoon avocado oil ¼ cup apple cider vinegar

1. Mix mussels with onion powder, ground cumin, avocado oil, and apple cider vinegar. 2. Put the mussels in the air fryer and cook at 395°F (202°C) for 2 minutes.

Asian Marinated Salmon

Prep time: 30 minutes | Cook time: 6 minutes | Serves 2

Marinade: ¼ cup wheat-free tamari or coconut aminos 2 tablespoons lime or lemon juice 2 tablespoons sesame oil 2 tablespoons Swerve confectioners'-style sweetener, or a few drops liquid stevia 2 teaspoons grated fresh ginger 2 cloves garlic, minced ½ teaspoon ground black pepper 2 (4-ounce / 113-g) salmon	fillets (about 1¼ inches thick) Sliced green onions, for garnish Sauce (Optional): ¼ cup beef broth ¼ cup wheat-free tamari 3 tablespoons Swerve confectioners'-style sweetener or equivalent amount of liquid or powdered sweetener 1 tablespoon tomato sauce 1 teaspoon stevia glycerite (optional) ⅛ teaspoon guar gum or xanthan gum (optional, for thickening)

1. Make the marinade: In a medium-sized shallow dish, stir together all the ingredients for the marinade until well combined. Place the salmon in the marinade. Cover and refrigerate for at least 2 hours or overnight. 2. Preheat the air fryer to 400°F (204°C). 3. Remove the salmon fillets from the marinade and place them in the air fryer, leaving space between them. Air fry for 6 minutes, or until the salmon is cooked through and flakes easily with a fork. 4. While the salmon cooks, make the sauce, if using: Place all the sauce ingredients except the guar gum in a medium-sized bowl and stir until well combined. Taste and adjust the sweetness to your liking. While whisking slowly, add the guar gum. Allow the sauce to thicken for 3 to 5 minutes. (The sauce can be made up to 3 days ahead and stored in an airtight container in the fridge.) Drizzle the sauce over the salmon before serving. 5. Garnish the salmon with sliced green onions before serving. Store leftovers in an airtight container in the fridge for up to 3 days. Reheat in a preheated 350°F (177°C) air fryer for 3 minutes, or until heated through.

Panko Catfish Nuggets

Prep time: 10 minutes | Cook time: 7 to 8 minutes | Serves 4

2 medium catfish fillets, cut into chunks (approximately 1 × 2 inch) Salt and pepper, to taste 2 eggs	2 tablespoons skim milk ½ cup cornstarch 1 cup panko bread crumbs Cooking spray

1. Preheat the air fryer to 390°F (199°C). 2. In a medium bowl, season the fish chunks with salt and pepper to taste. 3. In a small bowl, beat together the eggs with milk until well combined. 4. Place the cornstarch and bread crumbs into separate shallow dishes. 5. Dredge the fish chunks one at a time in the cornstarch, coating well on both sides, then dip in the egg mixture, shaking off any excess, finally press well into the bread crumbs. Spritz the fish chunks with cooking spray. 6. Arrange the fish chunks in the air fryer basket in a single layer. You may need to cook in batches depending on the size of your air fryer basket. 7. Fry the fish chunks for 7 to 8 minutes until they are no longer translucent in the center and golden brown. Shake the basket once during cooking. 8. Remove the fish chunks from the basket to a plate. Repeat with the remaining fish chunks. 9. Serve warm.

Crunchy Fish Sticks

Prep time: 30 minutes | Cook time: 9 minutes | Serves 4

1 pound (454 g) cod fillets 1½ cups finely ground blanched almond flour 2 teaspoons Old Bay seasoning ½ teaspoon paprika	Sea salt and freshly ground black pepper, to taste ¼ cup sugar-free mayonnaise 1 large egg, beaten Avocado oil spray Tartar sauce, for serving

1. Cut the fish into ¾-inch-wide strips. 2. In a shallow bowl, stir together the almond flour, Old Bay seasoning, paprika, and salt and pepper to taste. In another shallow bowl, whisk together the mayonnaise and egg. 3. Dip the cod strips in the egg mixture, then the almond flour, gently pressing with your fingers to help adhere to the coating. 4. Place the coated fish on a parchment paper-lined baking sheet and freeze for 30 minutes. 5. Spray the air fryer basket with oil. Set the air fryer to 400°F (204°C). Place the fish in the basket in a single layer, and spray each piece with oil. 6. Cook for 5 minutes. Flip and spray with more oil. Cook for 4 minutes more, until the internal temperature reaches 140°F (60°C). Serve with the tartar sauce.

Almond Pesto Salmon

Prep time: 5 minutes | Cook time: 12 minutes | Serves 2

¼ cup pesto	fillets (about 4 ounces / 113
¼ cup sliced almonds, roughly chopped	g each)
2 (1½-inch-thick) salmon	2 tablespoons unsalted butter, melted

1. In a small bowl, mix pesto and almonds. Set aside. 2. Place fillets into a round baking dish. 3. Brush each fillet with butter and place half of the pesto mixture on the top of each fillet. Place dish into the air fryer basket. 4. Adjust the temperature to 390ºF (199ºC) and set the timer for 12 minutes. 5. Salmon will easily flake when fully cooked and reach an internal temperature of at least 145ºF (63ºC). Serve warm.

Creamy Haddock

Prep time: 10 minutes | Cook time: 8 minutes | Serves 4

1 pound (454 g) haddock fillet	1 teaspoon coconut oil
1 teaspoon cayenne pepper	½ cup heavy cream
1 teaspoon salt	

1. Grease a baking pan with coconut oil. 2. Then put haddock fillet inside and sprinkle it with cayenne pepper, salt, and heavy cream. Put the baking pan in the air fryer basket and cook at 375ºF (191ºC) for 8 minutes.

Crunchy Air Fried Cod Fillets

Prep time: 10 minutes | Cook time: 12 minutes | Serves 2

⅓ cup panko bread crumbs	parsley
1 teaspoon vegetable oil	1 tablespoon mayonnaise
1 small shallot, minced	1 large egg yolk
1 small garlic clove, minced	¼ teaspoon grated lemon zest, plus lemon wedges for serving
½ teaspoon minced fresh thyme	2 (8-ounce / 227-g) skinless cod fillets, 1¼ inches thick
Salt and pepper, to taste	Vegetable oil spray
1 tablespoon minced fresh	

1. Preheat the air fryer to 300ºF (149ºC). 2. Make foil sling for air fryer basket by folding 1 long sheet of aluminum foil so it is 4 inches wide. Lay sheet of foil widthwise across basket, pressing foil into and up sides of basket. Fold excess foil as needed so that edges of foil are flush with top of basket. Lightly spray the foil and basket with vegetable oil spray. 3. Toss the panko with the oil in a bowl until evenly coated. Stir in the shallot, garlic, thyme, ¼ teaspoon salt, and ⅛ teaspoon pepper. Microwave, stirring frequently, until the panko is light golden brown, about 2 minutes. Transfer to a shallow dish and let cool slightly; stir in the parsley. Whisk the mayonnaise, egg yolk, lemon zest, and ⅛ teaspoon pepper together in another bowl. 4. Pat the cod dry with paper towels and season with salt and pepper. Arrange the fillets, skinned-side down, on plate and brush tops evenly with mayonnaise mixture. (Tuck thinner tail ends of fillets under themselves as needed to create uniform pieces.) Working with 1 fillet at a time, dredge the coated side in panko mixture, pressing gently to adhere. Arrange the fillets, crumb-side up, on sling in the prepared basket, spaced evenly apart. 5. Bake for 12 to 16 minutes, using a sling to rotate fillets halfway through cooking. Using a sling, carefully remove cod from air fryer. Serve with the lemon wedges.

Paprika Shrimp

Prep time: 5 minutes | Cook time: 6 minutes | Serves 2

8 ounces (227 g) medium shelled and deveined shrimp	½ teaspoon garlic powder
2 tablespoons salted butter, melted	¼ teaspoon onion powder
1 teaspoon paprika	½ teaspoon Old Bay seasoning

1. Toss all ingredients together in a large bowl. Place shrimp into the air fryer basket. 2. Adjust the temperature to 400ºF (204ºC) and set the timer for 6 minutes. 3. Turn the shrimp halfway through the cooking time to ensure even cooking. Serve immediately.

Asian Swordfish

Prep time: 10 minutes | Cook time: 6 to 11 minutes | Serves 4

4 (4-ounce / 113-g) swordfish steaks	ginger
½ teaspoon toasted sesame oil	½ teaspoon Chinese five-spice powder
1 jalapeño pepper, finely minced	⅛ teaspoon freshly ground black pepper
2 garlic cloves, grated	2 tablespoons freshly squeezed lemon juice
1 tablespoon grated fresh	

1. Place the swordfish steaks on a work surface and drizzle with the sesame oil. 2. In a small bowl, mix the jalapeño, garlic, ginger, five-spice powder, pepper, and lemon juice. Rub this mixture into the fish and let it stand for 10 minutes. 3. Roast the swordfish in the air fryer at 380ºF (193ºC) for 6 to 11 minutes, or until the swordfish reaches an internal temperature of at least 140ºF (60ºC) on a meat thermometer. Serve immediately.

Southern-Style Catfish

Prep time: 10 minutes | Cook time: 12 minutes | Serves 4

4 (7-ounce / 198-g) catfish fillets	2 teaspoons Old Bay seasoning
⅓ cup heavy whipping cream	½ teaspoon salt
1 tablespoon lemon juice	¼ teaspoon ground black pepper
1 cup blanched finely ground almond flour	

1. Place catfish fillets into a large bowl with cream and pour in lemon juice. Stir to coat. 2. In a separate large bowl, mix flour and Old Bay seasoning. 3. Remove each fillet and gently shake off excess cream. Sprinkle with salt and pepper. Press each fillet gently into flour mixture on both sides to coat. 4. Place fillets into ungreased air fryer basket. Adjust the temperature to 400ºF (204ºC) and air fry for 12 minutes, turning fillets halfway through cooking. Catfish will be golden brown and have an internal temperature of at least 145ºF (63ºC) when done. Serve warm.

Tuna Melt

Prep time: 3 minutes | Cook time: 10 minutes | Serves 1

Oil, for spraying
½ (5-ounce / 142-g) can tuna, drained
1 tablespoon mayonnaise
¼ teaspoon granulated garlic,

plus more for garnish
2 teaspoons unsalted butter
2 slices sandwich bread
2 slices Cheddar cheese

1. Line the air fryer basket with parchment and spray lightly with oil. 2. In a medium bowl, mix together the tuna, mayonnaise, and garlic. 3. Spread 1 teaspoon of butter on each slice of bread and place one slice butter-side down in the prepared basket. 4. Top with a slice of cheese, the tuna mixture, another slice of cheese, and the other slice of bread, butter-side up. 5. Air fry at 400ºF (204ºC) for 5 minutes, flip, and cook for another 5 minutes, until browned and crispy. 6. Sprinkle with additional garlic before cutting in half and serving.

Paprika Crab Burgers

Prep time: 30 minutes | Cook time: 14 minutes | Serves 3

2 eggs, beaten
1 shallot, chopped
2 garlic cloves, crushed
1 tablespoon olive oil
1 teaspoon yellow mustard
1 teaspoon fresh cilantro, chopped

10 ounces (283 g) crab meat
1 teaspoon smoked paprika
½ teaspoon ground black pepper
Sea salt, to taste
¾ cup Parmesan cheese

1. In a mixing bowl, thoroughly combine the eggs, shallot, garlic, olive oil, mustard, cilantro, crab meat, paprika, black pepper, and salt. Mix until well combined. 2. Shape the mixture into 6 patties. Roll the crab patties over grated Parmesan cheese, coating well on all sides. Place in your refrigerator for 2 hours. 3. Spritz the crab patties with cooking oil on both sides. Cook in the preheated air fryer at 360ºF (182ºC) for 14 minutes. Serve on dinner rolls if desired. Bon appétit!

Cheesy Tuna Patties

Prep time: 5 minutes | Cook time: 17 to 18 minutes | Serves 4

Tuna Patties:
1 pound (454 g) canned tuna, drained
1 egg, whisked
2 tablespoons shallots, minced
1 garlic clove, minced
1 cup grated Romano cheese
Sea salt and ground black

pepper, to taste
1 tablespoon sesame oil
Cheese Sauce:
1 tablespoon butter
1 cup beer
2 tablespoons grated Colby cheese

1. Mix together the canned tuna, whisked egg, shallots, garlic, cheese, salt, and pepper in a large bowl and stir to incorporate. 2. Divide the tuna mixture into four equal portions and form each portion into a patty with your hands. Refrigerate the patties for 2 hours. 3. When ready, brush both sides of each patty with sesame oil. 4. Preheat the air fryer to 360ºF (182ºC). 5. Place the patties in the air fryer basket and bake for 14 minutes, flipping the patties halfway through, or until lightly browned and cooked through. 6. Meanwhile, melt the butter

in a pan over medium heat. 7. Pour in the beer and whisk constantly, or until it begins to bubble. 8. Add the grated Colby cheese and mix well. Continue cooking for 3 to 4 minutes, or until the cheese melts. Remove the patties from the basket to a plate. Drizzle them with the cheese sauce and serve immediately.

Herbed Shrimp Pita

Prep time: 5 minutes | Cook time: 8 minutes | Serves 4

1 pound (454 g) medium shrimp, peeled and deveined
2 tablespoons olive oil
1 teaspoon dried oregano
½ teaspoon dried thyme
½ teaspoon garlic powder
¼ teaspoon onion powder
½ teaspoon salt

¼ teaspoon black pepper
4 whole wheat pitas
4 ounces (113 g) feta cheese, crumbled
1 cup shredded lettuce
1 tomato, diced
¼ cup black olives, sliced
1 lemon

1. Preheat the oven to 380ºF (193ºC). 2. In a medium bowl, combine the shrimp with the olive oil, oregano, thyme, garlic powder, onion powder, salt, and black pepper. 3. Pour shrimp in a single layer in the air fryer basket and roast for 6 to 8 minutes, or until cooked through. 4. Remove from the air fryer and divide into warmed pitas with feta, lettuce, tomato, olives, and a squeeze of lemon.

Crab Cakes with Bell Peppers

Prep time: 5 minutes | Cook time: 10 minutes | Serves 4

8 ounces (227 g) jumbo lump crab meat
1 egg, beaten
Juice of ½ lemon
⅓ cup bread crumbs
¼ cup diced green bell pepper

¼ cup diced red bell pepper
¼ cup mayonnaise
1 tablespoon Old Bay seasoning
1 teaspoon flour
Cooking spray

1. Preheat the air fryer to 375ºF (190ºC). 2. Make the crab cakes: Place all the ingredients except the flour and oil in a large bowl and stir until well incorporated. 3. Divide the crab mixture into four equal portions and shape each portion into a patty with your hands. Top each patty with a sprinkle of ¼ teaspoon of flour. 4. Arrange the crab cakes in the air fryer basket and spritz them with cooking spray. 5. Air fry for 10 minutes, flipping the crab cakes halfway through, or until they are cooked through. 6. Divide the crab cakes among four plates and serve.

Shrimp with Swiss Chard

Prep time: 10 minutes | Cook time: 10 minutes | Serves 4

1 pound (454 g) shrimp, peeled and deveined
½ teaspoon smoked paprika
½ cup Swiss chard, chopped

2 tablespoons apple cider vinegar
1 tablespoon coconut oil
¼ cup heavy cream

1. Mix shrimps with smoked paprika and apple cider vinegar. 2. Put the shrimps in the air fryer and add coconut oil. 3. Cook the shrimps at 350ºF (177ºC) for 10 minutes. 4. Then mix cooked shrimps with remaining ingredients and carefully mix.

Mustard-Crusted Fish Fillets

Prep time: 5 minutes | Cook time: 8 to 11 minutes | Serves 4

5 teaspoons low-sodium yellow mustard
1 tablespoon freshly squeezed lemon juice
4 (3½-ounce / 99-g) sole fillets
½ teaspoon dried thyme

½ teaspoon dried marjoram
⅛ teaspoon freshly ground black pepper
1 slice low-sodium whole-wheat bread, crumbled
2 teaspoons olive oil

1. In a small bowl, mix the mustard and lemon juice. Spread this evenly over the fillets. Place them in the air fryer basket. 2. In another small bowl, mix the thyme, marjoram, pepper, bread crumbs, and olive oil. Mix until combined. 3. Gently but firmly press the spice mixture onto the top of each fish fillet. 4. Bake at 320ºF (160ºC) for 8 to 11 minutes, or until the fish reaches an internal temperature of at least 145ºF (63ºC) on a meat thermometer and the topping is browned and crisp. Serve immediately.

Crab and Bell Pepper Cakes

Prep time: 5 minutes | Cook time: 10 minutes | Serves 4

8 ounces (227 g) jumbo lump crabmeat
1 tablespoon Old Bay seasoning
⅓ cup bread crumbs
¼ cup diced red bell pepper

¼ cup diced green bell pepper
1 egg
¼ cup mayonnaise
Juice of ½ lemon
1 teaspoon all-purpose flour
Cooking oil spray

1. Sort through the crabmeat, picking out any bits of shell or cartilage. 2. In a large bowl, stir together the Old Bay seasoning, bread crumbs, red and green bell peppers, egg, mayonnaise, and lemon juice. Gently stir in the crabmeat. 3. Insert the crisper plate into the basket and the basket into the unit. Preheat the unit by selecting AIR FRY, setting the temperature to 375ºF (191ºC), and setting the time to 3 minutes. Select START/STOP to begin. 4. Form the mixture into 4 patties. Sprinkle ¼ teaspoon of flour on top of each patty. 5. Once the unit is preheated, spray the crisper plate with cooking oil. Place the crab cakes into the basket and spray them with cooking oil. 6. Select AIR FRY, set the temperature to 375ºF (191ºC), and set the time to 10 minutes. Select START/STOP to begin. 7. When the cooking is complete, the crab cakes will be golden brown and firm.

BBQ Shrimp with Creole Butter Sauce

Prep time: 10 minutes | Cook time: 12 to 15 minutes | Serves 4

6 tablespoons unsalted butter
⅓ cup Worcestershire sauce
3 cloves garlic, minced
Juice of 1 lemon
1 teaspoon paprika

1 teaspoon Creole seasoning
1½ pounds (680 g) large uncooked shrimp, peeled and deveined
2 tablespoons fresh parsley

1. Preheat the air fryer to 370ºF (188ºC). 2. In a large microwave-safe bowl, combine the butter, Worcestershire, and garlic. Microwave on high for 1 to 2 minutes until the butter is melted. Stir in the lemon juice, paprika, and Creole seasoning. Add the shrimp and toss until thoroughly coated. 3. Transfer the mixture to a casserole dish or pan that fits in your air fryer. Pausing halfway through the cooking time to turn the shrimp, air fry for 12 to 15 minutes, until the shrimp are cooked through. Top with the parsley just before serving.

Tuna Patty Sliders

Prep time: 15 minutes | Cook time: 10 to 15 minutes | Serves 4

3 (5-ounce / 142-g) cans tuna, packed in water
⅔ cup whole-wheat panko bread crumbs
⅓ cup shredded Parmesan

cheese
1 tablespoon sriracha
¾ teaspoon black pepper
10 whole-wheat slider buns
Cooking spray

1. Preheat the air fryer to 350ºF (177ºC). 2. Spray the air fryer basket lightly with cooking spray. 3. In a medium bowl combine the tuna, bread crumbs, Parmesan cheese, sriracha, and black pepper and stir to combine. 4. Form the mixture into 10 patties. 5. Place the patties in the air fryer basket in a single layer. Spray the patties lightly with cooking spray. You may need to cook them in batches. 6. Air fry for 6 to 8 minutes. Turn the patties over and lightly spray with cooking spray. Air fry until golden brown and crisp, another 4 to 7 more minutes. Serve warm.

Bacon Halibut Steak

Prep time: 15 minutes | Cook time: 10 minutes | Serves 4

24 ounces (680 g) halibut steaks (6 ounces / 170 g each fillet)
1 teaspoon avocado oil

1 teaspoon ground black pepper
4 ounces bacon, sliced

1. Sprinkle the halibut steaks with avocado oil and ground black pepper. 2. Then wrap the fish in the bacon slices and put in the air fryer. 3. Cook the fish at 390ºF (199ºC) for 5 minutes per side.

Baked Monkfish

Prep time: 20 minutes | Cook time: 12 minutes | Serves 2

2 teaspoons olive oil
1 cup celery, sliced
2 bell peppers, sliced
1 teaspoon dried thyme
½ teaspoon dried marjoram
½ teaspoon dried rosemary
2 monkfish fillets

1 tablespoon coconut aminos
2 tablespoons lime juice
Coarse salt and ground black pepper, to taste
1 teaspoon cayenne pepper
½ cup Kalamata olives, pitted and sliced

1. In a nonstick skillet, heat the olive oil for 1 minute. Once hot, sauté the celery and peppers until tender, about 4 minutes. Sprinkle with thyme, marjoram, and rosemary and set aside. 2. Toss the fish fillets with the coconut aminos, lime juice, salt, black pepper, and cayenne pepper. Place the fish fillets in the lightly greased air fryer basket and bake at 390ºF (199ºC) for 8 minutes. 3. Turn them over, add the olives, and cook an additional 4 minutes. Serve with the sautéed vegetables on the side. Bon appétit!

Balsamic Tilapia

Prep time: 5 minutes | Cook time: 15 minutes | Serves 4

4 tilapia fillets, boneless	1 teaspoon avocado oil
2 tablespoons balsamic vinegar	1 teaspoon dried basil

1. Sprinkle the tilapia fillets with balsamic vinegar, avocado oil, and dried basil. 2. Then put the fillets in the air fryer basket and cook at 365ºF (185ºC) for 15 minutes.

Orange-Mustard Glazed Salmon

Prep time: 10 minutes | Cook time: 10 minutes | Serves 2

1 tablespoon orange marmalade	mustard
¼ teaspoon grated orange zest plus 1 tablespoon juice	2 (8-ounce / 227 -g) skin-on salmon fillets, 1½ inches thick
2 teaspoons whole-grain	Salt and pepper, to taste
	Vegetable oil spray

1. Preheat the air fryer to 400ºF (204ºC). 2. Make foil sling for air fryer basket by folding 1 long sheet of aluminum foil so it is 4 inches wide. Lay sheet of foil widthwise across basket, pressing foil into and up sides of basket. Fold excess foil as needed so that edges of foil are flush with top of basket. Lightly spray foil and basket with vegetable oil spray. 3. Combine marmalade, orange zest and juice, and mustard in bowl. Pat salmon dry with paper towels and season with salt and pepper. Brush tops and sides of fillets evenly with glaze. Arrange fillets skin side down on sling in prepared basket, spaced evenly apart. Air fry salmon until center is still translucent when checked with the tip of a paring knife and registers 125ºF (52ºC) (for medium-rare), 10 to 14 minutes, using sling to rotate fillets halfway through cooking. 4. Using the sling, carefully remove salmon from air fryer. Slide fish spatula along underside of fillets and transfer to individual serving plates, leaving skin behind. Serve.

Pecan-Crusted Catfish

Prep time: 5 minutes | Cook time: 12 minutes | Serves 4

½ cup pecan meal	fillets
1 teaspoon fine sea salt	For Garnish (Optional):
¼ teaspoon ground black pepper	Fresh oregano
	Pecan halves
4 (4-ounce / 113-g) catfish	

1. Spray the air fryer basket with avocado oil. Preheat the air fryer to 375ºF (191ºC). 2. In a large bowl, mix the pecan meal, salt, and pepper. One at a time, dredge the catfish fillets in the mixture, coating them well. Use your hands to press the pecan meal into the fillets. Spray the fish with avocado oil and place them in the air fryer basket. 3. Air fry the coated catfish for 12 minutes, or until it flakes easily and is no longer translucent in the center, flipping halfway through. 4. Garnish with oregano sprigs and pecan halves, if desired. 5. Store leftovers in an airtight container in the fridge for up to 3 days. Reheat in a preheated 350ºF (177ºC) air fryer for 4 minutes, or until heated through.

Tilapia Sandwiches with Tartar Sauce

Prep time: 8 minutes | Cook time: 17 minutes | Serves 4

¾ cup mayonnaise	⅓ cup all-purpose flour
2 tablespoons dried minced onion	1 egg, lightly beaten
1 dill pickle spear, finely chopped	1¾ cups panko bread crumbs
2 teaspoons pickle juice	2 teaspoons lemon pepper
¼ teaspoon salt	4 (6-ounce / 170-g) tilapia fillets
⅛ teaspoon freshly ground black pepper	Olive oil spray
	4 hoagie rolls
	4 butter lettuce leaves

1. To make the tartar sauce, in a small bowl, whisk the mayonnaise, dried onion, pickle, pickle juice, salt, and pepper until blended. Refrigerate while you make the fish. 2. Scoop the flour onto a plate; set aside. 3. Put the beaten egg in a medium shallow bowl. 4. On another plate, stir together the panko and lemon pepper. 5. Insert the crisper plate into the basket and the basket into the unit. Preheat the unit by selecting AIR FRY, setting the temperature to 400ºF (204ºC), and setting the time to 3 minutes. Select START/STOP to begin. 6. Dredge the tilapia fillets in the flour, in the egg, and press into the panko mixture to coat. 7. Once the unit is preheated, spray the crisper plate with olive oil and place a parchment paper liner into the basket. Place the prepared fillets on the liner in a single layer. Lightly spray the fillets with olive oil. 8. Select AIR FRY, set the temperature to 400ºF (204ºC), and set the time to 17 minutes. Select START/STOP to begin. 9. After 8 minutes, remove the basket, carefully flip the fillets, and spray them with more olive oil. Reinsert the basket to resume cooking. 10. When the cooking is complete, the fillets should be golden and crispy and a food thermometer should register 145ºF (63ºC). Place each cooked fillet in a hoagie roll, top with a little bit of tartar sauce and lettuce, and serve.

Cod with Avocado

Prep time: 30 minutes | Cook time: 10 minutes | Serves 2

1 cup shredded cabbage	1 teaspoon chili powder
¼ cup full-fat sour cream	1 teaspoon cumin
2 tablespoons full-fat mayonnaise	½ teaspoon paprika
¼ cup chopped pickled jalapeños	¼ teaspoon garlic powder
2 (3-ounce / 85-g) cod fillets	1 medium avocado, peeled, pitted, and sliced
	½ medium lime

1. In a large bowl, place cabbage, sour cream, mayonnaise, and jalapeños. Mix until fully coated. Let sit for 20 minutes in the refrigerator. 2. Sprinkle cod fillets with chili powder, cumin, paprika, and garlic powder. Place each fillet into the air fryer basket. 3. Adjust the temperature to 370ºF (188ºC) and set the timer for 10 minutes. 4. Flip the fillets halfway through the cooking time. When fully cooked, fish should have an internal temperature of at least 145ºF (63ºC). 5. To serve, divide slaw mixture into two serving bowls, break cod fillets into pieces and spread over the bowls, and top with avocado. Squeeze lime juice over each bowl. Serve immediately.

Garlic Shrimp

Prep time: 15 minutes | Cook time: 10 minutes | Serves 3

Shrimp:
Oil, for spraying
1 pound (454 g) medium raw shrimp, peeled and deveined
6 tablespoons unsalted butter, melted
1 cup panko bread crumbs
2 tablespoons granulated garlic

1 teaspoon salt
½ teaspoon freshly ground black pepper
Garlic Butter Sauce:
½ cup unsalted butter
2 teaspoons granulated garlic
¾ teaspoon salt (omit if using salted butter)

Make the Shrimp 1. Preheat the air fryer to 400ºF (204ºC). Line the air fryer basket with parchment and spray lightly with oil. 2. Place the shrimp and melted butter in a zip-top plastic bag, seal, and shake well, until evenly coated. 3. In a medium bowl, mix together the bread crumbs, garlic, salt, and black pepper. 4. Add the shrimp to the panko mixture and toss until evenly coated. Shake off any excess coating. 5. Place the shrimp in the prepared basket and spray lightly with oil. 6. Cook for 8 to 10 minutes, flipping and spraying with oil after 4 to 5 minutes, until golden brown and crispy. Make the Garlic Butter Sauce 7. In a microwave-safe bowl, combine the butter, garlic, and salt and microwave on 50% power for 30 to 60 seconds, stirring every 15 seconds, until completely melted. 8. Serve the shrimp immediately with the garlic butter sauce on the side for dipping.

Breaded Shrimp Tacos

Prep time: 10 minutes | Cook time: 9 minutes | Makes 8 tacos

2 large eggs
1 teaspoon prepared yellow mustard
1 pound (454 g) small shrimp, peeled, deveined, and tails removed
½ cup finely shredded Gouda or Parmesan cheese

½ cup pork dust
For Serving:
8 large Boston lettuce leaves
¼ cup pico de gallo
¼ cup shredded purple cabbage
1 lemon, sliced
Guacamole (optional)

1. Preheat the air fryer to 400ºF (204ºC). 2. Crack the eggs into a large bowl, add the mustard, and whisk until well combined. Add the shrimp and stir well to coat. 3. In a medium-sized bowl, mix together the cheese and pork dust until well combined. 4. One at a time, roll the coated shrimp in the pork dust mixture and use your hands to press it onto each shrimp. Spray the coated shrimp with avocado oil and place them in the air fryer basket, leaving space between them. 5. Air fry the shrimp for 9 minutes, or until cooked through and no longer translucent, flipping after 4 minutes. 6. To serve, place a lettuce leaf on a serving plate, place several shrimp on top, and top with 1½ teaspoons each of pico de gallo and purple cabbage. Squeeze some lemon juice on top and serve with guacamole, if desired. 7. Store leftover shrimp in an airtight container in the refrigerator for up to 3 days. Reheat in a preheated 400ºF (204ºC) air fryer for 5 minutes, or until warmed through.

Parmesan-Crusted Halibut Fillets

Prep time: 5 minutes | Cook time: 10 minutes | Serves 4

2 medium-sized halibut fillets
Dash of tabasco sauce
1 teaspoon curry powder
½ teaspoon ground coriander
½ teaspoon hot paprika
Kosher salt and freshly

cracked mixed peppercorns, to taste
2 eggs
1½ tablespoons olive oil
½ cup grated Parmesan cheese

1. Preheat the air fryer to 365ºF (185ºC). 2. On a clean work surface, drizzle the halibut fillets with the tabasco sauce. Sprinkle with the curry powder, coriander, hot paprika, salt, and cracked mixed peppercorns. Set aside. 3. In a shallow bowl, beat the eggs until frothy. In another shallow bowl, combine the olive oil and Parmesan cheese. 4. One at a time, dredge the halibut fillets in the beaten eggs, shaking off any excess, then roll them over the Parmesan cheese until evenly coated. 5. Arrange the halibut fillets in the air fryer basket in a single layer and air fry for 10 minutes, or until the fish is golden brown and crisp. 6. Cool for 5 minutes before serving.

Mouthwatering Cod over Creamy Leek Noodles

Prep time: 10 minutes | Cook time: 24 minutes | Serves 4

1 small leek, sliced into long thin noodles (about 2 cups)
½ cup heavy cream
2 cloves garlic, minced
1 teaspoon fine sea salt, divided
4 (4-ounce / 113-g) cod fillets (about 1 inch thick)
½ teaspoon ground black pepper

Coating:
¼ cup grated Parmesan cheese
2 tablespoons mayonnaise
2 tablespoons unsalted butter, softened
1 tablespoon chopped fresh thyme, or ½ teaspoon dried thyme leaves, plus more for garnish

1. Preheat the air fryer to 350ºF (177ºC). 2. Place the leek noodles in a casserole dish or a pan that will fit in your air fryer. 3. In a small bowl, stir together the cream, garlic, and ½ teaspoon of the salt. Pour the mixture over the leeks and cook in the air fryer for 10 minutes, or until the leeks are very tender. 4. Pat the fish dry and season with the remaining ½ teaspoon of salt and the pepper. When the leeks are ready, open the air fryer and place the fish fillets on top of the leeks. Air fry for 8 to 10 minutes, until the fish flakes easily with a fork (the thicker the fillets, the longer this will take). 5. While the fish cooks, make the coating: In a small bowl, combine the Parmesan, mayo, butter, and thyme. 6. When the fish is ready, remove it from the air fryer and increase the heat to 425ºF (218ºC) (or as high as your air fryer can go). Spread the fillets with a ½-inch-thick to ¾-inch-thick layer of the coating. 7. Place the fish back in the air fryer and air fry for 3 to 4 minutes, until the coating browns. 8. Garnish with fresh or dried thyme, if desired. Store leftovers in an airtight container in the refrigerator for up to 3 days. Reheat in a casserole dish in a preheated 350ºF (177ºC) air fryer for 6 minutes, or until heated through.

Chapter **5**

Poultry

Lettuce-Wrapped Turkey and Mushroom Meatballs

Prep time: 10 minutes | Cook time: 15 minutes | Serves 6

Sauce:
2 tablespoons tamari
2 tablespoons tomato sauce
1 tablespoon lime juice
¼ teaspoon peeled and grated fresh ginger
1 clove garlic, smashed to a paste
½ cup chicken broth
⅓ cup sugar
2 tablespoons toasted sesame oil
Cooking spray
Meatballs:
2 pounds (907 g) ground turkey
¾ cup finely chopped button

mushrooms
2 large eggs, beaten
1½ teaspoons tamari
¼ cup finely chopped green onions, plus more for garnish
2 teaspoons peeled and grated fresh ginger
1 clove garlic, smashed
2 teaspoons toasted sesame oil
2 tablespoons sugar
For Serving:
Lettuce leaves, for serving
Sliced red chiles, for garnish (optional)
Toasted sesame seeds, for garnish (optional)

1. Preheat the air fryer to 350°F (177°C). Spritz a baking pan with cooking spray. 2. Combine the ingredients for the sauce in a small bowl. Stir to mix well. Set aside. 3. Combine the ingredients for the meatballs in a large bowl. Stir to mix well, then shape the mixture in twelve 1½-inch meatballs. 4. Arrange the meatballs in a single layer on the baking pan, then baste with the sauce. You may need to work in batches to avoid overcrowding. 5. Arrange the pan in the air fryer. Air fry for 15 minutes or until the meatballs are golden brown. Flip the balls halfway through the cooking time. 6. Unfold the lettuce leaves on a large serving plate, then transfer the cooked meatballs on the leaves. Spread the red chiles and sesame seeds over the balls, then serve.

Coconut Chicken Meatballs

Prep time: 10 minutes | Cook time: 14 minutes | Serves 4

1 pound (454 g) ground chicken
2 scallions, finely chopped
1 cup chopped fresh cilantro leaves
¼ cup unsweetened shredded coconut

1 tablespoon hoisin sauce
1 tablespoon soy sauce
2 teaspoons Sriracha or other hot sauce
1 teaspoon toasted sesame oil
½ teaspoon kosher salt
1 teaspoon black pepper

1. In a large bowl, gently mix the chicken, scallions, cilantro, coconut, hoisin, soy sauce, Sriracha, sesame oil, salt, and pepper until thoroughly combined (the mixture will be wet and sticky). 2. Place a sheet of parchment paper in the air fryer basket. Using a small scoop or teaspoon, drop rounds of the mixture in a single layer onto the parchment paper. 3. Set the air fryer to 350°F (177°C) for 10 minutes, turning the meatballs halfway through the cooking time. Raise the air fryer temperature to 400°F (204°C) and cook for 4 minutes more to brown the outsides of the meatballs. Use a meat thermometer to ensure the meatballs have reached an internal temperature of 165°F (74°C). 4. Transfer the meatballs to a serving platter. Repeat with any remaining chicken mixture.

Peanut Butter Chicken Satay

Prep time: 12 minutes | Cook time: 12 to 18 minutes | Serves 4

½ cup crunchy peanut butter
⅓ cup chicken broth
3 tablespoons low-sodium soy sauce
2 tablespoons freshly squeezed lemon juice
2 garlic cloves, minced

2 tablespoons extra-virgin olive oil
1 teaspoon curry powder
1 pound (454 g) chicken tenders
Cooking oil spray

1. In a medium bowl, whisk the peanut butter, broth, soy sauce, lemon juice, garlic, olive oil, and curry powder until smooth. 2. Place 2 tablespoons of this mixture into a small bowl. Transfer the remaining sauce to a serving bowl and set aside. 3. Add the chicken tenders to the bowl with the 2 tablespoons of sauce and stir to coat. Let stand for a few minutes to marinate. 4. Insert the crisper plate into the basket and the basket into the unit. Preheat the unit by selecting AIR FRY, setting the temperature to 390°F (199°C), and setting the time to 3 minutes. Select START/STOP to begin. 5. Run a 6-inch bamboo skewer lengthwise through each chicken tender. 6. Once the unit is preheated, spray the crisper plate with cooking oil. Working in batches, place half the chicken skewers into the basket in a single layer without overlapping. 7. Select AIR FRY, set the temperature to 390°F (199°C), and set the time to 9 minutes. Select START/STOP to begin. 8. After 6 minutes, check the chicken. If a food thermometer inserted into the chicken registers 165°F (74°C), it is done. If not, resume cooking. 9. Repeat steps 6, 7, and 8 with the remaining chicken. 10. When the cooking is complete, serve the chicken with the reserved sauce.

South Indian Pepper Chicken

Prep time: 30 minutes | Cook time: 15 minutes | Serves 4

Spice Mix:
1 dried red chile, or ½ teaspoon dried red pepper flakes
1-inch piece cinnamon or cassia bark
1½ teaspoons coriander seeds
1 teaspoon fennel seeds
1 teaspoon cumin seeds
1 teaspoon black peppercorns
½ teaspoon cardamom seeds

¼ teaspoon ground turmeric
1 teaspoon kosher salt
Chicken:
1 pound (454 g) boneless, skinless chicken thighs, cut crosswise into thirds
2 medium onions, cut into ½-inch-thick slices
¼ cup olive oil
Cauliflower rice, steamed rice, or naan bread, for serving

1. For the spice mix: Combine the dried chile, cinnamon, coriander, fennel, cumin, peppercorns, and cardamom in a clean coffee or spice grinder. Grind, shaking the grinder lightly so all the seeds and bits get into the blades, until the mixture is broken down to a fine powder. Stir in the turmeric and salt. 2. For the chicken: Place the chicken and onions in resealable plastic bag. Add the oil and 1½ tablespoons of the spice mix. Seal the bag and massage until the chicken is well coated. Marinate at room temperature for 30 minutes or in the refrigerator for up to 24 hours. 3. Place the chicken and onions in the air fryer basket. Set the air fryer to 350°F (177°C) for 10 minutes, stirring once halfway through the cooking time. Increase the temperature to 400°F (204°C) for 5 minutes. Use a meat thermometer to ensure the chicken has reached an internal temperature of 165°F (74°C). 4. Serve with steamed rice, cauliflower rice, or naan.

Chicken Thighs with Cilantro

Prep time: 15 minutes | Cook time: 25 minutes | Serves 4

1 tablespoon olive oil	8 bone-in chicken thighs, skin
Juice of ½ lime	on
1 tablespoon coconut aminos	2 tablespoons chopped fresh
1½ teaspoons Montreal	cilantro
chicken seasoning	

1. In a gallon-size resealable bag, combine the olive oil, lime juice, coconut aminos, and chicken seasoning. Add the chicken thighs, seal the bag, and massage the bag to ensure the chicken is thoroughly coated. Refrigerate for at least 2 hours, preferably overnight. 2. Preheat the air fryer to 400ºF (204ºC). 3. Remove the chicken from the marinade (discard the marinade) and arrange in a single layer in the air fryer basket. Pausing halfway through the cooking time to flip the chicken, air fry for 20 to 25 minutes, until a thermometer inserted into the thickest part registers 165ºF (74ºC). 4. Transfer the chicken to a serving platter and top with the cilantro before serving.

Spicy Chicken Thighs and Gold Potatoes

Prep time: 5 minutes | Cook time: 25 minutes | Serves 4

4 bone-in, skin-on chicken	leaves
thighs	½ teaspoon dry mustard
½ teaspoon kosher salt or ¼	½ teaspoon granulated garlic
teaspoon fine salt	¼ teaspoon paprika
2 tablespoons melted unsalted	¼ teaspoon hot pepper sauce
butter	Cooking oil spray
2 teaspoons Worcestershire	4 medium Yukon gold
sauce	potatoes, chopped
2 teaspoons curry powder	1 tablespoon extra-virgin olive
1 teaspoon dried oregano	oil

1. Sprinkle the chicken thighs on both sides with salt. 2. In a medium bowl, stir together the melted butter, Worcestershire sauce, curry powder, oregano, dry mustard, granulated garlic, paprika, and hot pepper sauce. Add the thighs to the sauce and stir to coat. 3. Insert the crisper plate into the basket and the basket into the unit. Preheat the unit by selecting AIR FRY, setting the temperature to 400ºF (204ºC), and setting the time to 3 minutes. Select START/STOP to begin. 4. Once the unit is preheated, spray the crisper plate with cooking oil. In the basket, combine the potatoes and olive oil and toss to coat. 5. Add the wire rack to the air fryer and place the chicken thighs on top. 6. Select AIR FRY, set the temperature to 400ºF (204ºC), and set the time to 25 minutes. Select START/STOP to begin. 7. After 19 minutes check the chicken thighs. If a food thermometer inserted into the chicken registers 165ºF (74ºC), transfer them to a clean plate, and cover with aluminum foil to keep warm. If they aren't cooked to 165ºF (74ºC), resume cooking for another 1 to 2 minutes until they are done. Remove them from the unit along with the rack. 8. Remove the basket and shake it to distribute the potatoes. Reinsert the basket to resume cooking for 3 to 6 minutes, or until the potatoes are crisp and golden brown. 9. When the cooking is complete, serve the chicken with the potatoes.

Piri-Piri Chicken Thighs

Prep time: 5 minutes | Cook time: 25 minutes | Serves 4

¼ cup piri-piri sauce	oil
1 tablespoon freshly squeezed	4 bone-in, skin-on chicken
lemon juice	thighs, each weighing
2 tablespoons brown sugar,	approximately 7 to 8 ounces
divided	(198 to 227 g)
2 cloves garlic, minced	½ teaspoon cornstarch
1 tablespoon extra-virgin olive	

1. To make the marinade, whisk together the piri-piri sauce, lemon juice, 1 tablespoon of brown sugar, and the garlic in a small bowl. While whisking, slowly pour in the oil in a steady stream and continue to whisk until emulsified. Using a skewer, poke holes in the chicken thighs and place them in a small glass dish. Pour the marinade over the chicken and turn the thighs to coat them with the sauce. Cover the dish and refrigerate for at least 15 minutes and up to 1 hour. 2. Preheat the air fryer to 375ºF (191ºC). Remove the chicken thighs from the dish, reserving the marinade, and place them skin-side down in the air fryer basket. Air fry until the internal temperature reaches 165ºF (74ºC), 15 to 20 minutes. 3. Meanwhile, whisk the remaining brown sugar and the cornstarch into the marinade and microwave it on high power for 1 minute until it is bubbling and thickened to a glaze. 4. Once the chicken is cooked, turn the thighs over and brush them with the glaze. Air fry for a few additional minutes until the glaze browns and begins to char in spots. 5. Remove the chicken to a platter and serve with additional piri-piri sauce, if desired.

Israeli Chicken Schnitzel

Prep time: 5 minutes | Cook time: 10 minutes | Serves 4

2 large boneless, skinless	1 teaspoon black pepper
chicken breasts, each	1 teaspoon paprika
weighing about 1 pound (454	2 eggs beaten with 2
g)	tablespoons water
1 cup all-purpose flour	2 cups panko bread crumbs
2 teaspoons garlic powder	Vegetable oil spray
2 teaspoons kosher salt	Lemon juice, for serving

1. Preheat the air fryer to 375ºF (191ºC). 2. Place 1 chicken breast between 2 pieces of plastic wrap. Use a mallet or a rolling pin to pound the chicken until it is ¼ inch thick. Set aside. Repeat with the second breast. Whisk together the flour, garlic powder, salt, pepper, and paprika on a large plate. Place the panko in a separate shallow bowl or pie plate. 3. Dredge 1 chicken breast in the flour, shaking off any excess, then dip it in the egg mixture. Dredge the chicken breast in the panko, making sure to coat it completely. Shake off any excess panko. Place the battered chicken breast on a plate. Repeat with the second chicken breast. 4. Spray the air fryer basket with oil spray. Place 1 of the battered chicken breasts in the basket and spray the top with oil spray. Air fry until the top is browned, about 5 minutes. Flip the chicken and spray the second side with oil spray. Air fry until the second side is browned and crispy and the internal temperature reaches 165ºF (74ºC). Remove the first chicken breast from the air fryer and repeat with the second chicken breast. 5. Serve hot with lemon juice.

Bacon Lovers' Stuffed Chicken

Prep time: 10 minutes | Cook time: 20 minutes | Serves 4

4 (5-ounce / 142-g) boneless, skinless chicken breasts, pounded to ¼ inch thick	cheese style spread, softened, for dairy-free)
2 (5.2-ounce / 147-g) packages Boursin cheese (or Kite Hill brand chive cream	8 slices thin-cut bacon or beef bacon
	Sprig of fresh cilantro, for garnish (optional)

1. Spray the air fryer basket with avocado oil. Preheat the air fryer to 400ºF (204ºC). 2. Place one of the chicken breasts on a cutting board. With a sharp knife held parallel to the cutting board, make a 1-inch-wide incision at the top of the breast. Carefully cut into the breast to form a large pocket, leaving a ½-inch border along the sides and bottom. Repeat with the other 3 chicken breasts. 3. Snip the corner of a large resealable plastic bag to form a ¾-inch hole. Place the Boursin cheese in the bag and pipe the cheese into the pockets in the chicken breasts, dividing the cheese evenly among them. 4. Wrap 2 slices of bacon around each chicken breast and secure the ends with toothpicks. Place the bacon-wrapped chicken in the air fryer basket and air fry until the bacon is crisp and the chicken's internal temperature reaches 165ºF (74ºC), about 18 to 20 minutes, flipping after 10 minutes. Garnish with a sprig of cilantro before serving, if desired. 5. Store leftovers in an airtight container in the refrigerator for up to 4 days. Reheat in a preheated 400ºF (204ºC) air fryer for 5 minutes, or until warmed through.

Pickle Brined Fried Chicken

Prep time: 30 minutes | Cook time: 47 minutes | Serves 4

4 bone-in, skin-on chicken legs, cut into drumsticks and thighs (about 3½ pounds / 1.6 kg)	2 eggs
	1 cup fine bread crumbs
Pickle juice from 1 (24-ounce / 680-g) jar kosher dill pickles	1 teaspoon salt
	1 teaspoon freshly ground black pepper
½ cup flour	½ teaspoon ground paprika
Salt and freshly ground black pepper, to taste	⅛ teaspoon ground cayenne pepper
	Vegetable or canola oil

1. Place the chicken in a shallow dish and pour the pickle juice over the top. Cover and transfer the chicken to the refrigerator to brine in the pickle juice for 3 to 8 hours. 2. When you are ready to cook, remove the chicken from the refrigerator to let it come to room temperature while you set up a dredging station. Place the flour in a shallow dish and season well with salt and freshly ground black pepper. Whisk the eggs in a second shallow dish. In a third shallow dish, combine the bread crumbs, salt, pepper, paprika and cayenne pepper. 3. Preheat the air fryer to 370ºF (188ºC). 4. Remove the chicken from the pickle brine and gently dry it with a clean kitchen towel. Dredge each piece of chicken in the flour, then dip it into the egg mixture, and finally press it into the bread crumb mixture to coat all sides of the chicken. Place the breaded chicken on a plate or baking sheet and spray each piece all over with vegetable oil. 5. Air fry the chicken in two batches. Place two chicken thighs and two drumsticks into the air fryer basket. Air fry for 10 minutes. Then, gently turn the chicken pieces over and air fry for another 10 minutes. Remove the chicken pieces and let them rest on plate, do not cover. Repeat with the second batch of chicken,

air frying for 20 minutes, turning the chicken over halfway through. 6. Lower the temperature of the air fryer to 340ºF (171ºC). Place the first batch of chicken on top of the second batch already in the basket and air fry for an additional 7 minutes. Serve warm and enjoy.

Easy Chicken Fingers

Prep time: 20 minutes | Cook time: 30 minutes | Makes 12 chicken fingers

½ cup all-purpose flour	chicken breasts, each cut into 4 strips
2 cups panko breadcrumbs	
2 tablespoons canola oil	Kosher salt and freshly ground black pepper, to taste
1 large egg	
3 boneless and skinless	Cooking spray

1. Preheat the air fryer to 360ºF (182ºC). Spritz the air fryer basket with cooking spray. 2. Pour the flour in a large bowl. Combine the panko and canola oil on a shallow dish. Whisk the egg in a separate bowl. 3. Rub the chicken strips with salt and ground black pepper on a clean work surface, then dip the chicken in the bowl of flour. Shake the excess off and dunk the chicken strips in the bowl of whisked egg, then roll the strips over the panko to coat well. 4. Arrange 4 strips in the air fryer basket each time and air fry for 10 minutes or until crunchy and lightly browned. Flip the strips halfway through. Repeat with remaining ingredients. 5. Serve immediately.

Crispy Duck with Cherry Sauce

Prep time: 10 minutes | Cook time: 33 minutes | Serves 2 to 4

1 whole duck (up to 5 pounds / 2.3 kg), split in half, back and rib bones removed	1 shallot, minced
	½ cup sherry
	¾ cup cherry preserves
1 teaspoon olive oil	1 cup chicken stock
Salt and freshly ground black pepper, to taste	1 teaspoon white wine vinegar
	1 teaspoon fresh thyme leaves
Cherry Sauce:	Salt and freshly ground black pepper, to taste
1 tablespoon butter	

1. Preheat the air fryer to 400ºF (204ºC). 2. Trim some of the fat from the duck. Rub olive oil on the duck and season with salt and pepper. Place the duck halves in the air fryer basket, breast side up and facing the center of the basket. 3. Air fry the duck for 20 minutes. Turn the duck over and air fry for another 6 minutes. 4. While duck is air frying, make the cherry sauce. Melt the butter in a large sauté pan. Add the shallot and sauté until it is just starting to brown, about 2 to 3 minutes. Add the sherry and deglaze the pan by scraping up any brown bits from the bottom of the pan. Simmer the liquid for a few minutes, until it has reduced by half. Add the cherry preserves, chicken stock and white wine vinegar. Whisk well to combine all the ingredients. Simmer the sauce until it thickens and coats the back of a spoon, about 5 to 7 minutes. Season with salt and pepper and stir in the fresh thyme leaves. 5. When the air fryer timer goes off, spoon some cherry sauce over the duck and continue to air fry at 400ºF (204ºC) for 4 more minutes. Then, turn the duck halves back over so that the breast side is facing up. Spoon more cherry sauce over the top of the duck, covering the skin completely. Air fry for 3 more minutes and then remove the duck to a plate to rest for a few minutes. 6. Serve the duck in halves, or cut each piece in half again for a smaller serving. Spoon any additional sauce over the duck or serve it on the side.

Jalapeño Chicken Balls

Prep time: 10 minutes | Cook time: 25 minutes | Serves 4

1 medium red onion, minced	1 egg
2 garlic cloves, minced	1 teaspoon dried thyme
1 jalapeño pepper, minced	1 pound (454 g) ground
2 teaspoons extra-virgin olive	chicken breast
oil	Cooking oil spray
3 tablespoons ground almonds	

1. Insert the crisper plate into the basket and the basket into the unit. Preheat the unit by selecting BAKE, setting the temperature to 400°F (204°C), and setting the time to 3 minutes. Select START/STOP to begin. 2. In a 6-by-2-inch round pan, combine the red onion, garlic, jalapeño, and olive oil. 3. Once the unit is preheated, place the pan into the basket. 4. Select BAKE, set the temperature to 400°F (204°C), and set the time to 4 minutes. Select START/STOP to begin. 5. When the cooking is complete, the vegetables should be crisp-tender. Transfer to a medium bowl. 6. Mix the almonds, egg, and thyme into the vegetable mixture. Add the chicken and mix until just combined. Form the chicken mixture into about 24 (1-inch) balls. 7. Insert the crisper plate into the basket and the basket into the unit. Preheat the unit by selecting BAKE, setting the temperature to 400°F (204°C), and setting the time to 3 minutes. Select START/STOP to begin. 8. Once the unit is preheated, spray the crisper plate with cooking oil. Working in batches, place half the meatballs in a single layer, not touching, into the basket. 9. Select BAKE, set the temperature to 400°F (204°C), and set the time to 10 minutes. Select START/STOP to begin. 10. When the cooking is complete, a food thermometer inserted into the meatballs should register at least 165°F (74°C). 11. Repeat steps 8 and 9 with the remaining meatballs. Serve warm.

Buttermilk Breaded Chicken

Prep time: 7 minutes | Cook time: 20 to 25 minutes | Serves 4

1 cup all-purpose flour	2 tablespoons extra-virgin
2 teaspoons paprika	olive oil
Pinch salt	1½ cups bread crumbs
Freshly ground black pepper,	6 chicken pieces, drumsticks,
to taste	breasts, and thighs, patted dry
⅓ cup buttermilk	Cooking oil spray
2 eggs	

1. In a shallow bowl, stir together the flour, paprika, salt, and pepper. 2. In another bowl, beat the buttermilk and eggs until smooth. 3. In a third bowl, stir together the olive oil and bread crumbs until mixed. 4. Dredge the chicken in the flour, dip in the eggs to coat, and finally press into the bread crumbs, patting the crumbs firmly onto the chicken skin. 5. Insert the crisper plate into the basket and the basket into the unit. Preheat the unit by selecting AIR FRY, setting the temperature to 375°F (191°C), and setting the time to 3 minutes. Select START/STOP to begin. 6. Once the unit is preheated, spray the crisper plate with cooking oil. Place the chicken into the basket. 7. Select AIR FRY, set the temperature to 375°F (191°C), and set the time to 25 minutes. Select START/STOP to begin. 8. After 10 minutes, flip the chicken. Resume cooking. After 10 minutes more, check the chicken. If a food thermometer inserted into the chicken registers 165°F (74°C) and the chicken is brown and crisp, it is done. Otherwise, resume cooking for up to 5 minutes longer. 9. When the cooking is complete, let cool for 5 minutes, then serve.

Cheesy Pepperoni and Chicken Pizza

Prep time: 15 minutes | Cook time: 15 minutes | Serves 6

2 cups cooked chicken, cubed	1 cup shredded Mozzarella
1 cup pizza sauce	cheese
20 slices pepperoni	Cooking spray
¼ cup grated Parmesan cheese	

1. Preheat the air fryer to 375°F (191°C). Spritz a baking pan with cooking spray. 2. Arrange the chicken cubes in the prepared baking pan, then top the cubes with pizza sauce and pepperoni. Stir to coat the cubes and pepperoni with sauce. 3. Scatter the cheeses on top, then place the baking pan in the preheated air fryer. Air fryer for 15 minutes or until frothy and the cheeses melt. 4. Serve immediately.

Chicken with Lettuce

Prep time: 15 minutes | Cook time: 14 minutes | Serves 4

1 pound (454 g) chicken	and thinly sliced
breast tenders, chopped into	1 tablespoon olive oil
bite-size pieces	1 tablespoon fajita seasoning
½ onion, thinly sliced	1 teaspoon kosher salt
½ red bell pepper, seeded and	Juice of ½ lime
thinly sliced	8 large lettuce leaves
½ green bell pepper, seeded	1 cup prepared guacamole

1. Preheat the air fryer to 400°F (204°C). 2. In a large bowl, combine the chicken, onion, and peppers. Drizzle with the olive oil and toss until thoroughly coated. Add the fajita seasoning and salt and toss again. 3. Working in batches if necessary, arrange the chicken and vegetables in a single layer in the air fryer basket. Pausing halfway through the cooking time to shake the basket, air fry for 14 minutes, or until the vegetables are tender and a thermometer inserted into the thickest piece of chicken registers 165°F (74°C). 4. Transfer the mixture to a serving platter and drizzle with the fresh lime juice. Serve with the lettuce leaves and top with the guacamole.

Fajita Chicken Strips

Prep time: 10 minutes | Cook time: 15 minutes | Serves 4

1 pound (454 g) boneless,	1 onion, cut into chunks
skinless chicken tenderloins,	1 tablespoon olive oil
cut into strips	1 tablespoon fajita seasoning
3 bell peppers, any color, cut	mix
into chunks	Cooking spray

1. Preheat the air fryer to 370°F (188°C). 2. In a large bowl, mix together the chicken, bell peppers, onion, olive oil, and fajita seasoning mix until completely coated. 3. Spray the air fryer basket lightly with cooking spray. 4. Place the chicken and vegetables in the air fryer basket and lightly spray with cooking spray. 5. Air fry for 7 minutes. Shake the basket and air fry for an additional 5 to 8 minutes, until the chicken is cooked through and the veggies are starting to char. 6. Serve warm.

Blackened Chicken

Prep time: 10 minutes | Cook time: 20 minutes | Serves 4

1 large egg, beaten	chicken breasts (about 1
¾ cup Blackened seasoning	pound / 454 g each), halved
2 whole boneless, skinless	1 to 2 tablespoons oil

1. Place the beaten egg in one shallow bowl and the Blackened seasoning in another shallow bowl. 2. One at a time, dip the chicken pieces in the beaten egg and the Blackened seasoning, coating thoroughly. 3. Preheat the air fryer to 360ºF (182ºC). Line the air fryer basket with parchment paper. 4. Place the chicken pieces on the parchment and spritz with oil. 5. Cook for 10 minutes. Flip the chicken, spritz it with oil, and cook for 10 minutes more until the internal temperature reaches 165ºF (74ºC) and the chicken is no longer pink inside. Let sit for 5 minutes before serving.

Chicken Pesto Pizzas

Prep time: 10 minutes | Cook time: 12 minutes | Serves 4

1 pound (454 g) ground chicken thighs	¼ cup basil pesto
¼ teaspoon salt	1 cup shredded Mozzarella cheese
⅛ teaspoon ground black pepper	4 grape tomatoes, sliced

1. Cut four squares of parchment paper to fit into your air fryer basket. 2. Place ground chicken in a large bowl and mix with salt and pepper. Divide mixture into four equal sections. 3. Wet your hands with water to prevent sticking, then press each section into a 6-inch circle onto a piece of ungreased parchment. Place each chicken crust into air fryer basket, working in batches if needed. 4. Adjust the temperature to 350ºF (177ºC) and air fry for 10 minutes, turning crusts halfway through cooking. 5. Spread 1 tablespoon pesto across the top of each crust, then sprinkle with ¼ cup Mozzarella and top with 1 sliced tomato. Continue cooking at 350ºF (177ºC) for 2 minutes. Cheese will be melted and brown when done. Serve warm.

Air Fried Chicken Potatoes with Sun-Dried Tomato

Prep time: 15 minutes | Cook time: 25 minutes | Serves 2

2 teaspoons minced fresh oregano, divided	¼ cup oil-packed sun-dried tomatoes, patted dry and chopped
2 teaspoons minced fresh thyme, divided	1½ tablespoons red wine vinegar
2 teaspoons extra-virgin olive oil, plus extra as needed	1 tablespoon capers, rinsed and minced
1 pound (454 g) fingerling potatoes, unpeeled	1 small shallot, minced
2 (12-ounce / 340-g) bone-in split chicken breasts, trimmed	Salt and ground black pepper, to taste
1 garlic clove, minced	

1. Preheat the air fryer to 350ºF (177ºC). 2. Combine 1 teaspoon of oregano, 1 teaspoon of thyme, ¼ teaspoon of salt, ¼ teaspoon of ground black pepper, 1 teaspoons of olive oil in a large bowl. Add the potatoes and toss to coat well. 3. Combine the chicken with remaining thyme, oregano, and olive oil. Sprinkle with garlic, salt, and pepper. Toss to coat well. 4. Place the potatoes in the preheated air fryer, then arrange the chicken on top of the potatoes. 5. Air fry for 25 minutes or until the internal temperature of the chicken reaches at least 165ºF (74ºC) and the potatoes are wilted. Flip the chicken and potatoes halfway through. 6. Meanwhile, combine the sun-dried tomatoes, vinegar, capers, and shallot in a separate large bowl. Sprinkle with salt and ground black pepper. Toss to mix well. 7. Remove the chicken and potatoes from the air fryer and allow to cool for 10 minutes. Serve with the sun-dried tomato mix.

Pecan Turkey Cutlets

Prep time: 10 minutes | Cook time: 10 to 12 minutes per batch | Serves 4

¾ cup panko bread crumbs	1 egg, beaten
¼ teaspoon salt	1 pound (454 g) turkey cutlets, ½-inch thick
¼ teaspoon pepper	
¼ teaspoon dry mustard	Salt and pepper, to taste
¼ teaspoon poultry seasoning	Oil for misting or cooking spray
½ cup pecans	
¼ cup cornstarch	

1. Place the panko crumbs, ¼ teaspoon salt, ¼ teaspoon pepper, mustard, and poultry seasoning in food processor. Process until crumbs are finely crushed. Add pecans and process in short pulses just until nuts are finely chopped. Go easy so you don't overdo it! 2. Preheat the air fryer to 360ºF (182ºC). 3. Place cornstarch in one shallow dish and beaten egg in another. Transfer coating mixture from food processor into a third shallow dish. 4. Sprinkle turkey cutlets with salt and pepper to taste. 5. Dip cutlets in cornstarch and shake off excess. Then dip in beaten egg and roll in crumbs, pressing to coat well. Spray both sides with oil or cooking spray. 6. Place 2 cutlets in air fryer basket in a single layer and cook for 10 to 12 minutes or until juices run clear. 7. Repeat step 6 to cook remaining cutlets.

Chicken with Pineapple and Peach

Prep time: 10 minutes | Cook time: 14 to 15 minutes | Serves 4

1 pound (454 g) low-sodium boneless, skinless chicken breasts, cut into 1-inch pieces	safflower oil
1 medium red onion, chopped	1 peach, peeled, pitted, and cubed
1 (8-ounce / 227-g) can pineapple chunks, drained, ¼ cup juice reserved	1 tablespoon cornstarch
1 tablespoon peanut oil or	½ teaspoon ground ginger
	¼ teaspoon ground allspice
	Brown rice, cooked (optional)

1. Preheat the air fryer to 380ºF (193ºC). 2. In a medium metal bowl, mix the chicken, red onion, pineapple, and peanut oil. Bake in the air fryer for 9 minutes. Remove and stir. 3. Add the peach and return the bowl to the air fryer. Bake for 3 minutes more. Remove and stir again. 4. In a small bowl, whisk the reserved pineapple juice, the cornstarch, ginger, and allspice well. Add to the chicken mixture and stir to combine. 5. Bake for 2 to 3 minutes more, or until the chicken reaches an internal temperature of 165ºF (74ºC) on a meat thermometer and the sauce is slightly thickened. 6. Serve immediately over hot cooked brown rice, if desired.

Spice-Rubbed Chicken Thighs

Prep time: 10 minutes | Cook time: 25 minutes | Serves 4

4 (4-ounce / 113-g) bone-in, skin-on chicken thighs	2 teaspoons chili powder
½ teaspoon salt	1 teaspoon paprika
½ teaspoon garlic powder	1 teaspoon ground cumin
	1 small lime, halved

1. Pat chicken thighs dry and sprinkle with salt, garlic powder, chili powder, paprika, and cumin. 2. Squeeze juice from ½ lime over thighs. Place thighs into ungreased air fryer basket. Adjust the temperature to 380ºF (193ºC) and roast for 25 minutes, turning thighs halfway through cooking. Thighs will be crispy and browned with an internal temperature of at least 165ºF (74ºC) when done. 3. Transfer thighs to a large serving plate and drizzle with remaining lime juice. Serve warm.

Buttermilk-Fried Drumsticks

Prep time: 10 minutes | Cook time: 25 minutes | Serves 2

1 egg	¼ teaspoon ground black pepper (to mix into coating)
½ cup buttermilk	
¾ cup self-rising flour	4 chicken drumsticks, skin on
¾ cup seasoned panko bread crumbs	Oil for misting or cooking spray
1 teaspoon salt	

1. Beat together egg and buttermilk in shallow dish. 2. In a second shallow dish, combine the flour, panko crumbs, salt, and pepper. 3. Sprinkle chicken legs with additional salt and pepper to taste. 4. Dip legs in buttermilk mixture, then roll in panko mixture, pressing in crumbs to make coating stick. Mist with oil or cooking spray. 5. Spray the air fryer basket with cooking spray. 6. Cook drumsticks at 360ºF (182ºC) for 10 minutes. Turn pieces over and cook an additional 10 minutes. 7. Turn pieces to check for browning. If you have any white spots that haven't begun to brown, spritz them with oil or cooking spray. Continue cooking for 5 more minutes or until crust is golden brown and juices run clear. Larger, meatier drumsticks will take longer to cook than small ones.

Herb-Buttermilk Chicken Breast

Prep time: 5 minutes | Cook time: 40 minutes | Serves 2

1 large bone-in, skin-on chicken breast	½ teaspoon dried dill
	½ teaspoon onion powder
1 cup buttermilk	¼ teaspoon garlic powder
1½ teaspoons dried parsley	¼ teaspoon dried tarragon
1½ teaspoons dried chives	Cooking spray
¾ teaspoon kosher salt	

1. Place the chicken breast in a bowl and pour over the buttermilk, turning the chicken in it to make sure it's completely covered. Let the chicken stand at room temperature for at least 20 minutes or in the refrigerator for up to 4 hours. 2. Meanwhile, in a bowl, stir together the parsley, chives, salt, dill, onion powder, garlic powder, and tarragon. 3. Preheat the air fryer to 300ºF (149ºC). 4. Remove the chicken from the buttermilk, letting the excess drip off, then place the chicken skin-side up directly in the air fryer. Sprinkle the seasoning mix all over the top of the chicken breast, then let stand until the herb mix soaks into the buttermilk, at least 5 minutes. 5. Spray the top of the chicken with cooking spray. Bake for 10 minutes, then increase the temperature to 350ºF (177ºC) and bake until an instant-read thermometer inserted into the thickest part of the breast reads 160ºF (71ºC) and the chicken is deep golden brown, 30 to 35 minutes. 6. Transfer the chicken breast to a cutting board, let rest for 10 minutes, then cut the meat off the bone and cut into thick slices for serving.

General Tso's Chicken

Prep time: 10 minutes | Cook time: 14 minutes | Serves 4

1 tablespoon sesame oil	4 tablespoons cornstarch, divided
1 teaspoon minced garlic	
½ teaspoon ground ginger	4 boneless, skinless chicken breasts, cut into 1-inch pieces
1 cup chicken broth	
4 tablespoons soy sauce, divided	Olive oil spray
	2 medium scallions, sliced, green parts only
½ teaspoon sriracha, plus more for serving	
	Sesame seeds, for garnish
2 tablespoons hoisin sauce	

1. In a small saucepan over low heat, combine the sesame oil, garlic, and ginger and cook for 1 minute. 2. Add the chicken broth, 2 tablespoons of soy sauce, the sriracha, and hoisin. Whisk to combine. 3. Whisk in 2 tablespoons of cornstarch and continue cooking over low heat until the sauce starts to thicken, about 5 minutes. Remove the pan from the heat, cover it, and set aside. 4. Insert the crisper plate into the basket and the basket into the unit. Preheat the unit by selecting BAKE, setting the temperature to 400ºF (204ºC), and setting the time to 3 minutes. Select START/STOP to begin. 5. In a medium bowl, toss together the chicken, remaining 2 tablespoons of soy sauce, and remaining 2 tablespoons of cornstarch. 6. Once the unit is preheated, spray the crisper plate with olive oil. Place the chicken into the basket and spray it with olive oil. 7. Select BAKE, set the temperature to 400ºF (204ºC), and set the time to 9 minutes. Select START/STOP to begin. 8. After 5 minutes, remove the basket, shake, and spray the chicken with more olive oil. Reinsert the basket to resume cooking. 9. When the cooking is complete, a food thermometer inserted into the chicken should register at least 165ºF (74ºC). Transfer the chicken to a large bowl and toss it with the sauce. Garnish with the scallions and sesame seeds and serve.

Ginger Turmeric Chicken Thighs

Prep time: 5 minutes | Cook time: 25 minutes | Serves 4

4 (4-ounce / 113-g) boneless, skin-on chicken thighs	½ teaspoon salt
	½ teaspoon garlic powder
2 tablespoons coconut oil, melted	½ teaspoon ground ginger
	¼ teaspoon ground black pepper
½ teaspoon ground turmeric	

1. Place chicken thighs in a large bowl and drizzle with coconut oil. Sprinkle with remaining ingredients and toss to coat both sides of thighs. 2. Place thighs skin side up into ungreased air fryer basket. Adjust the temperature to 400ºF (204ºC) and air fry for 25 minutes. After 10 minutes, turn thighs. When 5 minutes remain, flip thighs once more. Chicken will be done when skin is golden brown and the internal temperature is at least 165ºF (74ºC). Serve warm.

Chicken and Avocado Fajitas

Prep time: 10 minutes | Cook time: 10 to 14 minutes | Serves 4

Cooking oil spray
4 boneless, skinless chicken breasts, sliced crosswise
1 small red onion, sliced
2 red bell peppers, seeded and sliced
½ cup spicy ranch salad
dressing, divided
½ teaspoon dried oregano
8 corn tortillas
2 cups torn butter lettuce leaves
2 avocados, peeled, pitted, and chopped

1. Insert the crisper plate into the basket and the basket into the unit. Preheat the unit by selecting BAKE, setting the temperature to 375ºF (191ºC), and setting the time to 3 minutes. Select START/STOP to begin. 2. Once the unit is preheated, spray the crisper plate with cooking oil. Place the chicken, red onion, and red bell pepper into the basket. Drizzle with 1 tablespoon of the salad dressing and season with the oregano. Toss to combine. 3. Select BAKE, set the temperature to 375ºF (191ºC), and set the time to 14 minutes. Select START/STOP to begin. 4. After 10 minutes, check the chicken. If a food thermometer inserted into the chicken registers at least 165ºF (74ºC), it is done. If not, resume cooking. 5. When the cooking is complete, transfer the chicken and vegetables to a bowl and toss with the remaining salad dressing. 6. Serve the chicken mixture family-style with the tortillas, lettuce, and avocados, and let everyone make their own plates.

Thai Tacos with Peanut Sauce

Prep time: 10 minutes | Cook time: 6 minutes | Serves 4

1 pound (454 g) ground chicken
¼ cup diced onions (about 1 small onion)
2 cloves garlic, minced
¼ teaspoon fine sea salt
Sauce:
¼ cup creamy peanut butter, room temperature
2 tablespoons chicken broth, plus more if needed
2 tablespoons lime juice
2 tablespoons grated fresh ginger
2 tablespoons wheat-free tamari or coconut aminos
1½ teaspoons hot sauce
5 drops liquid stevia (optional)
For Serving:
2 small heads butter lettuce, leaves separated
Lime slices (optional)
For Garnish (Optional):
Cilantro leaves
Shredded purple cabbage
Sliced green onions

1. Preheat the air fryer to 350ºF (177ºC). 2. Place the ground chicken, onions, garlic, and salt in a pie pan or a dish that will fit in your air fryer. Break up the chicken with a spatula. Place in the air fryer and bake for 5 minutes, or until the chicken is browned and cooked through. Break up the chicken again into small crumbles. 3. Make the sauce: In a medium-sized bowl, stir together the peanut butter, broth, lime juice, ginger, tamari, hot sauce, and stevia (if using) until well combined. If the sauce is too thick, add another tablespoon or two of broth. Taste and add more hot sauce if desired. 4. Add half of the sauce to the pan with the chicken. Cook for another minute, until heated through, and stir well to combine. 5. Assemble the tacos: Place several lettuce leaves on a serving plate. Place a few tablespoons of the chicken mixture in each lettuce leaf and garnish with cilantro leaves, purple cabbage, and sliced green onions, if desired. Serve the remaining sauce on the side. Serve with lime slices, if desired. 6. Store

leftover meat mixture in an airtight container in the refrigerator for up to 4 days; store leftover sauce, lettuce leaves, and garnishes separately. Reheat the meat mixture in a lightly greased pie pan in a preheated 350ºF (177ºC) air fryer for 3 minutes, or until heated through.

Bacon-Wrapped Chicken Breasts Rolls

Prep time: 10 minutes | Cook time: 15 minutes | Serves 4

¼ cup chopped fresh chives
2 tablespoons lemon juice
1 teaspoon dried sage
1 teaspoon fresh rosemary leaves
½ cup fresh parsley leaves
4 cloves garlic, peeled
1 teaspoon ground fennel
3 teaspoons sea salt
½ teaspoon red pepper flakes
4 (4-ounce / 113-g) boneless, skinless chicken breasts, pounded to ¼ inch thick
8 slices bacon
Sprigs of fresh rosemary, for garnish
Cooking spray

1. Preheat the air fryer to 340ºF (171ºC). Spritz the air fryer basket with cooking spray. 2. Put the chives, lemon juice, sage, rosemary, parsley, garlic, fennel, salt, and red pepper flakes in a food processor, then pulse to purée until smooth. 3. Unfold the chicken breasts on a clean work surface, then brush the top side of the chicken breasts with the sauce. 4. Roll the chicken breasts up from the shorter side, then wrap each chicken rolls with 2 bacon slices to cover. Secure with toothpicks. 5. Arrange the rolls in the preheated air fryer, then cook for 10 minutes. Flip the rolls halfway through. 6. Increase the heat to 390ºF (199ºC) and air fry for 5 more minutes or until the bacon is browned and crispy. 7. Transfer the rolls to a large plate. Discard the toothpicks and spread with rosemary sprigs before serving.

Stuffed Chicken Florentine

Prep time: 10 minutes | Cook time: 20 minutes | Serves 4

3 tablespoons pine nuts
¾ cup frozen spinach, thawed and squeezed dry
⅓ cup ricotta cheese
2 tablespoons grated Parmesan cheese
3 cloves garlic, minced
Salt and freshly ground black pepper, to taste
4 small boneless, skinless chicken breast halves (about 1½ pounds / 680 g)
8 slices bacon

1. Place the pine nuts in a small pan and set in the air fryer basket. Set the air fryer to 400ºF (204ºC) and air fry for 2 to 3 minutes until toasted. Remove the pine nuts to a mixing bowl and continue preheating the air fryer. 2. In a large bowl, combine the spinach, ricotta, Parmesan, and garlic. Season to taste with salt and pepper and stir well until thoroughly combined. 3. Using a sharp knife, cut into the chicken breasts, slicing them across and opening them up like a book, but be careful not to cut them all the way through. Sprinkle the chicken with salt and pepper. 4. Spoon equal amounts of the spinach mixture into the chicken, then fold the top of the chicken breast back over the top of the stuffing. Wrap each chicken breast with 2 slices of bacon. 5. Working in batches if necessary, air fry the chicken for 18 to 20 minutes until the bacon is crisp and a thermometer inserted into the thickest part of the chicken registers 165ºF (74ºC).

Honey-Glazed Chicken Thighs

Prep time: 5 minutes | Cook time: 14 minutes | Serves 4

Oil, for spraying	1 tablespoon balsamic vinegar
4 boneless, skinless chicken	2 teaspoons honey
thighs, fat trimmed	2 teaspoons minced garlic
3 tablespoons soy sauce	1 teaspoon ground ginger

1. Preheat the air fryer to 400ºF (204ºC). Line the air fryer basket with parchment and spray lightly with oil. 2. Place the chicken in the prepared basket. 3. Cook for 7 minutes, flip, and cook for another 7 minutes, or until the internal temperature reaches 165ºF (74ºC) and the juices run clear. 4. In a small saucepan, combine the soy sauce, balsamic vinegar, honey, garlic, and ginger and cook over low heat for 1 to 2 minutes, until warmed through. 5. Transfer the chicken to a serving plate and drizzle with the sauce just before serving.

Chicken and Gruyère Cordon Bleu

Prep time: 15 minutes | Cook time: 15 minutes | Serves 4

4 chicken breast filets	Freshly ground black pepper,
¼ cup chopped ham	to taste
⅓ cup grated Swiss cheese, or	½ teaspoon dried marjoram
Gruyère cheese	1 egg
¼ cup all-purpose flour	1 cup panko bread crumbs
Pinch salt	Olive oil spray

1. Put the chicken breast filets on a work surface and gently press them with the palm of your hand to make them a bit thinner. Don't tear the meat. 2. In a small bowl, combine the ham and cheese. Divide this mixture among the chicken filets. Wrap the chicken around the filling to enclose it, using toothpicks to hold the chicken together. 3. In a shallow bowl, stir together the flour, salt, pepper, and marjoram. 4. In another bowl, beat the egg. 5. Spread the panko on a plate. 6. Dip the chicken in the flour mixture, in the egg, and in the panko to coat thoroughly. Press the crumbs into the chicken so they stick well. 7. Insert the crisper plate into the basket and the basket into the unit. Preheat the unit by selecting BAKE, setting the temperature to 375ºF (191ºC), and setting the time to 3 minutes. Select START/STOP to begin. 8. Once the unit is preheated, spray the crisper plate with olive oil. Place the chicken into the basket and spray it with olive oil. 9. Select BAKE, set the temperature to 375ºF (191ºC), and set the time to 15 minutes. Select START/STOP to begin. 10. When the cooking is complete, the chicken should be cooked through and a food thermometer inserted into the chicken should register 165ºF (74ºC). Carefully remove the toothpicks and serve.

Fajita-Stuffed Chicken Breast

Prep time: 15 minutes | Cook time: 25 minutes | Serves 4

2 (6-ounce / 170-g) boneless,	seeded and sliced
skinless chicken breasts	1 tablespoon coconut oil
¼ medium white onion,	2 teaspoons chili powder
peeled and sliced	1 teaspoon ground cumin
1 medium green bell pepper,	½ teaspoon garlic powder

1. Slice each chicken breast completely in half lengthwise into two even pieces. Using a meat tenderizer, pound out the chicken until it's about ¼-inch thickness. 2. Lay each slice of chicken out and place three slices of onion and four slices of green pepper on the end closest to you. Begin rolling the peppers and onions tightly into the chicken. Secure the roll with either toothpicks or a couple pieces of butcher's twine. 3. Drizzle coconut oil over chicken. Sprinkle each side with chili powder, cumin, and garlic powder. Place each roll into the air fryer basket. 4. Adjust the temperature to 350ºF (177ºC) and air fry for 25 minutes. 5. Serve warm.

Buffalo Crispy Chicken Strips

Prep time: 15 minutes | Cook time: 13 to 17 minutes per batch | Serves 4

¾ cup all-purpose flour	black pepper
2 eggs	16 chicken breast strips, or
2 tablespoons water	3 large boneless, skinless
1 cup seasoned panko bread	chicken breasts, cut into
crumbs	1-inch strips
2 teaspoons granulated garlic	Olive oil spray
1 teaspoon salt	¼ cup Buffalo sauce, plus
1 teaspoon freshly ground	more as needed

1. Put the flour in a small bowl. 2. In another small bowl, whisk the eggs and the water. 3. In a third bowl, stir together the panko, granulated garlic, salt, and pepper. 4. Dip each chicken strip in the flour, in the egg, and in the panko mixture to coat. Press the crumbs onto the chicken with your fingers. 5. Insert the crisper plate into the basket and the basket into the unit. Preheat the unit by selecting AIR FRY, setting the temperature to 375ºF (191ºC), and setting the time to 3 minutes. Select START/STOP to begin. 6. Once the unit is preheated, place a parchment paper liner into the basket. Working in batches if needed, place the chicken strips into the basket. Do not stack unless using a wire rack for the second layer. Spray the top of the chicken with olive oil. 7. Select AIR FRY, set the temperature to 375ºF (191ºC), and set the time to 17 minutes. Select START/STOP to begin. 8. After 10 or 12 minutes, remove the basket, flip the chicken, and spray again with olive oil. Reinsert the basket to resume cooking. 9. When the cooking is complete, the chicken should be golden brown and crispy and a food thermometer inserted into the chicken should register 165ºF (74ºC). 10. Repeat steps 6, 7, and 8 with any remaining chicken. 11. Transfer the chicken to a large bowl. Drizzle the Buffalo sauce over the top of the cooked chicken, toss to coat, and serve.

Italian Chicken Thighs

Prep time: 5 minutes | Cook time: 20 minutes | Serves 2

4 bone-in, skin-on chicken	1 teaspoon dried basil
thighs	½ teaspoon garlic powder
2 tablespoons unsalted butter,	¼ teaspoon onion powder
melted	¼ teaspoon dried oregano
1 teaspoon dried parsley	

1. Brush chicken thighs with butter and sprinkle remaining ingredients over thighs. Place thighs into the air fryer basket. 2. Adjust the temperature to 380ºF (193ºC) and roast for 20 minutes. 3. Halfway through the cooking time, flip the thighs. 4. When fully cooked, internal temperature will be at least 165ºF (74ºC) and skin will be crispy. Serve warm.

Ethiopian Chicken with Cauliflower

Prep time: 15 minutes | Cook time: 28 minutes | Serves 6

2 handful fresh Italian parsley, roughly chopped
½ cup fresh chopped chives
2 sprigs thyme
6 chicken drumsticks
1½ small-sized head cauliflower, broken into large-sized florets
2 teaspoons mustard powder

⅓ teaspoon porcini powder
1½teaspoons berbere spice
⅓ teaspoon sweet paprika
½ teaspoon shallot powder
1teaspoon granulated garlic
1 teaspoon freshly cracked pink peppercorns
½ teaspoon sea salt

1. Simply combine all items for the berbere spice rub mix. After that, coat the chicken drumsticks with this rub mix on all sides. Transfer them to the baking dish. 2. Now, lower the cauliflower onto the chicken drumsticks. Add thyme, chives and Italian parsley and spritz everything with a pan spray. Transfer the baking dish to the preheated air fryer. 3. Next step, set the timer for 28 minutes; roast at 355ºF (179ºC), turning occasionally. Bon appétit!

Lemon-Dijon Boneless Chicken

Prep time: 30 minutes | Cook time: 13 to 16 minutes | Serves 6

½ cup sugar-free mayonnaise
1 tablespoon Dijon mustard
1 tablespoon freshly squeezed lemon juice (optional)
1 tablespoon coconut aminos
1 teaspoon Italian seasoning
1 teaspoon sea salt

½ teaspoon freshly ground black pepper
¼ teaspoon cayenne pepper
1½ pounds (680 g) boneless, skinless chicken breasts or thighs

1. In a small bowl, combine the mayonnaise, mustard, lemon juice (if using), coconut aminos, Italian seasoning, salt, black pepper, and cayenne pepper. 2. Place the chicken in a shallow dish or large zip-top plastic bag. Add the marinade, making sure all the pieces are coated. Cover and refrigerate for at least 30 minutes or up to 4 hours. 3. Set the air fryer to 400ºF (204ºC). Arrange the chicken in a single layer in the air fryer basket, working in batches if necessary. Air fry for 7 minutes. Flip the chicken and continue cooking for 6 to 9 minutes more, until an instant-read thermometer reads 160ºF (71ºC).

Chicken Rochambeau

Prep time: 15 minutes | Cook time: 20 minutes | Serves 4

1 tablespoon butter
4 chicken tenders, cut in half crosswise
Salt and pepper, to taste
¼ cup flour
Oil for misting
4 slices ham, ¼- to ⅜-inches thick and large enough to cover an English muffin
2 English muffins, split

Sauce:
2 tablespoons butter
½ cup chopped green onions
½ cup chopped mushrooms
2 tablespoons flour
1 cup chicken broth
¼ teaspoon garlic powder
1½ teaspoons Worcestershire sauce

1. Place 1 tablespoon of butter in a baking pan and air fry at 390ºF (199ºC) for 2 minutes to melt. 2. Sprinkle chicken tenders with salt and pepper to taste, then roll in the ¼ cup of flour. 3. Place chicken in baking pan, turning pieces to coat with melted butter. 4. Air fry at 390ºF (199ºC) for 5 minutes. Turn chicken pieces over, and spray tops lightly with olive oil. Cook 5 minutes longer or until juices run clear. The chicken will not brown. 5. While chicken is cooking, make the sauce: In a medium saucepan, melt the 2 tablespoons of butter. 6. Add onions and mushrooms and sauté until tender, about 3 minutes. 7. Stir in the flour. Gradually add broth, stirring constantly until you have a smooth gravy. 8. Add garlic powder and Worcestershire sauce and simmer on low heat until sauce thickens, about 5 minutes. 9. When chicken is cooked, remove baking pan from air fryer and set aside. 10. Place ham slices directly into air fryer basket and air fry at 390ºF (199ºC) for 5 minutes or until hot and beginning to sizzle a little. Remove and set aside on top of the chicken for now. 11. Place the English muffin halves in air fryer basket and air fry at 390ºF (199ºC) for 1 minute. 12. Open air fryer and place a ham slice on top of each English muffin half. Stack 2 pieces of chicken on top of each ham slice. Air fry for 1 to 2 minutes to heat through. 13. Place each English muffin stack on a serving plate and top with plenty of sauce.

Chicken Patties

Prep time: 15 minutes | Cook time: 12 minutes | Serves 4

1 pound (454 g) ground chicken thigh meat
½ cup shredded Mozzarella cheese
1 teaspoon dried parsley

½ teaspoon garlic powder
¼ teaspoon onion powder
1 large egg
2 ounces (57 g) pork rinds, finely ground

1. In a large bowl, mix ground chicken, Mozzarella, parsley, garlic powder, and onion powder. Form into four patties. 2. Place patties in the freezer for 15 to 20 minutes until they begin to firm up. 3. Whisk egg in a medium bowl. Place the ground pork rinds into a large bowl. 4. Dip each chicken patty into the egg and then press into pork rinds to fully coat. Place patties into the air fryer basket. 5. Adjust the temperature to 360ºF (182ºC) and air fry for 12 minutes. 6. Patties will be firm and cooked to an internal temperature of 165ºF (74ºC) when done. Serve immediately.

Pecan-Crusted Chicken Tenders

Prep time: 10 minutes | Cook time: 12 minutes | Serves 4

2 tablespoons mayonnaise
1 teaspoon Dijon mustard
1 pound (454 g) boneless, skinless chicken tenders
½ teaspoon salt

¼ teaspoon ground black pepper
½ cup chopped roasted pecans, finely ground

1. In a small bowl, whisk mayonnaise and mustard until combined. Brush mixture onto chicken tenders on both sides, then sprinkle tenders with salt and pepper. 2. Place pecans in a medium bowl and press each tender into pecans to coat each side. 3. Place tenders into ungreased air fryer basket in a single layer, working in batches if needed. Adjust the temperature to 375ºF (191ºC) and roast for 12 minutes, turning tenders halfway through cooking. Tenders will be golden brown and have an internal temperature of at least 165ºF (74ºC) when done. Serve warm.

Spanish Chicken and Mini Sweet Pepper Baguette

Prep time: 10 minutes | Cook time: 20 minutes | Serves 2

1¼ pounds (567 g) assorted small chicken parts, breasts cut into halves	½ pound (227 g) mini sweet peppers
¼ teaspoon salt	¼ cup light mayonnaise
¼ teaspoon ground black pepper	¼ teaspoon smoked paprika
2 teaspoons olive oil	½ clove garlic, crushed
	Baguette, for serving
	Cooking spray

1. Preheat air fryer to 375ºF (191ºC). Spritz the air fryer basket with cooking spray. 2. Toss the chicken with salt, ground black pepper, and olive oil in a large bowl. 3. Arrange the sweet peppers and chicken in the preheated air fryer and air fry for 10 minutes, then transfer the peppers on a plate. 4. Flip the chicken and air fry for 10 more minutes or until well browned. 5. Meanwhile, combine the mayo, paprika, and garlic in a small bowl. Stir to mix well. 6. Assemble the baguette with chicken and sweet pepper, then spread with mayo mixture and serve.

Simply Terrific Turkey Meatballs

Prep time: 10 minutes | Cook time: 7 to 10 minutes | Serves 4

1 red bell pepper, seeded and coarsely chopped	ground turkey
2 cloves garlic, coarsely chopped	1 egg, lightly beaten
¼ cup chopped fresh parsley	½ cup grated Parmesan cheese
1½ pounds (680 g) 85% lean	1 teaspoon salt
	½ teaspoon freshly ground black pepper

1. Preheat the air fryer to 400ºF (204ºC). 2. In a food processor fitted with a metal blade, combine the bell pepper, garlic, and parsley. Pulse until finely chopped. Transfer the vegetables to a large mixing bowl. 3. Add the turkey, egg, Parmesan, salt, and black pepper. Mix gently until thoroughly combined. Shape the mixture into 1¼-inch meatballs. 4. Working in batches if necessary, arrange the meatballs in a single layer in the air fryer basket; coat lightly with olive oil spray. Pausing halfway through the cooking time to shake the basket, air fry for 7 to 10 minutes, until lightly browned and a thermometer inserted into the center of a meatball registers 165ºF (74ºC).

Barbecue Chicken

Prep time: 10 minutes | Cook time: 18 to 20 minutes | Serves 4

⅓ cup no-salt-added tomato sauce	2 garlic cloves, minced
2 tablespoons low-sodium grainy mustard	1 jalapeño pepper, minced
2 tablespoons apple cider vinegar	3 tablespoons minced onion
1 tablespoon honey	4 (5-ounce / 142-g) low-sodium boneless, skinless chicken breasts

1. Preheat the air fryer to 370ºF (188ºC). 2. In a small bowl, stir together the tomato sauce, mustard, cider vinegar, honey, garlic, jalapeño, and onion. 3. Brush the chicken breasts with some sauce and air fry for 10

minutes. 4. Remove the air fryer basket and turn the chicken; brush with more sauce. Air fry for 5 minutes more. 5. Remove the air fryer basket and turn the chicken again; brush with more sauce. Air fry for 3 to 5 minutes more, or until the chicken reaches an internal temperature of 165ºF (74ºC) on a meat thermometer. Discard any remaining sauce. Serve immediately.

Tortilla Crusted Chicken Breast

Prep time: 10 minutes | Cook time: 12 minutes | Serves 2

⅓ cup flour	2 (3- to 4-ounce / 85- to 113-g) boneless chicken breasts
1 teaspoon salt	Vegetable oil
1½ teaspoons chili powder	½ cup salsa
1 teaspoon ground cumin	½ cup crumbled queso fresco
Freshly ground black pepper, to taste	Fresh cilantro leaves
1 egg, beaten	Sour cream or guacamole (optional)
¾ cup coarsely crushed yellow corn tortilla chips	

1. Set up a dredging station with three shallow dishes. Combine the flour, salt, chili powder, cumin and black pepper in the first shallow dish. Beat the egg in the second shallow dish. Place the crushed tortilla chips in the third shallow dish. 2. Dredge the chicken in the spiced flour, covering all sides of the breast. Then dip the chicken into the egg, coating the chicken completely. Finally, place the chicken into the tortilla chips and press the chips onto the chicken to make sure they adhere to all sides of the breast. Spray the coated chicken breasts on both sides with vegetable oil. 3. Preheat the air fryer to 380ºF (193ºC). 4. Air fry the chicken for 6 minutes. Then turn the chicken breasts over and air fry for another 6 minutes. (Increase the cooking time if you are using chicken breasts larger than 3 to 4 ounces / 85 to 113 g.) 5. When the chicken has finished cooking, serve each breast with a little salsa, the crumbled queso fresco and cilantro as the finishing touch. Serve some sour cream and/or guacamole at the table, if desired.

Chicken Shawarma

Prep time: 30 minutes | Cook time: 15 minutes | Serves 4

Shawarma Spice:	Chicken:
2 teaspoons dried oregano	1 pound (454 g) boneless, skinless chicken thighs, cut into large bite-size chunks
1 teaspoon ground cinnamon	
1 teaspoon ground cumin	
1 teaspoon ground coriander	2 tablespoons vegetable oil
1 teaspoon kosher salt	For Serving:
½ teaspoon ground allspice	Tzatziki
½ teaspoon cayenne pepper	Pita bread

1. For the shawarma spice: In a small bowl, combine the oregano, cayenne, cumin, coriander, salt, cinnamon, and allspice. 2. For the chicken: In a large bowl, toss together the chicken, vegetable oil, and shawarma spice to coat. Marinate at room temperature for 30 minutes or cover and refrigerate for up to 24 hours. 3. Place the chicken in the air fryer basket. Set the air fryer to 350ºF (177ºC) for 15 minutes, or until the chicken reaches an internal temperature of 165ºF (74ºC). 4. Transfer the chicken to a serving platter. Serve with tzatziki and pita bread.

Chicken, Zucchini, and Spinach Salad

Prep time: 10 minutes | Cook time: 20 minutes | Serves 4

3 (5-ounce / 142-g) boneless, skinless chicken breasts, cut into 1-inch cubes	1 red bell pepper, sliced
5 teaspoons extra-virgin olive oil	1 small zucchini, cut into strips
½ teaspoon dried thyme	3 tablespoons freshly squeezed lemon juice
1 medium red onion, sliced	6 cups fresh baby spinach leaves

1. Insert the crisper plate into the basket and the basket into the unit. Preheat the unit by selecting AIR ROAST, setting the temperature to 375ºF (191ºC), and setting the time to 3 minutes. Select START/STOP to begin. 2. In a large bowl, combine the chicken, olive oil, and thyme. Toss to coat. Transfer to a medium metal bowl that fits into the basket. 3. Once the unit is preheated, place the bowl into the basket. 4. Select AIR ROAST, set the temperature to 375ºF (191ºC), and set the time to 20 minutes. Select START/STOP to begin. 5. After 8 minutes, add the red onion, red bell pepper, and zucchini to the bowl. Resume cooking. After about 6 minutes more, stir the chicken and vegetables. Resume cooking. 6. When the cooking is complete, a food thermometer inserted into the chicken should register at least 165ºF (74ºC). Remove the bowl from the unit and stir in the lemon juice. 7. Put the spinach in a serving bowl and top with the chicken mixture. Toss to combine and serve immediately.

Sweet Chili Spiced Chicken

Prep time: 10 minutes | Cook time: 43 minutes | Serves 4

Spice Rub:	or kosher salt
2 tablespoons brown sugar	2 teaspoons coarsely ground black pepper
2 tablespoons paprika	
1 teaspoon dry mustard powder	1 tablespoon vegetable oil
1 teaspoon chili powder	1 (3½-pound / 1.6-kg) chicken, cut into 8 pieces
2 tablespoons coarse sea salt	

1. Prepare the spice rub by combining the brown sugar, paprika, mustard powder, chili powder, salt and pepper. Rub the oil all over the chicken pieces and then rub the spice mix onto the chicken, covering completely. This is done very easily in a zipper sealable bag. You can do this ahead of time and let the chicken marinate in the refrigerator, or just proceed with cooking right away. 2. Preheat the air fryer to 370ºF (188ºC). 3. Air fry the chicken in two batches. Place the two chicken thighs and two drumsticks into the air fryer basket. Air fry at 370ºF (188ºC) for 10 minutes. Then, gently turn the chicken pieces over and air fry for another 10 minutes. Remove the chicken pieces and let them rest on a plate while you cook the chicken breasts. Air fry the chicken breasts, skin side down for 8 minutes. Turn the chicken breasts over and air fry for another 12 minutes. 4. Lower the temperature of the air fryer to 340ºF (171ºC). Place the first batch of chicken on top of the second batch already in the basket and air fry for a final 3 minutes. 5. Let the chicken rest for 5 minutes and serve warm with some mashed potatoes and a green salad or vegetables.

Chicken Kiev

Prep time: 15 minutes | Cook time: 25 minutes | Serves 4

1 cup (2 sticks) unsalted butter, softened (or butter-flavored coconut oil for dairy-free)	1 teaspoon fine sea salt, divided
	4 (4-ounce / 113-g) boneless, skinless chicken breasts
2 tablespoons lemon juice	2 large eggs
2 tablespoons plus 1 teaspoon chopped fresh parsley leaves, divided, plus more for garnish	2 cups pork dust
	1 teaspoon ground black pepper
2 tablespoons chopped fresh tarragon leaves	Sprig of fresh parsley, for garnish
3 cloves garlic, minced	Lemon slices, for serving

1. Spray the air fryer basket with avocado oil. Preheat the air fryer to 350ºF (177ºC). 2. In a medium-sized bowl, combine the butter, lemon juice, 2 tablespoons of the parsley, the tarragon, garlic, and ¼ teaspoon of the salt. Cover and place in the fridge to harden for 7 minutes. 3. While the butter mixture chills, place one of the chicken breasts on a cutting board. With a sharp knife held parallel to the cutting board, make a 1-inch-wide incision at the top of the breast. Carefully cut into the breast to form a large pocket, leaving a ½-inch border along the sides and bottom. Repeat with the other 3 breasts. 4. Stuff one-quarter of the butter mixture into each chicken breast and secure the openings with toothpicks. 5. Beat the eggs in a small shallow dish. In another shallow dish, combine the pork dust, the remaining 1 teaspoon of parsley, the remaining ¾ teaspoon of salt, and the pepper. 6. One at a time, dip the chicken breasts in the egg, shake off the excess egg, and dredge the breasts in the pork dust mixture. Use your hands to press the pork dust onto each breast to form a nice crust. If you desire a thicker coating, dip it again in the egg and pork dust. As you finish, spray each coated chicken breast with avocado oil and place it in the air fryer basket. 7. Roast the chicken in the air fryer for 15 minutes, flip the breasts, and cook for another 10 minutes, or until the internal temperature of the chicken is 165ºF (74ºC) and the crust is golden brown. 8. Serve garnished with chopped fresh parsley and a parsley sprig, with lemon slices on the side. 9. Store leftovers in an airtight container in the refrigerator for up to 4 days or in the freezer for up to a month. Reheat in a preheated 350ºF (177ºC) air fryer for 5 minutes, or until heated through.

Cilantro Chicken Kebabs

Prep time: 30 minutes | Cook time: 10 minutes | Serves 4

Chutney:	1 jalapeño, seeded and roughly chopped
½ cup unsweetened shredded coconut	¼ to ¾ cup water, as needed
½ cup hot water	Juice of 1 lemon
2 cups fresh cilantro leaves, roughly chopped	Chicken:
	1 pound (454 g) boneless, skinless chicken thighs, cut crosswise into thirds
¼ cup fresh mint leaves, roughly chopped	
6 cloves garlic, roughly chopped	Olive oil spray

1. For the chutney: In a blender or food processor, combine the coconut and hot water; set aside to soak for 5 minutes. 2. To the processor, add the cilantro, mint, garlic, and jalapeño, along with ¼

cup water. Blend at low speed, stopping occasionally to scrape down the sides. Add the lemon juice. With the blender or processor running, add only enough additional water to keep the contents moving. Turn the blender to high once the contents are moving freely and blend until the mixture is puréed. 3. For the chicken: Place the chicken pieces in a large bowl. Add ¼ cup of the chutney and mix well to coat. Set aside the remaining chutney to use as a dip. Marinate the chicken for 15 minutes at room temperature. 4. Spray the air fryer basket with olive oil spray. Arrange the chicken in the air fryer basket. Set the air fryer to 350ºF (177ºC) for 10 minutes. Use a meat thermometer to ensure that the chicken has reached an internal temperature of 165ºF (74ºC). 5. Serve the chicken with the remaining chutney.

Chapter 6
Beef, Pork, and Lamb

Blackened Cajun Pork Roast

Prep time: 20 minutes | Cook time: 33 minutes | Serves 4

2 pounds (907 g) bone-in pork loin roast	½ cup diced onion
2 tablespoons oil	½ cup diced celery
¼ cup Cajun seasoning	½ cup diced green bell pepper
	1 tablespoon minced garlic

1. Cut 5 slits across the pork roast. Spritz it with oil, coating it completely. Evenly sprinkle the Cajun seasoning over the pork roast. 2. In a medium bowl, stir together the onion, celery, green bell pepper, and garlic until combined. Set aside. 3. Preheat the air fryer to 360°F (182°C). Line the air fryer basket with parchment paper. 4. Place the pork roast on the parchment and spritz with oil. 5. Cook for 5 minutes. Flip the roast and cook for 5 minutes more. Continue to flip and cook in 5-minute increments for a total cook time of 20 minutes. 6. Increase the air fryer temperature to 390°F (199°C). 7. Cook the roast for 8 minutes more and flip. Add the vegetable mixture to the basket and cook for a final 5 minutes. Let the roast sit for 5 minutes before serving.

Beef Chuck Cheeseburgers

Prep time: 10 minutes | Cook time: 15 minutes | Serves 4

¾ pound (340 g) ground beef chuck	ground black pepper, to taste
1 envelope onion soup mix	1 teaspoon paprika
Kosher salt and freshly	4 slices Monterey Jack cheese
	4 ciabatta rolls

1. In a bowl, stir together the ground chuck, onion soup mix, salt, black pepper, and paprika to combine well. 2. Preheat the air fryer to 385°F (196°C). 3. Take four equal portions of the mixture and mold each one into a patty. Transfer to the air fryer and air fry for 10 minutes. 4. Put the slices of cheese on the top of the burgers. 5. Air fry for another minute before serving on ciabatta rolls.

Pork Schnitzel with Dill Sauce

Prep time: 5 minutes | Cook time: 24 minutes | Serves 4 to 6

6 boneless, center cut pork chops (about 1½ pounds / 680 g)	3 tablespoons butter, melted
	2 tablespoons vegetable or olive oil
½ cup flour	lemon wedges
1½ teaspoons salt	Dill Sauce:
Freshly ground black pepper, to taste	1 cup chicken stock
2 eggs	1½ tablespoons cornstarch
½ cup milk	⅓ cup sour cream
1½ cups toasted fine bread crumbs	1½ tablespoons chopped fresh dill
1 teaspoon paprika	Salt and pepper, to taste

1. Trim the excess fat from the pork chops and pound each chop with a meat mallet between two pieces of plastic wrap until they are ½-inch thick. 2. Set up a dredging station. Combine the flour, salt, and black pepper in a shallow dish. Whisk the eggs and milk together in a second shallow dish. Finally, combine the bread crumbs and paprika in a third shallow dish. 3. Dip each flattened pork chop in the flour. Shake off the excess flour and dip each chop into the egg mixture. Finally dip them into the bread crumbs and press the bread crumbs onto the meat firmly. Place each finished chop on a baking sheet until they are all coated. 4. Preheat the air fryer to 400°F (204°C). 5. Combine the melted butter and the oil in a small bowl and lightly brush both sides of the coated pork chops. Do not brush the chops too heavily or the breading will not be as crispy. 6. Air fry one schnitzel at a time for 4 minutes, turning it over halfway through the cooking time. Hold the cooked schnitzels warm on a baking pan in a 170°F (77°C) oven while you finish air frying the rest. 7. While the schnitzels are cooking, whisk the chicken stock and cornstarch together in a small saucepan over medium-high heat on the stovetop. Bring the mixture to a boil and simmer for 2 minutes. Remove the saucepan from heat and whisk in the sour cream. Add the chopped fresh dill and season with salt and pepper. 8. Transfer the pork schnitzel to a platter and serve with dill sauce and lemon wedges.

Kielbasa and Cabbage

Prep time: 10 minutes | Cook time: 20 to 25 minutes | Serves 4

1 pound (454 g) smoked kielbasa sausage, sliced into ½-inch pieces	2 cloves garlic, chopped
	2 tablespoons olive oil
	½ teaspoon salt
1 head cabbage, very coarsely chopped	½ teaspoon freshly ground black pepper
½ yellow onion, chopped	¼ cup water

1. Preheat the air fryer to 400°F (204°C). 2. In a large bowl, combine the sausage, cabbage, onion, garlic, olive oil, salt, and black pepper. Toss until thoroughly combined. 3. Transfer the mixture to the basket of the air fryer and pour the water over the top. Pausing two or three times during the cooking time to shake the basket, air fry for 20 to 25 minutes, until the sausage is browned and the vegetables are tender.

Cheese Wine Pork Cutlets

Prep time: 30 minutes | Cook time: 15 minutes | Serves 2

1 cup water	½ teaspoon porcini powder
1 cup red wine	Sea salt and ground black pepper, to taste
1 tablespoon sea salt	
2 pork cutlets	1 egg
¼ cup almond meal	¼ cup yogurt
¼ cup flaxseed meal	1 teaspoon brown mustard
½ teaspoon baking powder	⅓ cup Parmesan cheese, grated
1 teaspoon shallot powder	

1. In a large ceramic dish, combine the water, wine and salt. Add the pork cutlets and put for 1 hour in the refrigerator. 2. In a shallow bowl, mix the almond meal, flaxseed meal, baking powder, shallot powder, porcini powder, salt, and ground pepper. In another bowl, whisk the eggs with yogurt and mustard. 3. In a third bowl, place the grated Parmesan cheese. 4. Dip the pork cutlets in the seasoned flour mixture and toss evenly; then, in the egg mixture. Finally, roll them over the grated Parmesan cheese. 5. Spritz the bottom of the air fryer basket with cooking oil. Add the breaded pork cutlets and cook at 395°F (202°C) and for 10 minutes. 6. Flip and cook for 5 minutes more on the other side. Serve warm.

Panko Pork Chops

Prep time: 10 minutes | Cook time: 12 minutes | Serves 4

4 center-cut boneless pork chops, excess fat trimmed	1½ teaspoons paprika
¼ teaspoon salt	½ teaspoon granulated garlic
2 eggs	½ teaspoon onion powder
1½ cups panko bread crumbs	1 teaspoon chili powder
3 tablespoons grated Parmesan cheese	¼ teaspoon freshly ground black pepper
	Olive oil spray

1. Sprinkle the pork chops with salt on both sides and let them sit while you prepare the seasonings and egg wash. 2. In a shallow medium bowl, beat the eggs. 3. In another shallow medium bowl, stir together the panko, Parmesan cheese, paprika, granulated garlic, onion powder, chili powder, and pepper. 4. Dip the pork chops in the egg and in the panko mixture to coat. Firmly press the crumbs onto the chops. 5. Insert the crisper plate into the basket and the basket into the unit. Preheat the unit by selecting AIR ROAST, setting the temperature to 400ºF (204ºC), and setting the time to 3 minutes. Select START/STOP to begin. 6. Once the unit is preheated, spray the crisper plate with olive oil. Place the pork chops into the basket and spray them with olive oil. 7. Select AIR ROAST, set the temperature to 400ºF (204ºC), and set the time to 12 minutes. Select START/STOP to begin. 8. After 6 minutes, flip the pork chops and spray them with more olive oil. Resume cooking. 9. When the cooking is complete, the chops should be golden and crispy and a food thermometer should register 145ºF (63ºC). Serve immediately.

Pork Medallions with Radicchio and Endive Salad

Prep time: 25 minutes | Cook time: 7 minutes | Serves 4

1 (8-ounce / 227-g) pork tenderloin	1 tablespoon Dijon mustard
Salt and freshly ground black pepper, to taste	juice of ½ lemon
¼ cup flour	2 tablespoons chopped chervil or flat-leaf parsley
2 eggs, lightly beaten	salt and freshly ground black pepper
¾ cup cracker meal	½ cup extra-virgin olive oil
1 teaspoon paprika	Radicchio and Endive Salad:
1 teaspoon dry mustard	1 heart romaine lettuce, torn into large pieces
1 teaspoon garlic powder	½ head radicchio, coarsely chopped
1 teaspoon dried thyme	2 heads endive, sliced
1 teaspoon salt	½ cup cherry tomatoes, halved
vegetable or canola oil, in spray bottle	3 ounces (85 g) fresh Mozzarella, diced
Vinaigrette:	Salt and freshly ground black pepper, to taste
¼ cup white balsamic vinegar	
2 tablespoons agave syrup (or honey or maple syrup)	

1. Slice the pork tenderloin into 1-inch slices. Using a meat pounder, pound the pork slices into thin ½-inch medallions. Generously season the pork with salt and freshly ground black pepper on both sides. 2. Set up a dredging station using three shallow dishes. Put the flour in one dish and the beaten eggs in a second dish. Combine the cracker meal, paprika, dry mustard, garlic powder, thyme and salt in a third dish. 3. Preheat the air fryer to 400ºF (204ºC). 4. Dredge the pork medallions in flour first and then into the beaten egg. Let the excess egg drip off and coat both sides of the medallions with the cracker meal crumb mixture. Spray both sides of the coated medallions with vegetable or canola oil. 5. Air fry the medallions in two batches at 400ºF (204ºC) for 5 minutes. Once you have air-fried all the medallions, flip them all over and return the first batch of medallions back into the air fryer on top of the second batch. Air fry at 400ºF (204ºC) for an additional 2 minutes. 6. While the medallions are cooking, make the salad and dressing. Whisk the white balsamic vinegar, agave syrup, Dijon mustard, lemon juice, chervil, salt and pepper together in a small bowl. Whisk in the olive oil slowly until combined and thickened. 7. Combine the romaine lettuce, radicchio, endive, cherry tomatoes, and Mozzarella cheese in a large salad bowl. Drizzle the dressing over the vegetables and toss to combine. Season with salt and freshly ground black pepper. 8. Serve the pork medallions warm on or beside the salad.

Sausage and Pork Meatballs

Prep time: 15 minutes | Cook time: 8 to 12 minutes | Serves 8

1 large egg	1 tablespoon tomato paste
1 teaspoon gelatin	1 teaspoon minced garlic
1 pound (454 g) ground pork	1 teaspoon dried oregano
½ pound (227 g) Italian sausage, casings removed, crumbled	¼ teaspoon red pepper flakes
	Sea salt and freshly ground black pepper, to taste
⅓ cup Parmesan cheese	Keto-friendly marinara sauce, for serving
¼ cup finely diced onion	

1. Beat the egg in a small bowl and sprinkle with the gelatin. Allow to sit for 5 minutes. 2. In a large bowl, combine the ground pork, sausage, Parmesan, onion, tomato paste, garlic, oregano, and red pepper flakes. Season with salt and black pepper. 3. Stir the gelatin mixture, then add it to the other ingredients and, using clean hands, mix to ensure that everything is well combined. Form into 1½-inch round meatballs. 4. Set the air fryer to 400ºF (204ºC). Place the meatballs in the air fryer basket in a single layer, cooking in batches as needed. Air fry for 5 minutes. Flip and cook for 3 to 7 minutes more, or until an instant-read thermometer reads 160ºF (71ºC).

Super Bacon with Meat

Prep time: 5 minutes | Cook time: 1 hour | Serves 4

30 slices thick-cut bacon	10 ounces (283 g) pork sausage
4 ounces (113 g) Cheddar cheese, shredded	Salt and ground black pepper, to taste
12 ounces (340 g) steak	

1. Preheat the air fryer to 400ºF (204ºC). 2. Lay out 30 slices of bacon in a woven pattern and bake for 20 minutes until crisp. Put the cheese in the center of the bacon. 3. Combine the steak and sausage to form a meaty mixture. 4. Lay out the meat in a rectangle of similar size to the bacon strips. Season with salt and pepper. 5. Roll the meat into a tight roll and refrigerate. 6. Preheat the air fryer to 400ºF (204ºC). 7. Make a 7×7 bacon weave and roll the bacon weave over the meat, diagonally. 8. Bake for 60 minutes or until the internal temperature reaches at least 165ºF (74ºC). 9. Let rest for 5 minutes before serving.

Beef and Goat Cheese Stuffed Peppers

Prep time: 10 minutes | Cook time: 30 minutes | Serves 4

1 pound (454 g) lean ground beef	1 teaspoon salt
½ cup cooked brown rice	½ teaspoon black pepper
2 Roma tomatoes, diced	¼ teaspoon ground allspice
3 garlic cloves, minced	2 bell peppers, halved and
½ yellow onion, diced	seeded
2 tablespoons fresh oregano, chopped	4 ounces (113 g) goat cheese
	¼ cup fresh parsley, chopped

1. Preheat the air fryer to 360°F(182°C). 2. In a large bowl, combine the ground beef, rice, tomatoes, garlic, onion, oregano, salt, pepper, and allspice. Mix well. 3. Divide the beef mixture equally into the halved bell peppers and top each with about 1 ounce (28 g a quarter of the total) of the goat cheese. 4. Place the peppers into the air fryer basket in a single layer, making sure that they don't touch each other. Bake for 30 minutes. 5. Remove the peppers from the air fryer and top with fresh parsley before serving.

Air Fryer Chicken-Fried Steak

Prep time: 5 minutes | Cook time: 20 minutes | Serves 4

1 pound beef chuck sirloin steak	2 medium egg whites
3 cups low-fat milk, divided	1 cup chickpea crumbs
1 teaspoon dried thyme	½ cup coconut flour
1 teaspoon dried rosemary	1 tablespoon Creole seasoning

1. In a bowl, marinate the steak in 2 cups of milk for 30 to 45 minutes. 2. Remove the steak from milk, shake off the excess liquid, and season with the thyme and rosemary. Discard the milk. 3. In a shallow bowl, beat the egg whites with the remaining 1 cup of milk. 4. In a separate shallow bowl, combine the chickpea crumbs, coconut flour, and seasoning. 5. Dip the steak in the egg white mixture then dredge in the chickpea crumb mixture, coating well. 6. Place the steak in the basket of an air fryer. 7. Set the air fryer to 390°F, close, and cook for 10 minutes. 8. Open the air fryer, turn the steaks, close, and cook for 10 minutes. Let rest for 5 minutes.

Beef Egg Rolls

Prep time: 15 minutes | Cook time: 12 minutes | Makes 8 egg rolls

½ chopped onion	½ can cilantro lime rotel
2 garlic cloves, chopped	16 egg roll wrappers
½ packet taco seasoning	1 cup shredded Mexican
Salt and ground black pepper, to taste	cheese
1 pound (454 g) lean ground beef	1 tablespoon olive oil
	1 teaspoon cilantro

1. Preheat the air fryer to 400°F (205°C). 2. Add onions and garlic to a skillet, cooking until fragrant. Then add taco seasoning, pepper, salt, and beef, cooking until beef is broke up into tiny pieces and cooked thoroughly. 3. Add rotel and stir well. 4. Lay out egg wrappers and brush with a touch of water to soften a bit. 5. Load wrappers with beef filling and add cheese to each. 6. Fold diagonally to close and use water to secure edges. 7. Brush filled egg wrappers with olive oil and add to the air fryer. 8. Air fry 8 minutes, flip, and air fry for another 4 minutes. 9. Serve sprinkled with cilantro.

German Rouladen-Style Steak

Prep time: 20 minutes | Cook time: 15 minutes | Serves 4

Onion Sauce:	parsley
2 medium onions, cut into	Rouladen:
½-inch-thick slices	¼ cup Dijon mustard
Kosher salt and black pepper, to taste	1 pound (454 g) flank or skirt steak, ¼ to ½ inch thick
½ cup sour cream	1 teaspoon black pepper
1 tablespoon tomato paste	4 slices bacon
2 teaspoons chopped fresh	¼ cup chopped fresh parsley

1. For the sauce: In a small bowl, mix together the onions with salt and pepper to taste. Place the onions in the air fryer basket. Set the air fryer to 400°F (204°C) for 6 minutes, or until the onions are softened and golden brown. 2. Set aside half of the onions to use in the rouladen. Place the rest in a small bowl and add the sour cream, tomato paste, parsley, ½ teaspoon salt, and ½ teaspoon pepper. Stir until well combined, adding 1 to 2 tablespoons of water, if necessary, to thin the sauce slightly. Set the sauce aside. 3. For the rouladen: Evenly spread the mustard over the meat. Sprinkle with the pepper. Top with the bacon slices, reserved onions, and parsley. Starting at the long end, roll up the steak as tightly as possible, ending seam side down. Use 2 or 3 wooden toothpicks to hold the roll together. Using a sharp knife, cut the roll in half so that it better fits in the air fryer basket. 4. Place the steak, seam side down, in the air fryer basket. Set the air fryer to 400°F (204°C) for 9 minutes. Use a meat thermometer to ensure the steak has reached an internal temperature of 145°F (63°C). (It is critical to not overcook flank steak, so as to not toughen the meat.) 5. Let the steak rest for 10 minutes before cutting into slices. Serve with the sauce.

Southern Chili

Prep time: 20 minutes | Cook time: 25 minutes | Serves 4

1 pound (454 g) ground beef (85% lean)	tomatoes with green chilies
1 cup minced onion	1 (15-ounce / 425-g) can light red kidney beans, rinsed and
1 (28-ounce / 794-g) can tomato purée	drained
1 (15-ounce / 425-g) can diced	¼ cup Chili seasoning

1. Preheat the air fryer to 400°F (204°C). 2. In a baking pan, mix the ground beef and onion. Place the pan in the air fryer. 3. Cook for 4 minutes. Stir and cook for 4 minutes more until browned. Remove the pan from the fryer. Drain the meat and transfer to a large bowl. 4. Reduce the air fryer temperature to 350°F (177°C). 5. To the bowl with the meat, add in the tomato purée, diced tomatoes and green chilies, kidney beans, and Chili seasoning. Mix well. Pour the mixture into the baking pan. 6. Cook for 25 minutes, stirring every 10 minutes, until thickened.

Beef and Spinach Rolls

Prep time: 10 minutes | Cook time: 14 minutes | Serves 2

3 teaspoons pesto	bell peppers
2 pounds (907 g) beef flank steak	¾ cup baby spinach
6 slices provolone cheese	1 teaspoon sea salt
3 ounces (85 g) roasted red	1 teaspoon black pepper

1. Preheat the air fryer to 400ºF (204ºC). 2. Spoon equal amounts of the pesto onto each flank steak and spread it across evenly. 3. Put the cheese, roasted red peppers and spinach on top of the meat, about three-quarters of the way down. 4. Roll the steak up, holding it in place with toothpicks. Sprinkle with the sea salt and pepper. 5. Put inside the air fryer and air fry for 14 minutes, turning halfway through the cooking time. 6. Allow the beef to rest for 10 minutes before slicing up and serving.

Pork and Pinto Bean Gorditas

Prep time: 20 minutes | Cook time: 21 minutes | Serves 4

1 pound (454 g) lean ground pork	pepper, to taste
2 tablespoons chili powder	2 cups grated Cheddar cheese
2 tablespoons ground cumin	5 (12-inch) flour tortillas
1 teaspoon dried oregano	4 (8-inch) crispy corn tortilla shells
2 teaspoons paprika	4 cups shredded lettuce
1 teaspoon garlic powder	1 tomato, diced
½ cup water	⅓ cup sliced black olives
1 (15-ounce / 425-g) can pinto beans, drained and rinsed	Sour cream, for serving
½ cup taco sauce	Tomato salsa, for serving
Salt and freshly ground black	Cooking spray

1. Preheat the air fryer to 400ºF (204ºC). Spritz the air fryer basket with cooking spray. 2. Put the ground pork in the air fryer basket and air fry at 400ºF (204ºC) for 10 minutes, stirring a few times to gently break up the meat. Combine the chili powder, cumin, oregano, paprika, garlic powder and water in a small bowl. Stir the spice mixture into the browned pork. Stir in the beans and taco sauce and air fry for an additional minute. Transfer the pork mixture to a bowl. Season with salt and freshly ground black pepper. 3. Sprinkle ½ cup of the grated cheese in the center of the flour tortillas, leaving a 2-inch border around the edge free of cheese and filling. Divide the pork mixture among the four tortillas, placing it on top of the cheese. Put a crunchy corn tortilla on top of the pork and top with shredded lettuce, diced tomatoes, and black olives. Cut the remaining flour tortilla into 4 quarters. These quarters of tortilla will serve as the bottom of the gordita. Put one quarter tortilla on top of each gordita and fold the edges of the bottom flour tortilla up over the sides, enclosing the filling. While holding the seams down, brush the bottom of the gordita with olive oil and place the seam side down on the countertop while you finish the remaining three gorditas. 4. Adjust the temperature to 380ºF (193ºC). 5. Air fry one gordita at a time. Transfer the gordita carefully to the air fryer basket, seam side down. Brush or spray the top tortilla with oil and air fry for 5 minutes. Carefully turn the gordita over and air fry for an additional 4 to 5 minutes until both sides are browned. When finished air frying all four gorditas, layer them back

into the air fryer for an additional minute to make sure they are all warm before serving with sour cream and salsa.

Stuffed Beef Tenderloin with Feta Cheese

Prep time: 10 minutes | Cook time: 10 minutes | Serves 4

1½ pounds (680 g) beef tenderloin, pounded to ¼ inch thick	2 ounces (57 g) creamy goat cheese
3 teaspoons sea salt	½ cup crumbled feta cheese
1 teaspoon ground black pepper	¼ cup finely chopped onions
	2 cloves garlic, minced
	Cooking spray

1. Preheat the air fryer to 400ºF (204ºC). Spritz the air fryer basket with cooking spray. 2. Unfold the beef tenderloin on a clean work surface. Rub the salt and pepper all over the beef tenderloin to season. 3. Make the filling for the stuffed beef tenderloins: Combine the goat cheese, feta, onions, and garlic in a medium bowl. Stir until well blended. 4. Spoon the mixture in the center of the tenderloin. Roll the tenderloin up tightly like rolling a burrito and use some kitchen twine to tie the tenderloin. 5. Arrange the tenderloin in the air fryer basket and air fry for 10 minutes, flipping the tenderloin halfway through to ensure even cooking, or until an instant-read thermometer inserted in the center of the tenderloin registers 135ºF (57ºC) for medium-rare. 6. Transfer to a platter and serve immediately.

Cheesy Low-Carb Lasagna

Prep time: 10 minutes | Cook time: 10 minutes | Serves 4

Meat Layer:	8 ounces (227 g) ricotta cheese
Extra-virgin olive oil	1 cup shredded Mozzarella cheese
1 pound (454 g) 85% lean ground beef	½ cup grated Parmesan cheese
1 cup prepared marinara sauce	2 large eggs
¼ cup diced celery	1 teaspoon dried Italian seasoning, crushed
¼ cup diced red onion	½ teaspoon each minced garlic, garlic powder, and black pepper
½ teaspoon minced garlic	
Kosher salt and black pepper, to taste	
Cheese Layer:	

1. For the meat layer: Grease a cake pan with 1 teaspoon olive oil. 2. In a large bowl, combine the ground beef, marinara, celery, onion, garlic, salt, and pepper. Place the seasoned meat in the pan. 3. Place the pan in the air fryer basket. Set the air fryer to 375ºF (191ºC) for 10 minutes. 4. Meanwhile, for the cheese layer: In a medium bowl, combine the ricotta, half the Mozzarella, the Parmesan, lightly beaten eggs, Italian seasoning, minced garlic, garlic powder, and pepper. Stir until well blended. 5. At the end of the cooking time, spread the cheese mixture over the meat mixture. Sprinkle with the remaining ½ cup Mozzarella. Set the air fryer to 375ºF (191ºC) for 10 minutes, or until the cheese is browned and bubbling. 6. At the end of the cooking time, use a meat thermometer to ensure the meat has reached an internal temperature of 160ºF (71ºC). 7. Drain the fat and liquid from the pan. Let stand for 5 minutes before serving.

Parmesan Herb Filet Mignon

Prep time: 20 minutes | Cook time: 13 minutes | Serves 4

1 pound (454 g) filet mignon	1 teaspoon dried thyme
Sea salt and ground black pepper, to taste	1 tablespoon sesame oil
½ teaspoon cayenne pepper	1 small-sized egg, well-whisked
1 teaspoon dried basil	½ cup Parmesan cheese, grated
1 teaspoon dried rosemary	

1. Season the filet mignon with salt, black pepper, cayenne pepper, basil, rosemary, and thyme. Brush with sesame oil. 2. Put the egg in a shallow plate. Now, place the Parmesan cheese in another plate. 3. Coat the filet mignon with the egg; then lay it into the Parmesan cheese. Set the air fryer to 360°F (182°C). 4. Cook for 10 to 13 minutes or until golden. Serve with mixed salad leaves and enjoy!

Garlic Butter Steak Bites

Prep time: 5 minutes | Cook time: 16 minutes | Serves 3

Oil, for spraying	sauce
1 pound (454 g) boneless steak, cut into 1-inch pieces	½ teaspoon granulated garlic
2 tablespoons olive oil	½ teaspoon salt
1 teaspoon Worcestershire	¼ teaspoon freshly ground black pepper

1. Preheat the air fryer to 400°F (204°C). Line the air fryer basket with parchment and spray lightly with oil. 2. In a medium bowl, combine the steak, olive oil, Worcestershire sauce, garlic, salt, and black pepper and toss until evenly coated. 3. Place the steak in a single layer in the prepared basket. You may have to work in batches, depending on the size of your air fryer. 4. Cook for 10 to 16 minutes, flipping every 3 to 4 minutes. The total cooking time will depend on the thickness of the meat and your preferred doneness. If you want it well done, it may take up to 5 additional minutes.

Sausage and Peppers

Prep time: 7 minutes | Cook time: 35 minutes | Serves 4

Oil, for spraying	1 onion, thinly sliced
2 pounds (907 g) hot or sweet Italian sausage links, cut into thick slices	1 tablespoon olive oil
	1 tablespoon chopped fresh parsley
4 large bell peppers of any color, seeded and cut into slices	1 teaspoon dried oregano
	1 teaspoon dried basil
	1 teaspoon balsamic vinegar

1. Line the air fryer basket with parchment and spray lightly with oil. 2. In a large bowl, combine the sausage, bell peppers, and onion. 3. In a small bowl, whisk together the olive oil, parsley, oregano, basil, and balsamic vinegar. Pour the mixture over the sausage and peppers and toss until evenly coated. 4. Using a slotted spoon, transfer the mixture to the prepared basket, taking care to drain out as much excess liquid as possible. 5. Air fry at 350°F (177°C) for 20 minutes, stir, and cook for another 15 minutes, or until the sausage is browned and the juices run clear.

Spinach and Provolone Steak Rolls

Prep time: 10 minutes | Cook time: 12 minutes | Makes 8 rolls

1 (1-pound / 454-g) flank steak, butterflied	1 cup fresh spinach leaves
8 (1-ounce / 28-g, ¼-inch-thick) deli slices provolone cheese	½ teaspoon salt
	¼ teaspoon ground black pepper

1. Place steak on a large plate. Place provolone slices to cover steak, leaving 1-inch at the edges. Lay spinach leaves over cheese. Gently roll steak and tie with kitchen twine or secure with toothpicks. Carefully slice into eight pieces. Sprinkle each with salt and pepper. 2. Place rolls into ungreased air fryer basket, cut side up. Adjust the temperature to 400°F (204°C) and air fry for 12 minutes. Steak rolls will be browned and cheese will be melted when done and have an internal temperature of at least 150°F (66°C) for medium steak and 180°F (82°C) for well-done steak. Serve warm.

Beef Steak Fingers

Prep time: 5 minutes | Cook time: 8 minutes | Serves 4

4 small beef cube steaks	½ cup flour
Salt and ground black pepper, to taste	Cooking spray

1. Preheat the air fryer to 390°F (199°C). 2. Cut cube steaks into 1-inch-wide strips. 3. Sprinkle lightly with salt and pepper to taste. 4. Roll in flour to coat all sides. 5. Spritz air fryer basket with cooking spray. 6. Put steak strips in air fryer basket in a single layer. Spritz top of steak strips with cooking spray. 7. Air fry for 4 minutes, turn strips over, and spritz with cooking spray. 8. Air fry 4 more minutes and test with fork for doneness. Steak fingers should be crispy outside with no red juices inside. 9. Repeat steps 5 through 7 to air fry remaining strips. 10. Serve immediately.

Garlic-Marinated Flank Steak

Prep time: 30 minutes | Cook time: 8 to 10 minutes | Serves 6

½ cup avocado oil	1½ teaspoons sea salt
¼ cup coconut aminos	1 teaspoon freshly ground black pepper
1 shallot, minced	¼ teaspoon red pepper flakes
1 tablespoon minced garlic	2 pounds (907 g) flank steak
2 tablespoons chopped fresh oregano, or 2 teaspoons dried	

1. In a blender, combine the avocado oil, coconut aminos, shallot, garlic, oregano, salt, black pepper, and red pepper flakes. Process until smooth. 2. Place the steak in a zip-top plastic bag or shallow dish with the marinade. Seal the bag or cover the dish and marinate in the refrigerator for at least 2 hours or overnight. 3. Remove the steak from the bag and discard the marinade. 4. Set the air fryer to 400°F (204°C). Place the steak in the air fryer basket (if needed, cut into sections and work in batches). Air fry for 4 to 6 minutes, flip the steak, and cook for another 4 minutes or until the internal temperature reaches 120°F (49°C) in the thickest part for medium-rare (or as desired).

Caraway Crusted Beef Steaks

Prep time: 5 minutes | Cook time: 10 minutes | Serves 4

4 beef steaks	to taste
2 teaspoons caraway seeds	1 tablespoon melted butter
2 teaspoons garlic powder	⅓ cup almond flour
Sea salt and cayenne pepper,	2 eggs, beaten

1. Preheat the air fryer to 355ºF (179ºC). 2. Add the beef steaks to a large bowl and toss with the caraway seeds, garlic powder, salt and pepper until well coated. 3. Stir together the melted butter and almond flour in a bowl. Whisk the eggs in a different bowl. 4. Dredge the seasoned steaks in the eggs, then dip in the almond and butter mixture. 5. Arrange the coated steaks in the air fryer basket. Air fryer for 10 minutes, or until the internal temperature of the beef steaks reaches at least 145ºF (63ºC) on a meat thermometer. Flip the steaks once halfway through to ensure even cooking. 6. Transfer the steaks to plates. Let cool for 5 minutes and serve hot.

Parmesan-Crusted Steak

Prep time: 30 minutes | Cook time: 12 minutes | Serves 6

½ cup (1 stick) unsalted butter, at room temperature	almond flour
1 cup finely grated Parmesan cheese	1½ pounds (680 g) New York strip steak
¼ cup finely ground blanched	Sea salt and freshly ground black pepper, to taste

1. Place the butter, Parmesan cheese, and almond flour in a food processor. Process until smooth. Transfer to a sheet of parchment paper and form into a log. Wrap tightly in plastic wrap. Freeze for 45 minutes or refrigerate for at least 4 hours. 2. While the butter is chilling, season the steak liberally with salt and pepper. Let the steak rest at room temperature for about 45 minutes. 3. Place the grill pan or basket in your air fryer, set it to 400ºF (204ºC), and let it preheat for 5 minutes. 4. Working in batches, if necessary, place the steak on the grill pan and air fry for 4 minutes. Flip and cook for 3 minutes more, until the steak is brown on both sides. 5. Remove the steak from the air fryer and arrange an equal amount of the Parmesan butter on top of each steak. Return the steak to the air fryer and continue cooking for another 5 minutes, until an instant-read thermometer reads 120ºF (49ºC) for medium-rare and the crust is golden brown (or to your desired doneness). 6. Transfer the cooked steak to a plate; let rest for 10 minutes before serving.

Short Ribs with Chimichurri

Prep time: 30 minutes | Cook time: 13 minutes | Serves 4

1 pound (454 g) boneless short ribs	1 tablespoon freshly squeezed lemon juice
1½ teaspoons sea salt, divided	½ teaspoon ground cumin
½ teaspoon freshly ground black pepper, divided	¼ teaspoon red pepper flakes
½ cup fresh parsley leaves	2 tablespoons extra-virgin olive oil
½ cup fresh cilantro leaves	Avocado oil spray
1 teaspoon minced garlic	

1. Pat the short ribs dry with paper towels. Sprinkle the ribs all over with 1 teaspoon salt and ¼ teaspoon black pepper. Let sit at room temperature for 45 minutes. 2. Meanwhile, place the parsley, cilantro, garlic, lemon juice, cumin, red pepper flakes, the remaining ½ teaspoon salt, and the remaining ¼ teaspoon black pepper in a blender or food processor. With the blender running, slowly drizzle in the olive oil. Blend for about 1 minute, until the mixture is smooth and well combined. 3. Set the air fryer to 400ºF (204ºC). Spray both sides of the ribs with oil. Place in the basket and air fry for 8 minutes. Flip and cook for another 5 minutes, until an instant-read thermometer reads 125ºF (52ºC) for medium-rare (or to your desired doneness). 4. Allow the meat to rest for 5 to 10 minutes, then slice. Serve warm with the chimichurri sauce.

Italian Sausages with Peppers and Onions

Prep time: 5 minutes | Cook time: 28 minutes | Serves 3

1 medium onion, thinly sliced	coconut oil
1 yellow or orange bell pepper, thinly sliced	1 teaspoon fine sea salt
1 red bell pepper, thinly sliced	6 Italian sausages
¼ cup avocado oil or melted	Dijon mustard, for serving (optional)

1. Preheat the air fryer to 400ºF (204ºC). 2. Place the onion and peppers in a large bowl. Drizzle with the oil and toss well to coat the veggies. Season with the salt. 3. Place the onion and peppers in a pie pan and cook in the air fryer for 8 minutes, stirring halfway through. Remove from the air fryer and set aside. 4. Spray the air fryer basket with avocado oil. Place the sausages in the air fryer basket and air fry for 20 minutes, or until crispy and golden brown. During the last minute or two of cooking, add the onion and peppers to the basket with the sausages to warm them through. 5. Place the onion and peppers on a serving platter and arrange the sausages on top. Serve Dijon mustard on the side, if desired. 6. Store leftovers in an airtight container in the fridge for up to 7 days or in the freezer for up to a month. Reheat in a preheated 390ºF (199ºC) air fryer for 3 minutes, or until heated through.

Air Fried Crispy Venison

Prep time: 10 minutes | Cook time: 20 minutes | Serves 4

2 eggs	pepper
¼ cup milk	1 pound (454 g) venison backstrap, sliced
1 cup whole wheat flour	Cooking spray
½ teaspoon salt	
¼ teaspoon ground black	

1. Preheat the air fryer to 360ºF (182ºC) and spritz with cooking spray. 2. Whisk the eggs with milk in a large bowl. Combine the flour with salt and ground black pepper in a shallow dish. 3. Dredge the venison in the flour first, then into the egg mixture. Shake the excess off and roll the venison back over the flour to coat well. 4. Arrange half of the venison in the preheated air fryer and spritz with cooking spray. 5. Air fry for 10 minutes or until the internal temperature of the venison reaches at least 145ºF (63ºC) for medium rare. Flip the venison halfway through. Repeat with remaining venison. 6. Serve immediately.

Smoky Pork Tenderloin

Prep time: 5 minutes | Cook time: 19 to 22 minutes | Serves 6

1½ pounds (680 g) pork tenderloin	1 teaspoon garlic powder
1 tablespoon avocado oil	1 teaspoon sea salt
1 teaspoon chili powder	1 teaspoon freshly ground black pepper
1 teaspoon smoked paprika	

1. Pierce the tenderloin all over with a fork and rub the oil all over the meat. 2. In a small dish, stir together the chili powder, smoked paprika, garlic powder, salt, and pepper. 3. Rub the spice mixture all over the tenderloin. 4. Set the air fryer to 400ºF (204ºC). Place the pork in the air fryer basket and air fry for 10 minutes. Flip the tenderloin and cook for 9 to 12 minutes more, until an instant-read thermometer reads at least 145ºF (63ºC). 5. Allow the tenderloin to rest for 5 minutes, then slice and serve.

Sausage-Stuffed Peppers

Prep time: 15 minutes | Cook time: 28 to 30 minutes | Serves 6

Avocado oil spray	black pepper, to taste
8 ounces (227 g) Italian sausage, casings removed	1 cup keto-friendly marinara sauce
½ cup chopped mushrooms	3 bell peppers, halved and seeded
¼ cup diced onion	
1 teaspoon Italian seasoning	3 ounces (85 g) provolone cheese, shredded
Sea salt and freshly ground	

1. Spray a large skillet with oil and place it over medium-high heat. Add the sausage and cook for 5 minutes, breaking up the meat with a wooden spoon. Add the mushrooms, onion, and Italian seasoning, and season with salt and pepper. Cook for 5 minutes more. Stir in the marinara sauce and cook until heated through. 2. Scoop the sausage filling into the bell pepper halves. 3. Set the air fryer to 350ºF (177ºC). Arrange the peppers in a single layer in the air fryer basket, working in batches if necessary. Air fry for 15 minutes. 4. Top the stuffed peppers with the cheese and air fry for 3 to 5 minutes more, until the cheese is melted and the peppers are tender.

Korean Beef Tacos

Prep time: 30 minutes | Cook time: 12 minutes | Serves 6

2 tablespoons gochujang (Korean red chile paste)	1½ pounds (680 g) thinly sliced beef (chuck, rib eye, or sirloin)
2 cloves garlic, minced	1 medium red onion, sliced
2 teaspoons minced fresh ginger	12 (6-inch) flour tortillas, warmed; or lettuce leaves
2 tablespoons toasted sesame oil	½ cup chopped green onions
1 tablespoon soy sauce	¼ cup chopped fresh cilantro (optional)
2 tablespoons sesame seeds	
2 teaspoons sugar	½ cup kimchi (optional)
½ teaspoon kosher salt	

1. In a small bowl, combine the gochujang, garlic, ginger, sesame oil, soy sauce, sesame seeds, sugar, and salt. Whisk until well combined.

Place the beef and red onion in a resealable plastic bag and pour the marinade over. Seal the bag and massage to coat all of the meat and onion. Marinate at room temperature for 30 minutes or in the refrigerator for up to 24 hours. 2. Place the meat and onion in the air fryer basket, leaving behind as much of the marinade as possible; discard the marinade. Set the air fryer to 400ºF (204ºC) for 12 minutes, shaking halfway through the cooking time. 3. To serve, place meat and onion in the tortillas. Top with the green onions and the cilantro and kimchi, if using, and serve.

Kheema Meatloaf

Prep time: 10 minutes | Cook time: 15 minutes | Serves 4

1 pound (454 g) 85% lean ground beef	1 tablespoon minced garlic
2 large eggs, lightly beaten	2 teaspoons garam masala
1 cup diced yellow onion	1 teaspoon kosher salt
¼ cup chopped fresh cilantro	1 teaspoon ground turmeric
1 tablespoon minced fresh ginger	1 teaspoon cayenne pepper
	½ teaspoon ground cinnamon
	⅛ teaspoon ground cardamom

1. In a large bowl, gently mix the ground beef, eggs, onion, cilantro, ginger, garlic, garam masala, salt, turmeric, cayenne, cinnamon, and cardamom until thoroughly combined. 2. Place the seasoned meat in a baking pan. Place the pan in the air fryer basket. Set the air fryer to 350ºF (177ºC) for 15 minutes. Use a meat thermometer to ensure the meat loaf has reached an internal temperature of 160ºF / 71ºC (medium). 3. Drain the fat and liquid from the pan and let stand for 5 minutes before slicing. 4. Slice and serve hot.

Bulgogi Burgers

Prep time: 30 minutes | Cook time: 10 minutes | Serves 4

Burgers:	1 tablespoon toasted sesame oil
1 pound (454 g) 85% lean ground beef	½ teaspoon kosher salt
¼ cup chopped scallions	Gochujang Mayonnaise:
2 tablespoons gochujang (Korean red chile paste)	¼ cup mayonnaise
1 tablespoon dark soy sauce	¼ cup chopped scallions
2 teaspoons minced garlic	1 tablespoon gochujang (Korean red chile paste)
2 teaspoons minced fresh ginger	1 tablespoon toasted sesame oil
	2 teaspoons sesame seeds
2 teaspoons sugar	4 hamburger buns

1. For the burgers: In a large bowl, mix the ground beef, scallions, gochujang, soy sauce, garlic, ginger, sugar, sesame oil, and salt. Marinate at room temperature for 30 minutes, or cover and refrigerate for up to 24 hours. 2. Divide the meat into four portions and form them into round patties. Make a slight depression in the middle of each patty with your thumb to prevent them from puffing up into a dome shape while cooking. 3. Place the patties in a single layer in the air fryer basket. Set the air fryer to 350ºF (177ºC) for 10 minutes. 4. Meanwhile, for the gochujang mayonnaise: Stir together the mayonnaise, scallions, gochujang, sesame oil, and sesame seeds. 5. At the end of the cooking time, use a meat thermometer to ensure the burgers have reached an internal temperature of 160ºF / 71ºC (medium). 6. To serve, place the burgers on the buns and top with the mayonnaise.

Cube Steak Roll-Ups

Prep time: 30 minutes | Cook time: 8 to 10 minutes | Serves 4

4 cube steaks (6 ounces / 170 g each)	½ cup finely chopped yellow onion
1 (16-ounce / 454-g) bottle Italian dressing	½ cup finely chopped green bell pepper
1 teaspoon salt	½ cup finely chopped mushrooms
½ teaspoon freshly ground black pepper	1 to 2 tablespoons oil

1. In a large resealable bag or airtight storage container, combine the steaks and Italian dressing. Seal the bag and refrigerate to marinate for 2 hours. 2. Remove the steaks from the marinade and place them on a cutting board. Discard the marinade. Evenly season the steaks with salt and pepper. 3. In a small bowl, stir together the onion, bell pepper, and mushrooms. Sprinkle the onion mixture evenly over the steaks. Roll up the steaks, jelly roll-style, and secure with toothpicks. 4. Preheat the air fryer to 400ºF (204ºC). 5. Place the steaks in the air fryer basket. 6. Cook for 4 minutes. Flip the steaks and spritz them with oil. Cook for 4 to 6 minutes more until the internal temperature reaches 145ºF (63ºC). Let rest for 5 minutes before serving.

Rosemary Ribeye Steaks

Prep time: 10 minutes | Cook time: 15 minutes | Serves 2

¼ cup butter	1½ tablespoons balsamic vinegar
1 clove garlic, minced	¼ cup rosemary, chopped
Salt and ground black pepper, to taste	2 ribeye steaks

1. Melt the butter in a skillet over medium heat. Add the garlic and fry until fragrant. 2. Remove the skillet from the heat and add the salt, pepper, and vinegar. Allow it to cool. 3. Add the rosemary, then pour the mixture into a Ziploc bag. 4. Put the ribeye steaks in the bag and shake well, coating the meat well. Refrigerate for an hour, then allow to sit for a further twenty minutes. 5. Preheat the air fryer to 400ºF (204ºC). 6. Air fry the ribeye steaks for 15 minutes. 7. Take care when removing the steaks from the air fryer and plate up. 8. Serve immediately.

Roast Beef with Horseradish Cream

Prep time: 5 minutes | Cook time: 35 to 45 minutes | Serves 6

2 pounds (907 g) beef roast top round or eye of round	Horseradish Cream:
1 tablespoon salt	⅓ cup heavy cream
2 teaspoons garlic powder	⅓ cup sour cream
1 teaspoon freshly ground black pepper	⅓ cup prepared horseradish
1 teaspoon dried thyme	2 teaspoons fresh lemon juice
	Salt and freshly ground black pepper, to taste

1. Preheat the air fryer to 400ºF (204ºC). 2. Season the beef with the salt, garlic powder, black pepper, and thyme. Place the beef fat-side down in the basket of the air fryer and lightly coat with olive oil. Pausing halfway through the cooking time to turn the meat, air fry for 35 to 45 minutes, until a thermometer inserted into the thickest part indicates the desired doneness, 125ºF (52ºC) (rare) to 150ºF (66ºC) (medium). Let the beef rest for 10 minutes before slicing. 3. To make the horseradish cream: In a small bowl, combine the heavy cream, sour cream, horseradish, and lemon juice. Whisk until thoroughly combined. Season to taste with salt and freshly ground black pepper. Serve alongside the beef.

Garlic Balsamic London Broil

Prep time: 30 minutes | Cook time: 8 to 10 minutes | Serves 8

2 pounds (907 g) London broil	2 tablespoons olive oil
3 large garlic cloves, minced	Sea salt and ground black pepper, to taste
3 tablespoons balsamic vinegar	½ teaspoon dried hot red pepper flakes
3 tablespoons whole-grain mustard	

1. Score both sides of the cleaned London broil. 2. Thoroughly combine the remaining ingredients; massage this mixture into the meat to coat it on all sides. Let it marinate for at least 3 hours. 3. Set the air fryer to 400ºF (204ºC); Then cook the London broil for 15 minutes. Flip it over and cook another 10 to 12 minutes. Bon appétit!

Sausage and Zucchini Lasagna

Prep time: 25 minutes | Cook time: 56 minutes | Serves 4

1 zucchini	¾ cup ricotta cheese
Avocado oil spray	1 cup shredded fontina cheese, divided
6 ounces (170 g) hot Italian sausage, casings removed	½ cup finely grated Parmesan cheese
2 ounces (57 g) mushrooms, stemmed and sliced	Sea salt and freshly ground black pepper, to taste
1 teaspoon minced garlic	Fresh basil, for garnish
1 cup keto-friendly marinara sauce	

1. Cut the zucchini into long thin slices using a mandoline slicer or sharp knife. Spray both sides of the slices with oil. 2. Place the slices in a single layer in the air fryer basket, working in batches if necessary. Set the air fryer to 325ºF (163ºC) and air fry for 4 to 6 minutes, until most of the moisture has been released from the zucchini. 3. Place a large skillet over medium-high heat. Crumble the sausage into the hot skillet and cook for 6 minutes, breaking apart the meat with the back of a spoon. Remove the sausage from the skillet, leaving any fats that remain. Add the mushrooms to the skillet and cook for 10 minutes, until the liquid nearly evaporates. Add the garlic and cook for 1 minute more. Stir in the marinara and cook for 2 more minutes. 4. In a medium bowl, combine the ricotta cheese, ½ cup of fontina cheese, Parmesan cheese, and salt and pepper to taste. 5. Spread ¼ cup of the meat sauce in the bottom of a deep pan (or other pan that fits inside your air fryer). Top with half of the zucchini slices. Add half of the cheese mixture. Top the cheese with half of the remaining meat sauce. Layer the remaining zucchini over the meat sauce and top with the remaining cheese mixture. Top the lasagna with the remaining ½ cup of fontina cheese. 6. Cover the lasagna with aluminum foil or parchment paper and place it in the air fryer. Bake for 25 minutes. Remove the foil and cook for 8 to 10 minutes more. 7. Allow the lasagna to rest for 15 minutes before cutting and serving. Garnish with basil.

New York Strip with Honey-Mustard Butter

Prep time: 5 minutes | Cook time: 14 minutes | Serves 4

2 pounds (907 g) New York Strip	½ stick butter, softened
1 teaspoon cayenne pepper	Sea salt and freshly ground black pepper, to taste
1 tablespoon honey	Cooking spray
1 tablespoon Dijon mustard	

1. Preheat the air fryer to 400ºF (204ºC) and spritz with cooking spray. 2. Sprinkle the New York Strip with cayenne pepper, salt, and black pepper on a clean work surface. 3. Arrange the New York Strip in the preheated air fryer and spritz with cooking spray. 4. Air fry for 14 minutes or until browned and reach your desired doneness. Flip the New York Strip halfway through. 5. Meanwhile, combine the honey, mustard, and butter in a small bowl. Stir to mix well. 6. Transfer the air fried New York Strip onto a plate and baste with the honey-mustard butter before serving.

Cheese Crusted Chops

Prep time: 10 minutes | Cook time: 12 minutes | Serves 4 to 6

¼ teaspoon pepper	½ teaspoons onion powder
½ teaspoons salt	1 teaspoon smoked paprika
4 to 6 thick boneless pork chops	2 beaten eggs
1 cup pork rind crumbs	3 tablespoons grated Parmesan cheese
¼ teaspoon chili powder	Cooking spray

1. Preheat the air fryer to 400ºF (205ºC). 2. Rub the pepper and salt on both sides of pork chops. 3. In a food processor, pulse pork rinds into crumbs. Mix crumbs with chili powder, onion powder, and paprika in a bowl. 4. Beat eggs in another bowl. 5. Dip pork chops into eggs then into pork rind crumb mixture. 6. Spritz the air fryer basket with cooking spray and add pork chops to the basket. 7. Air fry for 12 minutes. 8. Serve garnished with the Parmesan cheese.

Cinnamon-Beef Kofta

Prep time: 10 minutes | Cook time: 13 minutes per batch | Makes 12 koftas

1½ pounds (680 g) lean ground beef	1 teaspoon ground cumin
1 teaspoon onion powder	¾ teaspoon salt
¾ teaspoon ground cinnamon	¼ teaspoon cayenne
¾ teaspoon ground dried turmeric	12 (3½- to 4-inch-long) cinnamon sticks
	Cooking spray

1. Preheat the air fryer to 375ºF (191ºC). Spritz the air fryer basket with cooking spray. 2. Combine all the ingredients, except for the cinnamon sticks, in a large bowl. Toss to mix well. 3. Divide and shape the mixture into 12 balls, then wrap each ball around each cinnamon stick and leave a quarter of the length uncovered. 4. Arrange the beef-cinnamon sticks in the preheated air fryer and spritz with cooking spray. Work in batches to avoid overcrowding. 5. Air fry for 13 minutes or until the beef is browned. Flip the sticks halfway through. 6. Serve immediately.

Mediterranean Beef Steaks

Prep time: 20 minutes | Cook time: 20 minutes | Serves 4

2 tablespoons coconut aminos	pepper
3 heaping tablespoons fresh chives	½ teaspoon dried basil
2 tablespoons olive oil	½ teaspoon dried rosemary
3 tablespoons dry white wine	1 teaspoon freshly ground black pepper
4 small-sized beef steaks	1 teaspoon sea salt, or more to taste
2 teaspoons smoked cayenne	

1. Firstly, coat the steaks with the cayenne pepper, black pepper, salt, basil, and rosemary. 2. Drizzle the steaks with olive oil, white wine, and coconut aminos. 3. Finally, roast in the air fryer for 20 minutes at 340ºF (171ºC). Serve garnished with fresh chives. Bon appétit!

Pork Loin Roast

Prep time: 30 minutes | Cook time: 55 minutes | Serves 6

1½ pounds (680 g) boneless pork loin roast, washed	¾ teaspoon sea salt flakes
1 teaspoon mustard seeds	1 teaspoon red pepper flakes, crushed
1 teaspoon garlic powder	2 dried sprigs thyme, crushed
1 teaspoon porcini powder	2 tablespoons lime juice
1 teaspoon shallot powder	

1. Firstly, score the meat using a small knife; make sure to not cut too deep. 2. In a small-sized mixing dish, combine all seasonings in the order listed above; mix to combine well. 3. Massage the spice mix into the pork meat to evenly distribute. Drizzle with lemon juice. 4. Set the air fryer to 360ºF (182ºC). Place the pork in the air fryer basket; roast for 25 to 30 minutes. Pause the machine, check for doneness and cook for 25 minutes more.

Indian Mint and Chile Kebabs

Prep time: 30 minutes | Cook time: 15 minutes | Serves 4

1 pound (454 g) ground lamb	½ teaspoon ground turmeric
½ cup finely minced onion	½ teaspoon cayenne pepper
¼ cup chopped fresh mint	¼ teaspoon ground cardamom
¼ cup chopped fresh cilantro	¼ teaspoon ground cinnamon
1 tablespoon minced garlic	1 teaspoon kosher salt

1. In the bowl of a stand mixer fitted with the paddle attachment, combine the lamb, onion, mint, cilantro, garlic, turmeric, cayenne, cardamom, cinnamon, and salt. Mix on low speed until you have a sticky mess of spiced meat. If you have time, let the mixture stand at room temperature for 30 minutes (or cover and refrigerate for up to a day or two, until you're ready to make the kebabs). 2. Divide the meat into eight equal portions. Form each into a long sausage shape. Place the kebabs in a single layer in the air fryer basket. Set the air fryer to 350ºF (177ºC) for 10 minutes. Increase the air fryer temperature to 400ºF (204ºC) and cook for 3 to 4 minutes more to brown the kebabs. Use a meat thermometer to ensure the kebabs have reached an internal temperature of 160ºF / 71ºC (medium).

Pork Chops with Caramelized Onions

Prep time: 20 minutes | Cook time: 23 to 34 minutes | Serves 4

4 bone-in pork chops (8 ounces / 227 g each)
1 to 2 tablespoons oil
2 tablespoons Cajun seasoning, divided
1 yellow onion, thinly sliced
1 green bell pepper, thinly sliced
2 tablespoons light brown sugar

1. Spritz the pork chops with oil. Sprinkle 1 tablespoon of Cajun seasoning on one side of the chops. 2. Preheat the air fryer to 400°F (204°C). Line the air fryer basket with parchment paper and spritz the parchment with oil. 3. Place 2 pork chops, spice-side up, on the paper. 4. Cook for 4 minutes. Flip the chops, sprinkle with the remaining 1 tablespoon of Cajun seasoning, and cook for 4 to 8 minutes more until the internal temperature reaches 145°F (63°C), depending on the chops' thickness. Remove and keep warm while you cook the remaining 2 chops. Set the chops aside. 5. In a baking pan, combine the onion, bell pepper, and brown sugar, stirring until the vegetables are coated. Place the pan in the air fryer basket and cook for 4 minutes. 6. Stir the vegetables. Cook for 3 to 6 minutes more to your desired doneness. Spoon the vegetable mixture over the chops to serve.

London Broil with Herb Butter

Prep time: 30 minutes | Cook time: 20 to 25 minutes | Serves 4

1½ pounds (680 g) London broil top round steak
¼ cup olive oil
2 tablespoons balsamic vinegar
1 tablespoon Worcestershire sauce
4 cloves garlic, minced
Herb Butter:
6 tablespoons unsalted butter, softened
1 tablespoon chopped fresh parsley
¼ teaspoon salt
¼ teaspoon dried ground rosemary or thyme
¼ teaspoon garlic powder
Pinch of red pepper flakes

1. Place the beef in a gallon-size resealable bag. In a small bowl, whisk together the olive oil, balsamic vinegar, Worcestershire sauce, and garlic. Pour the marinade over the beef, massaging gently to coat, and seal the bag. Let sit at room temperature for an hour or refrigerate overnight. 2. To make the herb butter: In a small bowl, mix the butter with the parsley, salt, rosemary, garlic powder, and red pepper flakes until smooth. Cover and refrigerate until ready to use. 3. Preheat the air fryer to 400°F (204°C). 4. Remove the beef from the marinade (discard the marinade) and place the beef in the air fryer basket. Pausing halfway through the cooking time to turn the meat, air fry for 20 to 25 minutes, until a thermometer inserted into the thickest part indicates the desired doneness, 125°F / 52°C (rare) to 150°F / 66°C (medium). Let the beef rest for 10 minutes before slicing. Serve topped with the herb butter.

Steak Gyro Platter

Prep time: 30 minutes | Cook time: 8 to 10 minutes | Serves 4

1 pound (454 g) flank steak
1 teaspoon garlic powder
1 teaspoon ground cumin
½ teaspoon sea salt
½ teaspoon freshly ground black pepper
5 ounces (142 g) shredded romaine lettuce
½ cup crumbled feta cheese
½ cup peeled and diced cucumber
⅓ cup sliced red onion
¼ cup seeded and diced tomato
2 tablespoons pitted and sliced black olives
Tzatziki sauce, for serving

1. Pat the steak dry with paper towels. In a small bowl, combine the garlic powder, cumin, salt, and pepper. Sprinkle this mixture all over the steak, and allow the steak to rest at room temperature for 45 minutes. 2. Preheat the air fryer to 400°F (204°C). Place the steak in the air fryer basket and air fry for 4 minutes. Flip the steak and cook 4 to 6 minutes more, until an instant-read thermometer reads 120°F (49°C) at the thickest point for medium-rare (or as desired). Remove the steak from the air fryer and let it rest for 5 minutes. 3. Divide the romaine among plates. Top with the feta, cucumber, red onion, tomato, and olives.

Hoisin BBQ Pork Chops

Prep time: 5 minutes | Cook time: 22 minutes | Serves 2 to 3

3 tablespoons hoisin sauce
¼ cup honey
1 tablespoon soy sauce
3 tablespoons rice vinegar
2 tablespoons brown sugar
1½ teaspoons grated fresh ginger
1 to 2 teaspoons Sriracha sauce, to taste
2 to 3 bone-in center cut pork chops, 1-inch thick (about 1¼ pounds / 567 g)
Chopped scallions, for garnish

1. Combine the hoisin sauce, honey, soy sauce, rice vinegar, brown sugar, ginger, and Sriracha sauce in a small saucepan. Whisk the ingredients together and bring the mixture to a boil over medium-high heat on the stovetop. Reduce the heat and simmer the sauce until it has reduced in volume and thickened slightly, about 10 minutes. 2. Preheat the air fryer to 400°F (204°C). 3. Place the pork chops into the air fryer basket and pour half the hoisin BBQ sauce over the top. Air fry for 6 minutes. Then, flip the chops over, pour the remaining hoisin BBQ sauce on top and air fry for 5 to 6 more minutes, depending on the thickness of the pork chops. The internal temperature of the pork chops should be 155°F (68°C) when tested with an instant read thermometer. 4. Let the pork chops rest for 5 minutes before serving. You can spoon a little of the sauce from the bottom drawer of the air fryer over the top if desired. Sprinkle with chopped scallions and serve.

Italian Steak Rolls

Prep time: 30 minutes | Cook time: 9 minutes | Serves 4

1 tablespoon vegetable oil
2 cloves garlic, minced
2 teaspoons dried Italian seasoning
1 teaspoon kosher salt
1 teaspoon black pepper

1 pound (454 g) flank or skirt steak, ¼ to ½ inch thick
1 (10-ounce / 283-g) package frozen spinach, thawed and squeezed dry
½ cup diced jarred roasted red pepper
1 cup shredded Mozzarella cheese

1. In a large bowl, combine the oil, garlic, Italian seasoning, salt, and pepper. Whisk to combine. Add the steak to the bowl, turning to ensure the entire steak is covered with the seasonings. Cover and marinate at room temperature for 30 minutes or in the refrigerator for up to 24 hours. 2. Lay the steak on a flat surface. Spread the spinach evenly over the steak, leaving a ¼-inch border at the edge. Evenly top each steak with the red pepper and cheese. 3. Starting at a long end, roll up the steak as tightly as possible, ending seam side down. Use 2 or 3 wooden toothpicks to hold the roll together. Using a sharp knife, cut the roll in half so that it better fits in the air fryer basket. 4. Place the steak roll, seam side down, in the air fryer basket. Set the air fryer to 400ºF (204ºC) for 9 minutes. Use a meat thermometer to ensure the steak has reached an internal temperature of 145ºF (63ºC). (It is critical to not overcook flank steak, so as to not toughen the meat.) 5. Let the steak rest for 10 minutes before cutting into slices to serve.

Chapter 7

Snacks and Appetizers

Asian Five-Spice Wings

Prep time: 30 minutes | Cook time: 13 to 15 minutes | Serves 4

2 pounds (907 g) chicken wings	dressing
½ cup Asian-style salad	2 tablespoons Chinese five-spice powder

1. Cut off wing tips and discard or freeze for stock. Cut remaining wing pieces in two at the joint. 2. Place wing pieces in a large sealable plastic bag. Pour in the Asian dressing, seal bag, and massage the marinade into the wings until well coated. Refrigerate for at least an hour. 3. Remove wings from bag, drain off excess marinade, and place wings in air fryer basket. 4. Air fry at 360ºF (182ºC) for 13 to 15 minutes or until juices run clear. About halfway through cooking time, shake the basket or stir wings for more even cooking. 5. Transfer cooked wings to plate in a single layer. Sprinkle half of the Chinese five-spice powder on the wings, turn, and sprinkle other side with remaining seasoning.

Goat Cheese and Garlic Crostini

Prep time: 3 minutes | Cook time: 5 minutes | Serves 4

1 whole wheat baguette	4 ounces (113 g) goat cheese
¼ cup olive oil	2 tablespoons fresh basil, minced
2 garlic cloves, minced	

1. Preheat the air fryer to 380°F(193ºC). 2. Cut the baguette into ½-inch-thick slices. 3. In a small bowl, mix together the olive oil and garlic, then brush it over one side of each slice of bread. 4. Place the olive-oil-coated bread in a single layer in the air fryer basket and bake for 5 minutes. 5. Meanwhile, in a small bowl, mix together the goat cheese and basil. 6. Remove the toast from the air fryer, then spread a thin layer of the goat cheese mixture over the top of each piece and serve.

Cream Cheese Stuffed Jalapeño Poppers

Prep time: 12 minutes | Cook time: 6 to 8 minutes | Serves 10

8 ounces (227 g) cream cheese, at room temperature	minced
1 cup panko bread crumbs, divided	1 teaspoon chili powder
	10 jalapeño peppers, halved and seeded
2 tablespoons fresh parsley,	Cooking oil spray

1. In a small bowl, whisk the cream cheese, ½ cup of panko, the parsley, and chili powder until combined. Stuff the cheese mixture into the jalapeño halves. 2. Sprinkle the tops of the stuffed jalapeños with the remaining ½ cup of panko and press it lightly into the filling. 3. Insert the crisper plate into the basket and the basket into the unit. Preheat the unit by selecting AIR FRY, setting the temperature to 375ºF (191ºC), and setting the time to 3 minutes. Select START/STOP to begin. 4. Once the unit is preheated, spray the crisper plate with cooking oil. Place the poppers into the basket. 5. Select AIR FRY, set the temperature to 375ºF (191ºC), and set the time to 8 minutes. Select START/STOP to begin. 6. After 6 minutes, check the poppers.

If they are softened and the cheese is melted, they are done. If not, resume cooking. 7. When the cooking is complete, serve warm.

Cheesy Steak Fries

Prep time: 5 minutes | Cook time: 20 minutes | Serves 5

1 (28-ounce / 794-g) bag frozen steak fries	1 cup shredded Mozzarella cheese
Cooking spray	2 scallions, green parts only, chopped
Salt and pepper, to taste	
½ cup beef gravy	

1. Preheat the air fryer to 400ºF (204ºC). 2. Place the frozen steak fries in the air fryer. Air fry for 10 minutes. Shake the basket and spritz the fries with cooking spray. Sprinkle with salt and pepper. Air fry for an additional 8 minutes. 3. Pour the beef gravy into a medium, microwave-safe bowl. Microwave for 30 seconds, or until the gravy is warm. 4. Sprinkle the fries with the cheese. Air fry for an additional 2 minutes, until the cheese is melted. 5. Transfer the fries to a serving dish. Drizzle the fries with gravy and sprinkle the scallions on top for a green garnish. Serve.

Sweet Bacon Tater Tots

Prep time: 5 minutes | Cook time: 7 minutes | Serves 4

24 frozen tater tots	1 cup shredded Cheddar cheese
6 slices cooked bacon	
2 tablespoons maple syrup	

1. Preheat the air fryer to 400ºF (204ºC). 2. Put the tater tots in the air fryer basket. Air fry for 10 minutes, shaking the basket halfway through the cooking time. 3. Meanwhile, cut the bacon into 1-inch pieces. 4. Remove the tater tots from the air fryer basket and put into a baking pan. Top with the bacon and drizzle with the maple syrup. Air fry for 5 minutes, or until the tots and bacon are crisp. 5. Top with the cheese and air fry for 2 minutes, or until the cheese is melted. 6. Serve hot.

Spiced Nuts

Prep time: 5 minutes | Cook time: 25 minutes | Makes 3 cups

1 egg white, lightly beaten	¼ teaspoon ground allspice
¼ cup sugar	Pinch ground cayenne pepper
1 teaspoon salt	1 cup pecan halves
½ teaspoon ground cinnamon	1 cup cashews
¼ teaspoon ground cloves	1 cup almonds

1. Combine the egg white with the sugar and spices in a bowl. 2. Preheat the air fryer to 300ºF (149ºC). 3. Spray or brush the air fryer basket with vegetable oil. Toss the nuts together in the spiced egg white and transfer the nuts to the air fryer basket. 4. Air fry for 25 minutes, stirring the nuts in the basket a few times during the cooking process. Taste the nuts (carefully because they will be very hot) to see if they are crunchy and nicely toasted. Air fry for a few more minutes if necessary. 5. Serve warm or cool to room temperature and store in an airtight container for up to two weeks.

Grilled Ham and Cheese on Raisin Bread

Prep time: 5 minutes | Cook time: 10 minutes | Serves 1

2 slices raisin bread	ham (about 3 ounces / 85 g)
2 tablespoons butter, softened	4 slices Muenster cheese
2 teaspoons honey mustard	(about 3 ounces / 85 g)
3 slices thinly sliced honey	2 toothpicks

1. Preheat the air fryer to 370ºF (188ºC). 2. Spread the softened butter on one side of both slices of raisin bread and place the bread, buttered side down on the counter. Spread the honey mustard on the other side of each slice of bread. Layer 2 slices of cheese, the ham and the remaining 2 slices of cheese on one slice of bread and top with the other slice of bread. Remember to leave the buttered side of the bread on the outside. 3. Transfer the sandwich to the air fryer basket and secure the sandwich with toothpicks. 4. Air fry for 5 minutes. Flip the sandwich over, remove the toothpicks and air fry for another 5 minutes. Cut the sandwich in half and enjoy!

Egg Roll Pizza Sticks

Prep time: 10 minutes | Cook time: 5 minutes | Serves 4

Olive oil	24 slices turkey pepperoni
8 pieces reduced-fat string	Marinara sauce, for dipping
cheese	(optional)
8 egg roll wrappers	

1. Spray the air fryer basket lightly with olive oil. Fill a small bowl with water. 2. Place each egg roll wrapper diagonally on a work surface. It should look like a diamond. 3. Place 3 slices of turkey pepperoni in a vertical line down the center of the wrapper. 4. Place 1 Mozzarella cheese stick on top of the turkey pepperoni. 5. Fold the top and bottom corners of the egg roll wrapper over the cheese stick. 6. Fold the left corner over the cheese stick and roll the cheese stick up to resemble a spring roll. Dip a finger in the water and seal the edge of the roll 7. Repeat with the rest of the pizza sticks. 8. Place them in the air fryer basket in a single layer, making sure to leave a little space between each one. Lightly spray the pizza sticks with oil. You may need to cook these in batches. 9. Air fry at 375ºF (191ºC) until the pizza sticks are lightly browned and crispy, about 5 minutes. 10. These are best served hot while the cheese is melted. Accompany with a small bowl of marinara sauce, if desired.

Lebanese Muhammara

Prep time: 15 minutes | Cook time: 15 minutes | Serves 6

2 large red bell peppers	1 teaspoon ground cumin
¼ cup plus 2 tablespoons	1 teaspoon kosher salt
extra-virgin olive oil	1 teaspoon red pepper flakes
1 cup walnut halves	Raw vegetables (such as
1 tablespoon agave nectar or	cucumber, carrots, zucchini
honey	slices, or cauliflower) or
1 teaspoon fresh lemon juice	toasted pita chips, for serving

1. Drizzle the peppers with 2 tablespoons of the olive oil and place

in the air fryer basket. Set the air fryer to 400ºF (204ºC) for 10 minutes. 2. Add the walnuts to the basket, arranging them around the peppers. Set the air fryer to 400ºF (204ºC) for 5 minutes. 3. Remove the peppers, seal in a resealable plastic bag, and let rest for 5 to 10 minutes. Transfer the walnuts to a plate and set aside to cool. 4. Place the softened peppers, walnuts, agave, lemon juice, cumin, salt, and ½ teaspoon of the pepper flakes in a food processor and purée until smooth. 5. Transfer the dip to a serving bowl and make an indentation in the middle. Pour the remaining ¼ cup olive oil into the indentation. Garnish the dip with the remaining ½ teaspoon pepper flakes. 6. Serve with vegetables or toasted pita chips.

Sausage Balls with Cheese

Prep time: 10 minutes | Cook time: 10 to 11 minutes | Serves 8

12 ounces (340 g) mild	cheese
ground sausage	3 ounces (85 g) cream cheese,
1½ cups baking mix	at room temperature
1 cup shredded mild Cheddar	1 to 2 tablespoons olive oil

1. Preheat the air fryer to 325ºF (163ºC). Line the air fryer basket with parchment paper. 2. Mix together the ground sausage, baking mix, Cheddar cheese, and cream cheese in a large bowl and stir to incorporate. 3. Divide the sausage mixture into 16 equal portions and roll them into 1-inch balls with your hands. 4. Arrange the sausage balls on the parchment, leaving space between each ball. You may need to work in batches to avoid overcrowding. 5. Brush the sausage balls with the olive oil. Bake for 10 to 11 minutes, shaking the basket halfway through, or until the balls are firm and lightly browned on both sides. 6. Remove from the basket to a plate and repeat with the remaining balls. 7. Serve warm.

Asian Rice Logs

Prep time: 30 minutes | Cook time: 5 minutes | Makes 8 rice logs

1½ cups cooked jasmine or	⅓ cup plain bread crumbs
sushi rice	¾ cup panko bread crumbs
¼ teaspoon salt	2 tablespoons sesame seeds
2 teaspoons five-spice powder	Orange Marmalade Dipping
2 teaspoons diced shallots	Sauce:
1 tablespoon tamari sauce	½ cup all-natural orange
1 egg, beaten	marmalade
1 teaspoon sesame oil	1 tablespoon soy sauce
2 teaspoons water	

1. Make the rice according to package instructions. While the rice is cooking, make the dipping sauce by combining the marmalade and soy sauce and set aside. 2. Stir together the cooked rice, salt, five-spice powder, shallots, and tamari sauce. 3. Divide rice into 8 equal pieces. With slightly damp hands, mold each piece into a log shape. Chill in freezer for 10 to 15 minutes. 4. Mix the egg, sesame oil, and water together in a shallow bowl. 5. Place the plain bread crumbs on a sheet of wax paper. 6. Mix the panko bread crumbs with the sesame seeds and place on another sheet of wax paper. 7. Roll the rice logs in plain bread crumbs, then dip in egg wash, and then dip in the panko and sesame seeds. 8. Cook the logs at 390ºF (199ºC) for approximately 5 minutes, until golden brown. 9. Cool slightly before serving with Orange Marmalade Dipping Sauce.

Pork and Cabbage Egg Rolls

Prep time: 15 minutes | Cook time: 12 minutes | Makes 12 egg rolls

Cooking oil spray	fresh ginger
2 garlic cloves, minced	2 cups shredded green
12 ounces (340 g) ground	cabbage
pork	4 scallions, green parts (white
1 teaspoon sesame oil	parts optional), chopped
¼ cup soy sauce	24 egg roll wrappers
2 teaspoons grated peeled	

1. Spray a skillet with the cooking oil and place it over medium-high heat. Add the garlic and cook for 1 minute until fragrant. 2. Add the ground pork to the skillet. Using a spoon, break the pork into smaller chunks. 3. In a small bowl, whisk the sesame oil, soy sauce, and ginger until combined. Add the sauce to the skillet. Stir to combine and continue cooking for about 5 minutes until the pork is browned and thoroughly cooked. 4. Stir in the cabbage and scallions. Transfer the pork mixture to a large bowl. 5. Lay the egg roll wrappers on a flat surface. Dip a basting brush in water and glaze each egg roll wrapper along the edges with the wet brush. This will soften the dough and make it easier to roll. 6. Stack 2 egg roll wrappers (it works best if you double-wrap the egg rolls). Scoop 1 to 2 tablespoons of the pork mixture into the center of each wrapper stack. 7. Roll one long side of the wrappers up over the filling. Press firmly on the area with the filling, tucking it in lightly to secure it in place. Fold in the left and right sides. Continue rolling to close. Use the basting brush to wet the seam and seal the egg roll. Repeat with the remaining ingredients. 8. Insert the crisper plate into the basket and the basket into the unit. Preheat the unit by selecting AIR FRY, setting the temperature to 400ºF (204ºC), and setting the time to 3 minutes. Select START/STOP to begin. 9. Once the unit is preheated, spray the crisper plate with cooking oil. Place the egg rolls into the basket. It is okay to stack them. Spray them with cooking oil. 10. Select AIR FRY, set the temperature to 400ºF (204ºC), and set the time to 12 minutes. Insert the basket into the unit. Select START/STOP to begin. 11. After 8 minutes, use tongs to flip the egg rolls. Reinsert the basket to resume cooking. 12. When the cooking is complete, serve the egg rolls hot.

Old Bay Chicken Wings

Prep time: 10 minutes | Cook time: 12 to 15 minutes | Serves 4

2 tablespoons Old Bay	2 pounds (907 g) chicken
seasoning	wings, patted dry
2 teaspoons baking powder	Cooking spray
2 teaspoons salt	

1. Preheat the air fryer to 400ºF (204ºC). Lightly spray the air fryer basket with cooking spray. 2. Combine the Old Bay seasoning, baking powder, and salt in a large zip-top plastic bag. Add the chicken wings, seal, and shake until the wings are thoroughly coated in the seasoning mixture. 3. Lay the chicken wings in the air fryer basket in a single layer and lightly mist with cooking spray. You may need to work in batches to avoid overcrowding. 4. Air fry for 12 to 15 minutes, flipping the wings halfway through, or until the wings are lightly browned and the internal temperature reaches at least 165ºF (74ºC) on a meat thermometer. 5. Remove from the basket to a plate and repeat with the remaining chicken wings. 6. Serve hot.

Skinny Fries

Prep time: 10 minutes | Cook time: 15 minutes per batch | Serves 2

2 to 3 russet potatoes, peeled	vegetable oil
and cut into ¼-inch sticks	Salt, to taste
2 to 3 teaspoons olive or	

1. Cut the potatoes into ¼-inch strips. (A mandolin with a julienne blade is really helpful here.) Rinse the potatoes with cold water several times and let them soak in cold water for at least 10 minutes or as long as overnight. 2. Preheat the air fryer to 380ºF (193ºC). 3. Drain and dry the potato sticks really well, using a clean kitchen towel. Toss the fries with the oil in a bowl and then air fry the fries in two batches at 380ºF (193ºC) for 15 minutes, shaking the basket a couple of times while they cook. 4. Add the first batch of French fries back into the air fryer basket with the finishing batch and let everything warm through for a few minutes. As soon as the fries are done, season them with salt and transfer to a plate or basket. Serve them warm with ketchup or your favorite dip.

Fried Peaches

Prep time: 15 minutes | Cook time: 6 to 8 minutes | Serves 4

2 egg whites	2 medium, very firm peaches,
1 tablespoon water	peeled and pitted
¼ cup sliced almonds	¼ cup cornstarch
2 tablespoons brown sugar	Oil for misting or cooking
½ teaspoon almond extract	spray
1 cup crisp rice cereal	

1. Preheat the air fryer to 390ºF (199ºC). 2. Beat together egg whites and water in a shallow dish. 3. In a food processor, combine the almonds, brown sugar, and almond extract. Process until ingredients combine well and the nuts are finely chopped. 4. Add cereal and pulse just until cereal crushes. Pour crumb mixture into a shallow dish or onto a plate. 5. Cut each peach into eighths and place in a plastic bag or container with lid. Add cornstarch, seal, and shake to coat. 6. Remove peach slices from bag or container, tapping them hard to shake off the excess cornstarch. Dip in egg wash and roll in crumbs. Spray with oil. 7. Place in air fryer basket and cook for 5 minutes. Shake basket, separate any that have stuck together, and spritz a little oil on any spots that aren't browning. 8. Cook for 1 to 3 minutes longer, until golden brown and crispy.

Air Fryer Popcorn with Garlic Salt

Prep time: 3 minutes | Cook time: 10 minutes | Serves 2

2 tablespoons olive oil	1 teaspoon garlic salt
¼ cup popcorn kernels	

1. Preheat the air fryer to 380ºF(193ºC). 2. Tear a square of aluminum foil the size of the bottom of the air fryer and place into the air fryer. 3. Drizzle olive oil over the top of the foil, and then pour in the popcorn kernels. 4. Roast for 8 to 10 minutes, or until the popcorn stops popping. 5. Transfer the popcorn to a large bowl and sprinkle with garlic salt before serving.

Homemade Sweet Potato Chips

Prep time: 5 minutes | Cook time: 15 minutes | Serves 2

1 large sweet potato, sliced thin	⅛ teaspoon salt
	2 tablespoons olive oil

1. Preheat the air fryer to 380°F(193°C). 2. In a small bowl, toss the sweet potatoes, salt, and olive oil together until the potatoes are well coated. 3. Put the sweet potato slices into the air fryer and spread them out in a single layer. 4. Fry for 10 minutes. Stir, then air fry for 3 to 5 minutes more, or until the chips reach the preferred level of crispiness.

Mozzarella Arancini

Prep time: 5 minutes | Cook time: 8 to 11 minutes | Makes 16 arancini

2 cups cooked rice, cooled	2 tablespoons minced fresh
2 eggs, beaten	basil
1½ cups panko bread crumbs, divided	16¾-inch cubes Mozzarella cheese
½ cup grated Parmesan cheese	2 tablespoons olive oil

1. Preheat the air fryer to 400°F (204°C). 2. In a medium bowl, combine the rice, eggs, ½ cup of the bread crumbs, Parmesan cheese, and basil. Form this mixture into 16 1½-inch balls. 3. Poke a hole in each of the balls with your finger and insert a Mozzarella cube. Form the rice mixture firmly around the cheese. 4. On a shallow plate, combine the remaining 1 cup of the bread crumbs with the olive oil and mix well. Roll the rice balls in the bread crumbs to coat. 5. Air fry the arancini in batches for 8 to 11 minutes or until golden brown. 6. Serve hot.

Mexican Potato Skins

Prep time: 10 minutes | Cook time: 55 minutes | Serves 6

Olive oil	beans
6 medium russet potatoes, scrubbed	1 tablespoon taco seasoning
	½ cup salsa
Salt and freshly ground black pepper, to taste	¾ cup reduced-fat shredded Cheddar cheese
1 cup fat-free refried black	

1. Spray the air fryer basket lightly with olive oil. 2. Spray the potatoes lightly with oil and season with salt and pepper. Pierce each potato a few times with a fork. 3. Place the potatoes in the air fryer basket. Air fry at 400°F (204°C) until fork-tender, 30 to 40 minutes. The cooking time will depend on the size of the potatoes. You can cook the potatoes in the microwave or a standard oven, but they won't get the same lovely crispy skin they will get in the air fryer. 4. While the potatoes are cooking, in a small bowl, mix together the beans and taco seasoning. Set aside until the potatoes are cool enough to handle. 5. Cut each potato in half lengthwise. Scoop out most of the insides, leaving about ¼ inch in the skins so the potato skins hold their shape. 6. Season the insides of the potato skins with salt and black pepper. Lightly spray the insides of the potato skins with oil. You may need to cook them in batches. 7. Place them into the air fryer basket, skin-side down, and air fry until crisp and golden, 8 to 10 minutes. 8. Transfer the skins to a work surface and spoon ½ tablespoon of seasoned refried black beans into each one. Top each with 2 teaspoons salsa and 1 tablespoon shredded Cheddar cheese. 9. Place filled potato skins in the air fryer basket in a single layer. Lightly spray with oil. 10. Air fry until the cheese is melted and bubbly, 2 to 3 minutes.

Cream Cheese Wontons

Prep time: 15 minutes | Cook time: 6 minutes | Makes 20 wontons

Oil, for spraying	4 ounces (113 g) cream cheese
20 wonton wrappers	

1. Line the air fryer basket with parchment and spray lightly with oil. 2. Pour some water in a small bowl. 3. Lay out a wonton wrapper and place 1 teaspoon of cream cheese in the center. 4. Dip your finger in the water and moisten the edge of the wonton wrapper. Fold over the opposite corners to make a triangle and press the edges together. 5. Pinch the corners of the triangle together to form a classic wonton shape. Place the wonton in the prepared basket. Repeat with the remaining wrappers and cream cheese. You may need to work in batches, depending on the size of your air fryer. 6. Air fry at 400°F (204°C) for 6 minutes, or until golden brown around the edges.

Poutine with Waffle Fries

Prep time: 10 minutes | Cook time: 15 to 17 minutes | Serves 4

2 cups frozen waffle cut fries	2 green onions, sliced
2 teaspoons olive oil	1 cup shredded Swiss cheese
1 red bell pepper, chopped	½ cup bottled chicken gravy

1. Preheat the air fryer to 380°F (193°C). 2. Toss the waffle fries with the olive oil and place in the air fryer basket. Air fry for 10 to 12 minutes, or until the fries are crisp and light golden brown, shaking the basket halfway through the cooking time. 3. Transfer the fries to a baking pan and top with the pepper, green onions, and cheese. Air fry for 3 minutes, or until the vegetables are crisp and tender. 4. Remove the pan from the air fryer and drizzle the gravy over the fries. Air fry for 2 minutes, or until the gravy is hot. 5. Serve immediately.

Bacon-Wrapped Pickle Spears

Prep time: 10 minutes | Cook time: 8 minutes | Serves 4

8 to 12 slices bacon	cheese
¼ cup (2 ounces / 57 g) cream cheese, softened	8 dill pickle spears
	½ cup ranch dressing
¼ cup shredded Mozzarella	

1. Lay the bacon slices on a flat surface. In a medium bowl, combine the cream cheese and Mozzarella. Stir until well blended. Spread the cheese mixture over the bacon slices. 2. Place a pickle spear on a bacon slice and roll the bacon around the pickle in a spiral, ensuring the pickle is fully covered. (You may need to use more than one slice of bacon per pickle to fully cover the spear.) Tuck in the ends to ensure the bacon stays put. Repeat to wrap all the pickles. 3. Place the wrapped pickles in the air fryer basket in a single layer. Set the air fryer to 400°F (204°C) for 8 minutes, or until the bacon is cooked through and crisp on the edges. 4. Serve the pickle spears with ranch dressing on the side.

61

Red Pepper Tapenade

Prep time: 5 minutes | Cook time: 5 minutes | Serves 4

1 large red bell pepper	and roughly chopped
2 tablespoons plus 1 teaspoon olive oil, divided	1 garlic clove, minced
½ cup Kalamata olives, pitted	½ teaspoon dried oregano
	1 tablespoon lemon juice

1. Preheat the air fryer to 380°F(193ºC). 2. Brush the outside of a whole red pepper with 1 teaspoon olive oil and place it inside the air fryer basket. Roast for 5 minutes. 3. Meanwhile, in a medium bowl combine the remaining 2 tablespoons of olive oil with the olives, garlic, oregano, and lemon juice. 4. Remove the red pepper from the air fryer, then gently slice off the stem and remove the seeds. Roughly chop the roasted pepper into small pieces. 5. Add the red pepper to the olive mixture and stir all together until combined. 6. Serve with pita chips, crackers, or crusty bread.

Kale Chips with Tex-Mex Dip

Prep time: 10 minutes | Cook time: 5 to 6 minutes | Serves 8

1 cup Greek yogurt	1 bunch curly kale
1 tablespoon chili powder	1 teaspoon olive oil
⅓ cup low-sodium salsa, well drained	¼ teaspoon coarse sea salt

1. In a small bowl, combine the yogurt, chili powder, and drained salsa; refrigerate. 2. Rinse the kale thoroughly, and pat dry. Remove the stems and ribs from the kale, using a sharp knife. Cut or tear the leaves into 3-inch pieces. 3. Toss the kale with the olive oil in a large bowl. 4. Air fry the kale in small batches at 390°F (199ºC) until the leaves are crisp. This should take 5 to 6 minutes. Shake the basket once during cooking time. 5. As you remove the kale chips, sprinkle them with a bit of the sea salt. 6. When all of the kale chips are done, serve with the dip.

Baked Spanakopita Dip

Prep time: 10 minutes | Cook time: 15 minutes | Serves 2

Olive oil cooking spray	4 ounces (113 g) feta cheese,
3 tablespoons olive oil, divided	divided
	Zest of 1 lemon
2 tablespoons minced white onion	¼ teaspoon ground nutmeg
	1 teaspoon dried dill
2 garlic cloves, minced	½ teaspoon salt
4 cups fresh spinach	Pita chips, carrot sticks,
4 ounces (113 g) cream cheese, softened	or sliced bread for serving (optional)

1. Preheat the air fryer to 360°F(182ºC). Coat the inside of a 6-inch ramekin or baking dish with olive oil cooking spray. 2. In a large skillet over medium heat, heat 1 tablespoon of the olive oil. Add the onion, then cook for 1 minute. 3. Add in the garlic and cook, stirring for 1 minute more. 4. Reduce the heat to low and mix in the spinach and water. Let this cook for 2 to 3 minutes, or until the spinach has wilted. Remove the skillet from the heat. 5. In a medium bowl, combine the cream cheese, 2 ounces (57 g) of the feta, and the remaining 2 tablespoons of olive oil, along with the lemon zest, nutmeg, dill, and salt. Mix until just combined. 6. Add the vegetables to the cheese base and stir until combined. 7. Pour the dip mixture into the prepared ramekin and top with the remaining 2 ounces (57 g) of feta cheese. 8. Place the dip into the air fryer basket and cook for 10 minutes, or until heated through and bubbling. 9. Serve with pita chips, carrot sticks, or sliced bread.

Parmesan French Fries

Prep time: 10 minutes | Cook time: 25 minutes | Serves 2 to 3

2 to 3 large russet potatoes, peeled and cut into ½-inch sticks	½ teaspoon salt
	Freshly ground black pepper, to taste
2 teaspoons vegetable or canola oil	1 teaspoon fresh chopped parsley
¾ cup grated Parmesan cheese	

1. Bring a large saucepan of salted water to a boil on the stovetop while you peel and cut the potatoes. Blanch the potatoes in the boiling salted water for 4 minutes while you preheat the air fryer to 400°F (204ºC). Strain the potatoes and rinse them with cold water. Dry them well with a clean kitchen towel. 2. Toss the dried potato sticks gently with the oil and place them in the air fryer basket. Air fry for 25 minutes, shaking the basket a few times while the fries cook to help them brown evenly. 3. Combine the Parmesan cheese, salt and pepper. With 2 minutes left on the air fryer cooking time, sprinkle the fries with the Parmesan cheese mixture. Toss the fries to coat them evenly with the cheese mixture and continue to air fry for the final 2 minutes, until the cheese has melted and just starts to brown. Sprinkle the finished fries with chopped parsley, a little more grated Parmesan cheese if you like, and serve.

Crispy Mozzarella Sticks

Prep time: 8 minutes | Cook time: 5 minutes | Serves 4

½ cup all-purpose flour	½ teaspoon garlic salt
1 egg, beaten	6 Mozzarella sticks, halved
½ cup panko bread crumbs	crosswise
½ cup grated Parmesan cheese	Olive oil spray
1 teaspoon Italian seasoning	

1. Put the flour in a small bowl. 2. Put the beaten egg in another small bowl. 3. In a medium bowl, stir together the panko, Parmesan cheese, Italian seasoning, and garlic salt. 4. Roll a Mozzarella-stick half in the flour, dip it into the egg, and then roll it in the panko mixture to coat. Press the coating lightly to make. sure the bread crumbs stick to the cheese. Repeat with the remaining 11 Mozzarella sticks. 5. Insert the crisper plate into the basket and the basket into the unit. Preheat the unit by selecting AIR FRY, setting the temperature to 400ºF (204ºC), and setting the time to 3 minutes. Select START/STOP to begin. 6. Once the unit is preheated, spray the crisper plate with olive oil and place a parchment paper liner in the basket. Place the Mozzarella sticks into the basket and lightly spray them with olive oil. 7. Select AIR FRY, set the temperature to 400ºF (204ºC), and set the time to 5 minutes. Select START/STOP to begin. 8. When the cooking is complete, the Mozzarella sticks should be golden and crispy. Let the sticks stand for 1 minute before transferring them to a serving plate. Serve warm.

Garlic-Roasted Tomatoes and Olives

Prep time: 5 minutes | Cook time: 20 minutes | Serves 6

2 cups cherry tomatoes	1 tablespoon fresh basil,
4 garlic cloves, roughly	minced
chopped	1 tablespoon fresh oregano,
½ red onion, roughly chopped	minced
1 cup black olives	2 tablespoons olive oil
1 cup green olives	¼ to ½ teaspoon salt

1. Preheat the air fryer to 380°F(193°C). 2. In a large bowl, combine all of the ingredients and toss together so that the tomatoes and olives are coated well with the olive oil and herbs. 3. Pour the mixture into the air fryer basket, and roast for 10 minutes. Stir the mixture well, then continue roasting for an additional 10 minutes. 4. Remove from the air fryer, transfer to a serving bowl, and enjoy.

Lemon Shrimp with Garlic Olive Oil

Prep time: 5 minutes | Cook time: 6 minutes | Serves 4

1 pound (454 g) medium	½ teaspoon salt
shrimp, cleaned and deveined	¼ teaspoon red pepper flakes
¼ cup plus 2 tablespoons	Lemon wedges, for serving
olive oil, divided	(optional)
Juice of ½ lemon	Marinara sauce, for dipping
3 garlic cloves, minced and	(optional)
divided	

1. Preheat the air fryer to 380°F(193°C). 2. In a large bowl, combine the shrimp with 2 tablespoons of the olive oil, as well as the lemon juice, ⅓ of the minced garlic, salt, and red pepper flakes. Toss to coat the shrimp well. 3. In a small ramekin, combine the remaining ¼ cup of olive oil and the remaining minced garlic. 4. Tear off a 12-by-12-inch sheet of aluminum foil. Pour the shrimp into the center of the foil, then fold the sides up and crimp the edges so that it forms an aluminum foil bowl that is open on top. Place this packet into the air fryer basket. 5. Roast the shrimp for 4 minutes, then open the air fryer and place the ramekin with oil and garlic in the basket beside the shrimp packet. Cook for 2 more minutes. 6. Transfer the shrimp on a serving plate or platter with the ramekin of garlic olive oil on the side for dipping. You may also serve with lemon wedges and marinara sauce, if desired.

Polenta Fries with Chili-Lime Mayo

Prep time: 10 minutes | Cook time: 28 minutes | Serves 4

Polenta Fries:	½ cup mayonnaise
2 teaspoons vegetable or olive	1 teaspoon chili powder
oil	1 teaspoon chopped fresh
¼ teaspoon paprika	cilantro
1 pound (454 g) prepared	¼ teaspoon ground cumin
polenta, cut into 3-inch ×	Juice of ½ lime
½-inch strips	Salt and freshly ground black
Chili-Lime Mayo:	pepper, to taste

1. Preheat the air fryer to 400°F (204°C). 2. Mix the oil and paprika in a bowl. Add the polenta strips and toss until evenly coated. 3. Transfer the polenta strips to the air fry basket and air fry for 28 minutes until the fries are golden brown, shaking the basket once during cooking. Season as desired with salt and pepper. 4. Meanwhile, whisk together all the ingredients for the chili-lime mayo in a small bowl. 5. Remove the polenta fries from the air fryer to a plate and serve alongside the chili-lime mayo as a dipping sauce.

Peppery Chicken Meatballs

Prep time: 5 minutes | Cook time: 13 to 20 minutes | Makes 16 meatballs

2 teaspoons olive oil	1 egg white
¼ cup minced onion	½ teaspoon dried thyme
¼ cup minced red bell pepper	½ pound (227 g) ground
2 vanilla wafers, crushed	chicken breast

1. Preheat the air fryer to 370°F (188°C). 2. In a baking pan, mix the olive oil, onion, and red bell pepper. Put the pan in the air fryer. Air fry for 3 to 5 minutes, or until the vegetables are tender. 3. In a medium bowl, mix the cooked vegetables, crushed wafers, egg white, and thyme until well combined 4. Mix in the chicken, gently but thoroughly, until everything is combined. 5. Form the mixture into 16 meatballs and place them in the air fryer basket. Air fry for 10 to 15 minutes, or until the meatballs reach an internal temperature of 165°F (74°C) on a meat thermometer. 6. Serve immediately.

Sea Salt Potato Chips

Prep time: 30 minutes | Cook time: 27 minutes | Serves 4

Oil, for spraying	1 tablespoon oil
4 medium yellow potatoes	⅛ to ¼ teaspoon fine sea salt

1. Line the air fryer basket with parchment and spray lightly with oil. 2. Using a mandoline or a very sharp knife, cut the potatoes into very thin slices. 3. Place the slices in a bowl of cold water and let soak for about 20 minutes. 4. Drain the potatoes, transfer them to a plate lined with paper towels, and pat dry. 5. Drizzle the oil over the potatoes, sprinkle with the salt, and toss to combine. Transfer to the prepared basket. 6. Air fry at 200°F (93°C) for 20 minutes. Toss the chips, increase the heat to 400°F (204°C), and cook for another 5 to 7 minutes, until crispy.

Crunchy Tex-Mex Tortilla Chips

Prep time: 5 minutes | Cook time: 5 minutes | Serves 4

Olive oil	½ teaspoon paprika
½ teaspoon salt	Pinch cayenne pepper
½ teaspoon ground cumin	8 (6-inch) corn tortillas, each
½ teaspoon chili powder	cut into 6 wedges

1. Spray fryer basket lightly with olive oil. 2. In a small bowl, combine the salt, cumin, chili powder, paprika, and cayenne pepper. 3. Place the tortilla wedges in the air fryer basket in a single layer. Spray the tortillas lightly with oil and sprinkle with some of the seasoning mixture. You will need to cook the tortillas in batches. 4. Air fry at 375°F (191°C) for 2 to 3 minutes. Shake the basket and cook until the chips are light brown and crispy, an additional 2 to 3 minutes. Watch the chips closely so they do not burn.

Crispy Cajun Dill Pickle Chips

Prep time: 5 minutes | Cook time: 10 minutes | Makes 16 slices

¼ cup all-purpose flour	2 large dill pickles, sliced into
½ cup panko bread crumbs	8 rounds each
1 large egg, beaten	Cooking spray
2 teaspoons Cajun seasoning	

1. Preheat the air fryer to 390ºF (199ºC). 2. Place the all-purpose flour, panko bread crumbs, and egg into 3 separate shallow bowls, then stir the Cajun seasoning into the flour. 3. Dredge each pickle chip in the flour mixture, then the egg, and finally the bread crumbs. Shake off any excess, then place each coated pickle chip on a plate. 4. Spritz the air fryer basket with cooking spray, then place 8 pickle chips in the basket and air fry for 5 minutes, or until crispy and golden brown. Repeat this process with the remaining pickle chips. 5. Remove the chips and allow to slightly cool on a wire rack before serving.

Crispy Green Tomatoes with Horseradish

Prep time: 18 minutes | Cook time: 10 to 15 minutes | Serves 4

2 eggs	Horseradish Sauce:
¼ cup buttermilk	¼ cup sour cream
½ cup bread crumbs	¼ cup mayonnaise
½ cup cornmeal	2 teaspoons prepared
¼ teaspoon salt	horseradish
1½ pounds (680 g) firm green	½ teaspoon lemon juice
tomatoes, cut into ¼-inch	½ teaspoon Worcestershire
slices	sauce
Cooking spray	⅛ teaspoon black pepper

1. Preheat air fryer to 390ºF (199ºC). Spritz the air fryer basket with cooking spray. 2. In a small bowl, whisk together all the ingredients for the horseradish sauce until smooth. Set aside. 3. In a shallow dish, beat the eggs and buttermilk. 4. In a separate shallow dish, thoroughly combine the bread crumbs, cornmeal, and salt. 5. Dredge the tomato slices, one at a time, in the egg mixture, then roll in the bread crumb mixture until evenly coated. 6. Working in batches, place the tomato slices in the air fryer basket in a single layer. Spray them with cooking spray. 7. Air fry for 10 to 15 minutes, flipping the slices halfway through, or until the tomato slices are nicely browned and crisp. 8. Remove from the basket to a platter and repeat with the remaining tomato slices. 9. Serve drizzled with the prepared horseradish sauce.

Cheesy Zucchini Tots

Prep time: 15 minutes | Cook time: 6 minutes | Serves 8

2 medium zucchini (about 12	½ cup panko bread crumbs
ounces / 340 g), shredded	¼ teaspoon black pepper
1 large egg, whisked	1 clove garlic, minced
½ cup grated pecorino romano	Cooking spray
cheese	

1. Using your hands, squeeze out as much liquid from the zucchini as possible. In a large bowl, mix the zucchini with the remaining ingredients except the oil until well incorporated. 2. Make the zucchini tots: Use a spoon or cookie scoop to place tablespoonfuls of the zucchini mixture onto a lightly floured cutting board and form into 1-inch logs. 3. Preheat air fryer to 375ºF (191ºC). Spritz the air fryer basket with cooking spray. 4. Place the tots in the basket. You may need to cook in batches to avoid overcrowding. 5. Air fry for 6 minutes until golden brown. 6. Remove from the basket to a serving plate and repeat with the remaining zucchini tots. 7. Serve immediately.

Garlicky and Cheesy French Fries

Prep time: 5 minutes | Cook time: 20 to 25 minutes | Serves 4

3 medium russet potatoes,	½ teaspoon salt
rinsed, dried, and cut into thin	¼ teaspoon freshly ground
wedges or classic fry shapes	black pepper
2 tablespoons extra-virgin	Cooking oil spray
olive oil	2 tablespoons finely chopped
1 tablespoon granulated garlic	fresh parsley (optional)
⅓ cup grated Parmesan cheese	

1. In a large bowl combine the potato wedges or fries and the olive oil. Toss to coat. 2. Sprinkle the potatoes with the granulated garlic, Parmesan cheese, salt, and pepper, and toss again. 3. Insert the crisper plate into the basket and the basket into the unit. Preheat the unit by selecting AIR FRY, setting the temperature to 400ºF (204ºC), and setting the time to 3 minutes. Select START/STOP to begin. 4. Once the unit is preheated, spray the crisper plate with cooking oil. Place the potatoes into the basket. 5. Select AIR FRY, set the temperature to 400ºF (204ºC), and set the time to 20 to 25 minutes. Select START/STOP to begin. 6. After about 10 minutes, remove the basket and shake it so the fries at the bottom come up to the top. Reinsert the basket to resume cooking. 7. When the cooking is complete, top the fries with the parsley (if using) and serve hot.

Pepperoni Pizza Dip

Prep time: 10 minutes | Cook time: 10 minutes | Serves 6

6 ounces (170 g) cream	½ cup sliced miniature
cheese, softened	pepperoni
¾ cup shredded Italian cheese	¼ cup sliced black olives
blend	1 tablespoon thinly sliced
¼ cup sour cream	green onion
1½ teaspoons dried Italian	Cut-up raw vegetables,
seasoning	toasted baguette slices, pita
¼ teaspoon garlic salt	chips, or tortilla chips, for
¼ teaspoon onion powder	serving
¾ cup pizza sauce	

1. In a small bowl, combine the cream cheese, ¼ cup of the shredded cheese, the sour cream, Italian seasoning, garlic salt, and onion powder. Stir until smooth and the ingredients are well blended. 2. Spread the mixture in a baking pan. Top with the pizza sauce, spreading to the edges. Sprinkle with the remaining ½ cup shredded cheese. Arrange the pepperoni slices on top of the cheese. Top with the black olives and green onion. 3. Place the pan in the air fryer basket. Set the air fryer to 350ºF (177ºC) for 10 minutes, or until the pepperoni is beginning to brown on the edges and the cheese is bubbly and lightly browned. 4. Let stand for 5 minutes before serving with vegetables, toasted baguette slices, pita chips, or tortilla chips.

Greek Yogurt Deviled Eggs

Prep time: 15 minutes | Cook time: 15 minutes | Serves 4

4 eggs	⅛ teaspoon paprika
¼ cup nonfat plain Greek yogurt	⅛ teaspoon garlic powder
1 teaspoon chopped fresh dill	Chopped fresh parsley, for garnish
⅛ teaspoon salt	

1. Preheat the air fryer to 260°F(127°C). 2. Place the eggs in a single layer in the air fryer basket and cook for 15 minutes. 3. Quickly remove the eggs from the air fryer and place them into a cold water bath. Let the eggs cool in the water for 10 minutes before removing and peeling them. 4. After peeling the eggs, cut them in half. 5. Spoon the yolk into a small bowl. Add the yogurt, dill, salt, paprika, and garlic powder and mix until smooth. 6. Spoon or pipe the yolk mixture into the halved egg whites. Serve with a sprinkle of fresh parsley on top.

String Bean Fries

Prep time: 15 minutes | Cook time: 5 to 6 minutes | Serves 4

½ pound (227 g) fresh string beans	¼ teaspoon ground black pepper
2 eggs	¼ teaspoon dry mustard (optional)
4 teaspoons water	Oil for misting or cooking spray
½ cup white flour	
½ cup bread crumbs	
¼ teaspoon salt	

1. Preheat the air fryer to 360°F (182°C). 2. Trim stem ends from string beans, wash, and pat dry. 3. In a shallow dish, beat eggs and water together until well blended. 4. Place flour in a second shallow dish. 5. In a third shallow dish, stir together the bread crumbs, salt, pepper, and dry mustard if using. 6. Dip each string bean in egg mixture, flour, egg mixture again, then bread crumbs. 7. When you finish coating all the string beans, open air fryer and place them in basket. 8. Cook for 3 minutes. 9. Stop and mist string beans with oil or cooking spray. 10. Cook for 2 to 3 more minutes or until string beans are crispy and nicely browned.

Shishito Peppers with Herb Dressing

Prep time: 10 minutes | Cook time: 6 minutes | Serves 2 to 4

6 ounces (170 g) shishito peppers	fresh flat-leaf parsley
1 tablespoon vegetable oil	1 tablespoon finely chopped fresh tarragon
Kosher salt and freshly ground black pepper, to taste	1 tablespoon finely chopped fresh chives
½ cup mayonnaise	Finely grated zest of ½ lemon
2 tablespoons finely chopped fresh basil leaves	1 tablespoon fresh lemon juice
2 tablespoons finely chopped	Flaky sea salt, for serving

1. Preheat the air fryer to 400°F (204°C). 2. In a bowl, toss together the shishitos and oil to evenly coat and season with kosher salt and black pepper. Transfer to the air fryer and air fry for 6 minutes, shaking the basket halfway through, or until the shishitos are blistered and lightly charred. 3. Meanwhile, in a small bowl, whisk together the mayonnaise, basil, parsley, tarragon, chives, lemon zest, and lemon juice. 4. Pile the peppers on a plate, sprinkle with flaky sea salt, and serve hot with the dressing.

Spiced Roasted Cashews

Prep time: 5 minutes | Cook time: 10 minutes | Serves 4

2 cups raw cashews	¼ teaspoon chili powder
2 tablespoons olive oil	⅛ teaspoon garlic powder
¼ teaspoon salt	⅛ teaspoon smoked paprika

1. Preheat the air fryer to 360°F(182°C). 2. In a large bowl, toss all of the ingredients together. 3. Pour the cashews into the air fryer basket and roast them for 5 minutes. Shake the basket, then cook for 5 minutes more. 4. Serve immediately.

Fried Artichoke Hearts

Prep time: 10 minutes | Cook time: 12 minutes | Serves 10

Oil, for spraying	1 cup panko bread crumbs
3 (14-ounce / 397-g) cans quartered artichokes, drained and patted dry	⅓ cup grated Parmesan cheese
½ cup mayonnaise	Salt and freshly ground black pepper, to taste

1. Line the air fryer basket with parchment and spray lightly with oil. 2. Place the artichokes on a plate. Put the mayonnaise and bread crumbs in separate bowls. 3. Working one at a time, dredge each artichoke piece in the mayonnaise, then in the bread crumbs to cover. 4. Place the artichokes in the prepared basket. You may need to work in batches, depending on the size of your air fryer. 5. Air fry at 370°F (188°C) for 10 to 12 minutes, or until crispy and golden brown. 6. Sprinkle with the Parmesan cheese and season with salt and black pepper. Serve immediately.

Rumaki

Prep time: 30 minutes | Cook time: 10 to 12 minutes per batch | Makes about 24 rumaki

10 ounces (283 g) raw chicken livers	¼ cup low-sodium teriyaki sauce
1 can sliced water chestnuts, drained	12 slices turkey bacon

1. Cut livers into 1½-inch pieces, trimming out tough veins as you slice. 2. Place livers, water chestnuts, and teriyaki sauce in small container with lid. If needed, add another tablespoon of teriyaki sauce to make sure livers are covered. Refrigerate for 1 hour. 3. When ready to cook, cut bacon slices in half crosswise. 4. Wrap 1 piece of liver and 1 slice of water chestnut in each bacon strip. Secure with toothpick. 5. When you have wrapped half of the livers, place them in the air fryer basket in a single layer. 6. Air fry at 390°F (199°C) for 10 to 12 minutes, until liver is done and bacon is crispy. 7. While first batch cooks, wrap the remaining livers. Repeat step 6 to cook your second batch.

Veggie Shrimp Toast

Prep time: 15 minutes | Cook time: 3 to 6 minutes | Serves 4

8 large raw shrimp, peeled and finely chopped
1 egg white
2 garlic cloves, minced
3 tablespoons minced red bell pepper

1 medium celery stalk, minced
2 tablespoons cornstarch
¼ teaspoon Chinese five-spice powder
3 slices firm thin-sliced no-sodium whole-wheat bread

1. Preheat the air fryer to 350ºF (177ºC). 2. In a small bowl, stir together the shrimp, egg white, garlic, red bell pepper, celery, cornstarch, and five-spice powder. Top each slice of bread with one-third of the shrimp mixture, spreading it evenly to the edges. With a sharp knife, cut each slice of bread into 4 strips. 3. Place the shrimp toasts in the air fryer basket in a single layer. You may need to cook them in batches. Air fry for 3 to 6 minutes, until crisp and golden brown. 4. Serve hot.

Buffalo Bites

Prep time: 15 minutes | Cook time: 11 to 12 minutes per batch | Makes 16 meatballs

1½ cups cooked jasmine or sushi rice
¼ teaspoon salt
1 pound (454 g) ground chicken

8 tablespoons buffalo wing sauce
2 ounces (57 g) Gruyère cheese, cut into 16 cubes
1 tablespoon maple syrup

1. Mix 4 tablespoons buffalo wing sauce into all the ground chicken. 2. Shape chicken into a log and divide into 16 equal portions. 3. With slightly damp hands, mold each chicken portion around a cube of cheese and shape into a firm ball. When you have shaped 8 meatballs, place them in air fryer basket. 4. Air fry at 390ºF (199ºC) for approximately 5 minutes. Shake basket, reduce temperature to 360ºF (182ºC), and cook for 5 to 6 minutes longer. 5. While the first batch is cooking, shape remaining chicken and cheese into 8 more meatballs. 6. Repeat step 4 to cook second batch of meatballs. 7. In a medium bowl, mix the remaining 4 tablespoons of buffalo wing sauce with the maple syrup. Add all the cooked meatballs and toss to coat. 8. Place meatballs back into air fryer basket and air fry at 390ºF (199ºC) for 2 to 3 minutes to set the glaze. Skewer each with a toothpick and serve.

Cheese-Stuffed Blooming Onion

Prep time: 10 minutes | Cook time: 15 minutes | Serves 2

1 large yellow onion (14 ounces / 397 g)
1 tablespoon olive oil
Kosher salt and freshly ground black pepper, to taste
¼ cup plus 2 tablespoons panko bread crumbs
¼ cup grated Parmesan cheese

3 tablespoons mayonnaise
1 tablespoon fresh lemon juice
1 tablespoon chopped fresh flat-leaf parsley
2 teaspoons whole-grain Dijon mustard
1 garlic clove, minced

1. Place the onion on a cutting board and trim the top off and peel off the outer skin. Turn the onion upside down and use a paring knife, cut vertical slits halfway through the onion at ½-inch intervals around the onion, keeping the root intact. When you turn the onion right side up, it should open up like the petals of a flower. Drizzle the cut sides of the onion with the olive oil and season with salt and pepper. Place petal-side up in the air fryer and air fry at 350ºF (177ºC) for 10 minutes. 2. Meanwhile, in a bowl, stir together the panko, Parmesan, mayonnaise, lemon juice, parsley, mustard, and garlic until incorporated into a smooth paste. 3. Remove the onion from the fryer and stuff the paste all over and in between the onion "petals." Return the onion to the air fryer and air fry at 375ºF (191ºC) until the onion is tender in the center and the bread crumb mixture is golden brown, about 5 minutes. Remove the onion from the air fryer, transfer to a plate, and serve hot.

Shrimp Toasts with Sesame Seeds

Prep time: 15 minutes | Cook time: 6 to 8 minutes | Serves 4 to 6

½ pound (227 g) raw shrimp, peeled and deveined
1 egg, beaten
2 scallions, chopped, plus more for garnish
2 tablespoons chopped fresh cilantro
2 teaspoons grated fresh ginger

1 to 2 teaspoons sriracha sauce
1 teaspoon soy sauce
½ teaspoon toasted sesame oil
6 slices thinly sliced white sandwich bread
½ cup sesame seeds
Cooking spray
Thai chili sauce, for serving

1. Preheat the air fryer to 400ºF (204ºC). Spritz the air fryer basket with cooking spray. 2. In a food processor, add the shrimp, egg, scallions, cilantro, ginger, sriracha sauce, soy sauce and sesame oil, and pulse until chopped finely. You'll need to stop the food processor occasionally to scrape down the sides. Transfer the shrimp mixture to a bowl. 3. On a clean work surface, cut the crusts off the sandwich bread. Using a brush, generously brush one side of each slice of bread with shrimp mixture. 4. Place the sesame seeds on a plate. Press bread slices, shrimp-side down, into sesame seeds to coat evenly. Cut each slice diagonally into quarters. 5. Spread the coated slices in a single layer in the air fryer basket. 6. Air fry in batches for 6 to 8 minutes, or until golden and crispy. Flip the bread slices halfway through. Repeat with the remaining bread slices. 7. Transfer to a plate and let cool for 5 minutes. Top with the chopped scallions and serve warm with Thai chili sauce.

Tortellini with Spicy Dipping Sauce

Prep time: 5 minutes | Cook time: 20 minutes | Serves 4

¾ cup mayonnaise
2 tablespoons mustard
1 egg
½ cup flour

½ teaspoon dried oregano
1½ cups bread crumbs
2 tablespoons olive oil
2 cups frozen cheese tortellini

1. Preheat the air fryer to 380ºF (193ºC). 2. In a small bowl, combine the mayonnaise and mustard and mix well. Set aside. 3. In a shallow bowl, beat the egg. In a separate bowl, combine the flour and oregano. In another bowl, combine the bread crumbs and olive oil, and mix well. 4. Drop the tortellini, a few at a time, into the egg, then into the flour, then into the egg again, and then into the bread crumbs to coat. Put into the air fryer basket, cooking in batches. 5. Air fry for about 10 minutes, shaking halfway through the cooking time, or until the tortellini are crisp and golden brown on the outside. Serve with the mayonnaise mixture.

Parmesan Cauliflower

Prep time: 15 minutes | Cook time: 15 minutes | Makes 5 cups

8 cups small cauliflower florets (about 1¼ pounds / 567 g)
3 tablespoons olive oil
1 teaspoon garlic powder

½ teaspoon salt
½ teaspoon turmeric
¼ cup shredded Parmesan cheese

1. Preheat the air fryer to 390ºF (199ºC). 2. In a bowl, combine the cauliflower florets, olive oil, garlic powder, salt, and turmeric and toss to coat. 3. Transfer to the air fryer basket and air fry for 15 minutes, or until the florets are crisp-tender. Shake the basket twice during cooking. 4. Remove from the basket to a plate. Sprinkle with the shredded Parmesan cheese and toss well. Serve warm.

Chapter **8**

Vegetables and Sides

Garlic-Parmesan Crispy Baby Potatoes

Prep time: 10 minutes | Cook time: 15 minutes | Serves 4

Oil, for spraying
1 pound (454 g) baby potatoes
½ cup grated Parmesan cheese, divided
3 tablespoons olive oil
2 teaspoons granulated garlic
½ teaspoon onion powder
½ teaspoon salt
¼ teaspoon freshly ground black pepper
¼ teaspoon paprika
2 tablespoons chopped fresh parsley, for garnish

1. Line the air fryer basket with parchment and spray lightly with oil. 2. Rinse the potatoes, pat dry with paper towels, and place in a large bowl. 3. In a small bowl, mix together ¼ cup of Parmesan cheese, the olive oil, garlic, onion powder, salt, black pepper, and paprika. Pour the mixture over the potatoes and toss to coat. 4. Transfer the potatoes to the prepared basket and spread them out in an even layer, taking care to keep them from touching. You may need to work in batches, depending on the size of your air fryer. 5. Air fry at 400°F (204°C) for 15 minutes, stirring after 7 to 8 minutes, or until easily pierced with a fork. Continue to cook for another 1 to 2 minutes, if needed. 6. Sprinkle with the parsley and the remaining Parmesan cheese and serve.

Corn Croquettes

Prep time: 10 minutes | Cook time: 12 to 14 minutes | Serves 4

½ cup leftover mashed potatoes
2 cups corn kernels (if frozen, thawed, and well drained)
¼ teaspoon onion powder
⅛ teaspoon ground black
pepper
¼ teaspoon salt
½ cup panko bread crumbs
Oil for misting or cooking spray

1. Place the potatoes and half the corn in food processor and pulse until corn is well chopped. 2. Transfer mixture to large bowl and stir in remaining corn, onion powder, pepper and salt. 3. Shape mixture into 16 balls. 4. Roll balls in panko crumbs, mist with oil or cooking spray, and place in air fryer basket. 5. Air fry at 360°F (182°C) for 12 to 14 minutes, until golden brown and crispy.

Grits Casserole

Prep time: 5 minutes | Cook time: 28 to 30 minutes | Serves 4

10 fresh asparagus spears, cut into 1-inch pieces
2 cups cooked grits, cooled to room temperature
1 egg, beaten
2 teaspoons Worcestershire sauce
½ teaspoon garlic powder
¼ teaspoon salt
2 slices provolone cheese (about 1½ ounces / 43 g)
Oil for misting or cooking spray

1. Mist asparagus spears with oil and air fry at 390°F (199°C) for 5 minutes, until crisp-tender. 2. In a medium bowl, mix together the grits, egg, Worcestershire, garlic powder, and salt. 3. Spoon half of grits mixture into a baking pan and top with asparagus. 4. Tear cheese slices into pieces and layer evenly on top of asparagus. 5. Top with remaining grits. 6. Bake at 360°F (182°C) for 23 to 25 minutes. The casserole will rise a little as it cooks. When done, the top will have browned lightly with just a hint of crispiness.

Rosemary-Roasted Red Potatoes

Prep time: 5 minutes | Cook time: 20 minutes | Serves 6

1 pound (454 g) red potatoes, quartered
¼ cup olive oil
½ teaspoon kosher salt
¼ teaspoon black pepper
1 garlic clove, minced
4 rosemary sprigs

1. Preheat the air fryer to 360°F (182°C). 2. In a large bowl, toss the potatoes with the olive oil, salt, pepper, and garlic until well coated. 3. Pour the potatoes into the air fryer basket and top with the sprigs of rosemary. 4. Roast for 10 minutes, then stir or toss the potatoes and roast for 10 minutes more. 5. Remove the rosemary sprigs and serve the potatoes. Season with additional salt and pepper, if needed.

Asparagus Fries

Prep time: 15 minutes | Cook time: 5 to 7 minutes per batch | Serves 4

12 ounces (340 g) fresh asparagus spears with tough ends trimmed off
2 egg whites
¼ cup water
¾ cup panko bread crumbs
¼ cup grated Parmesan cheese, plus 2 tablespoons
¼ teaspoon salt
Oil for misting or cooking spray

1. Preheat the air fryer to 390°F (199°C). 2. In a shallow dish, beat egg whites and water until slightly foamy. 3. In another shallow dish, combine panko, Parmesan, and salt. 4. Dip asparagus spears in egg, then roll in crumbs. Spray with oil or cooking spray. 5. Place a layer of asparagus in air fryer basket, leaving just a little space in between each spear. Stack another layer on top, crosswise. Air fry at 390°F (199°C) for 5 to 7 minutes, until crispy and golden brown. 6. Repeat to cook remaining asparagus.

Garlic Parmesan-Roasted Cauliflower

Prep time: 5 minutes | Cook time: 15 minutes | Serves 6

1 medium head cauliflower, leaves and core removed, cut into florets
2 tablespoons salted butter, melted
½ tablespoon salt
2 cloves garlic, peeled and finely minced
½ cup grated Parmesan cheese, divided

1. Toss cauliflower in a large bowl with butter. Sprinkle with salt, garlic, and ¼ cup Parmesan. 2. Place florets into ungreased air fryer basket. Adjust the temperature to 350°F (177°C) and roast for 15 minutes, shaking basket halfway through cooking. Cauliflower will be browned at the edges and tender when done. 3. Transfer florets to a large serving dish and sprinkle with remaining Parmesan. Serve warm.

Gorgonzola Mushrooms with Horseradish Mayo

Prep time: 15 minutes | Cook time: 10 minutes | Serves 5

½ cup bread crumbs	removed
2 cloves garlic, pressed	½ cup grated Gorgonzola
2 tablespoons chopped fresh coriander	cheese
⅓ teaspoon kosher salt	¼ cup low-fat mayonnaise
½ teaspoon crushed red pepper flakes	1 teaspoon prepared horseradish, well-drained
1½ tablespoons olive oil	1 tablespoon finely chopped fresh parsley
20 medium mushrooms, stems	

1. Preheat the air fryer to 380ºF (193ºC). 2. Combine the bread crumbs together with the garlic, coriander, salt, red pepper, and olive oil. 3. Take equal-sized amounts of the bread crumb mixture and use them to stuff the mushroom caps. Add the grated Gorgonzola on top of each. 4. Put the mushrooms in a baking pan and transfer to the air fryer. 5. Air fry for 10 minutes, ensuring the stuffing is warm throughout. 6. In the meantime, prepare the horseradish mayo. Mix the mayonnaise, horseradish and parsley. 7. When the mushrooms are ready, serve with the mayo.

Lemon-Garlic Mushrooms

Prep time: 10 minutes | Cook time: 10 to 15 minutes | Serves 6

12 ounces (340 g) sliced mushrooms	1 teaspoon minced garlic
1 tablespoon avocado oil	1 teaspoon freshly squeezed lemon juice
Sea salt and freshly ground black pepper, to taste	½ teaspoon red pepper flakes
3 tablespoons unsalted butter	2 tablespoons chopped fresh parsley

1. Place the mushrooms in a medium bowl and toss with the oil. Season to taste with salt and pepper. 2. Place the mushrooms in a single layer in the air fryer basket. Set your air fryer to 375ºF (191ºC) and roast for 10 to 15 minutes, until the mushrooms are tender. 3. While the mushrooms cook, melt the butter in a small pot or skillet over medium-low heat. Stir in the garlic and cook for 30 seconds. Remove the pot from the heat and stir in the lemon juice and red pepper flakes. 4. Toss the mushrooms with the lemon-garlic butter and garnish with the parsley before serving.

Buffalo Cauliflower with Blue Cheese

Prep time: 15 minutes | Cook time: 5 to 7 minutes per batch | Serves 6

1 large head cauliflower, rinsed and separated into small florets	⅓ cup hot wing sauce
	⅔ cup nonfat Greek yogurt
1 tablespoon extra-virgin olive oil	¼ cup buttermilk
	½ teaspoon hot sauce
½ teaspoon garlic powder	1 celery stalk, chopped
Cooking oil spray	2 tablespoons crumbled blue cheese

1. Insert the crisper plate into the basket and the basket into the unit. Preheat the unit by selecting AIR FRY, setting the temperature to 375ºF (191ºC), and setting the time to 3 minutes. Select START/STOP to begin. 2. In a large bowl, toss together the cauliflower florets and olive oil. Sprinkle with the garlic powder and toss again to coat. 3. Once the unit is preheated, spray the crisper plate with cooking oil. Put half the cauliflower into the basket. 4. Select AIR FRY, set the temperature to 375ºF (191ºC), and set the time to 7 minutes. Select START/STOP to begin. 5. After 3 minutes, remove the basket and shake the cauliflower. Reinsert the basket to resume cooking. After 2 minutes, check the cauliflower. It is done when it is browned. If not, resume cooking. 6. When the cooking is complete, transfer the cauliflower to a serving bowl and toss with half the hot wing sauce. 7. Repeat steps 4, 5, and 6 with the remaining cauliflower and hot wing sauce. 8. In a small bowl, stir together the yogurt, buttermilk, hot sauce, celery, and blue cheese. Drizzle the sauce over the finished cauliflower and serve.

Lebanese Baba Ghanoush

Prep time: 15 minutes | Cook time: 20 minutes | Serves 4

1 medium eggplant	½ teaspoon kosher salt
2 tablespoons vegetable oil	1 tablespoon extra-virgin olive oil
2 tablespoons tahini (sesame paste)	½ teaspoon smoked paprika
2 tablespoons fresh lemon juice	2 tablespoons chopped fresh parsley

1. Rub the eggplant all over with the vegetable oil. Place the eggplant in the air fryer basket. Set the air fryer to 400ºF (204ºC) for 20 minutes, or until the eggplant skin is blistered and charred. 2. Transfer the eggplant to a resealable plastic bag, seal, and set aside for 15 minutes (the eggplant will finish cooking in the residual heat trapped in the bag). 3. Transfer the eggplant to a large bowl. Peel off and discard the charred skin. Roughly mash the eggplant flesh. Add the tahini, lemon juice, and salt. Stir to combine. 4. Transfer the mixture to a serving bowl. Drizzle with the olive oil. Sprinkle with the paprika and parsley and serve.

Zucchini Fritters

Prep time: 10 minutes | Cook time: 10 minutes | Serves 4

2 zucchini, grated (about 1 pound / 454 g)	¼ teaspoon dried thyme
	¼ teaspoon ground turmeric
1 teaspoon salt	¼ teaspoon freshly ground black pepper
¼ cup almond flour	
¼ cup grated Parmesan cheese	1 tablespoon olive oil
1 large egg	½ lemon, sliced into wedges

1. Preheat the air fryer to 400ºF (204ºC). Cut a piece of parchment paper to fit slightly smaller than the bottom of the air fryer. 2. Place the zucchini in a large colander and sprinkle with the salt. Let sit for 5 to 10 minutes. Squeeze as much liquid as you can from the zucchini and place in a large mixing bowl. Add the almond flour, Parmesan, egg, thyme, turmeric, and black pepper. Stir gently until thoroughly combined. 3. Shape the mixture into 8 patties and arrange on the parchment paper. Brush lightly with the olive oil. Pausing halfway through the cooking time to turn the patties, air fry for 10 minutes until golden brown. Serve warm with the lemon wedges.

Sesame-Ginger Broccoli

Prep time: 10 minutes | Cook time: 15 minutes | Serves 4

3 tablespoons toasted sesame oil	½ teaspoon kosher salt
2 teaspoons sesame seeds	½ teaspoon black pepper
1 tablespoon chili-garlic sauce	1 (16-ounce / 454-g) package frozen broccoli florets (do not thaw)
2 teaspoons minced fresh ginger	

1. In a large bowl, combine the sesame oil, sesame seeds, chili-garlic sauce, ginger, salt, and pepper. Stir until well combined. Add the broccoli and toss until well coated. 2. Arrange the broccoli in the air fryer basket. Set the air fryer to 325ºF (163ºC) for 15 minutes, or until the broccoli is crisp, tender, and the edges are lightly browned, gently tossing halfway through the cooking time.

Butter and Garlic Fried Cabbage

Prep time: 5 minutes | Cook time: 9 minutes | Serves 2

Oil, for spraying	1 teaspoon granulated garlic
½ head cabbage, cut into bite-size pieces	½ teaspoon coarse sea salt
2 tablespoons unsalted butter, melted	¼ teaspoon freshly ground black pepper

1. Line the air fryer basket with parchment and spray lightly with oil. 2. In a large bowl, mix together the cabbage, butter, garlic, salt, and black pepper until evenly coated. 3. Transfer the cabbage to the prepared basket and spray lightly with oil. 4. Air fry at 375ºF (191ºC) for 5 minutes, toss, and cook for another 3 to 4 minutes, or until lightly crispy.

Chiles Rellenos with Red Chile Sauce

Prep time: 20 minutes | Cook time: 20 minutes | Serves 2

Peppers:	½ cup finely chopped yellow onion
2 poblano peppers, rinsed and dried	2 teaspoons minced garlic
⅔ cup thawed frozen or drained canned corn kernels	1 (6-ounce / 170-g) can tomato paste
1 scallion, sliced	2 tablespoons ancho chile powder
2 tablespoons chopped fresh cilantro	1 teaspoon dried oregano
½ teaspoon kosher salt	1 teaspoon ground cumin
¼ teaspoon black pepper	½ teaspoon kosher salt
⅔ cup grated Monterey Jack cheese	2 cups chicken broth
Sauce:	2 tablespoons fresh lemon juice
3 tablespoons extra-virgin olive oil	Mexican crema or sour cream, for serving

1. For the peppers: Place the peppers in the air fryer basket. Set the air fryer to 400ºF (204ºC) for 10 minutes, turning the peppers halfway through the cooking time, until their skins are charred. Transfer the peppers to a resealable plastic bag, seal, and set aside to steam for 5 minutes. Peel the peppers and discard the skins. Cut a slit down the center of each pepper, starting at the stem and continuing to the tip. Remove the seeds, being careful not to tear the chile. 2. In a medium bowl, combine the corn, scallion, cilantro, salt, black pepper, and cheese; set aside. 3. Meanwhile, for the sauce: In a large skillet, heat the olive oil over medium-high heat. Add the onion and cook, stirring, until tender, about 5 minutes. Add the garlic and cook, stirring, for 30 seconds. Stir in the tomato paste, chile powder, oregano, and cumin, and salt. Cook, stirring, for 1 minute. Whisk in the broth and lemon juice. Bring to a simmer and cook, stirring occasionally, while the stuffed peppers finish cooking. 4. Cut a slit down the center of each poblano pepper, starting at the stem and continuing to the tip. Remove the seeds, being careful not to tear the chile. 5. Carefully stuff each pepper with half the corn mixture. Place the stuffed peppers in a baking pan. Place the pan in the air fryer basket. Set the air fryer to 400ºF (204ºC) for 10 minutes, or until the cheese has melted. 6. Transfer the stuffed peppers to a serving platter and drizzle with the sauce and some crema.

Radish Chips

Prep time: 10 minutes | Cook time: 5 minutes | Serves 4

2 cups water	½ teaspoon garlic powder
1 pound (454 g) radishes	2 tablespoons coconut oil, melted
¼ teaspoon onion powder	
¼ teaspoon paprika	

1. Place water in a medium saucepan and bring to a boil on stovetop. 2. Remove the top and bottom from each radish, then use a mandoline to slice each radish thin and uniformly. You may also use the slicing blade in the food processor for this step. 3. Place the radish slices into the boiling water for 5 minutes or until translucent. Remove them from the water and place them into a clean kitchen towel to absorb excess moisture. 4. Toss the radish chips in a large bowl with remaining ingredients until fully coated in oil and seasoning. Place radish chips into the air fryer basket. 5. Adjust the temperature to 320ºF (160ºC) and air fry for 5 minutes. 6. Shake the basket two or three times during the cooking time. Serve warm.

Fig, Chickpea, and Arugula Salad

Prep time: 15 minutes | Cook time: 20 minutes | Serves 4

8 fresh figs, halved	olive oil, plus more for greasing
1½ cups cooked chickpeas	Salt and ground black pepper, to taste
1 teaspoon crushed roasted cumin seeds	
4 tablespoons balsamic vinegar	3 cups arugula rocket, washed and dried
2 tablespoons extra-virgin	

1. Preheat the air fryer to 375ºF (191ºC). 2. Cover the air fryer basket with aluminum foil and grease lightly with oil. Put the figs in the air fryer basket and air fry for 10 minutes. 3. In a bowl, combine the chickpeas and cumin seeds. 4. Remove the air fried figs from the air fryer and replace with the chickpeas. Air fry for 10 minutes. Leave to cool. 5. In the meantime, prepare the dressing. Mix the balsamic vinegar, olive oil, salt and pepper. 6. In a salad bowl, combine the arugula rocket with the cooled figs and chickpeas. 7. Toss with the sauce and serve.

Ricotta Potatoes

Prep time: 15 minutes | Cook time: 15 minutes | Serves 4

4 potatoes	1 tablespoon minced coriander
2 tablespoons olive oil	2 ounces (57 g) Cheddar
½ cup Ricotta cheese, at room	cheese, preferably freshly
temperature	grated
2 tablespoons chopped	1 teaspoon celery seeds
scallions	½ teaspoon salt
1 tablespoon roughly chopped	½ teaspoon garlic pepper
fresh parsley	

1. Preheat the air fryer to 350ºF (177ºC). 2. Pierce the skin of the potatoes with a knife. 3. Air fry in the air fryer basket for 13 minutes. If they are not cooked through by this time, leave for 2 to 3 minutes longer. 4. In the meantime, make the stuffing by combining all the other ingredients. 5. Cut halfway into the cooked potatoes to open them. 6. Spoon equal amounts of the stuffing into each potato and serve hot.

Parmesan Mushrooms

Prep time: 5 minutes | Cook time: 15 minutes | Serves 4

Oil, for spraying	mix
1 pound (454 g) cremini	½ teaspoon salt
mushrooms, stems trimmed	¼ teaspoon freshly ground
2 tablespoons olive oil	black pepper
2 teaspoons granulated garlic	⅓ cup grated Parmesan
1 teaspoon dried onion soup	cheese, divided

1. Line the air fryer basket with parchment and spray lightly with oil. 2. In a large bowl, toss the mushrooms with the olive oil, garlic, onion soup mix, salt, and black pepper until evenly coated. 3. Place the mushrooms in the prepared basket. 4. Roast at 370ºF (188ºC) for 13 minutes. 5. Sprinkle half of the cheese over the mushrooms and cook for another 2 minutes. 6. Transfer the mushrooms to a serving bowl, add the remaining Parmesan cheese, and toss until evenly coated. Serve immediately.

Lemon-Thyme Asparagus

Prep time: 5 minutes | Cook time: 4 to 8 minutes | Serves 4

1 pound (454 g) asparagus,	black pepper, to taste
woody ends trimmed off	2 ounces (57 g) goat cheese,
1 tablespoon avocado oil	crumbled
½ teaspoon dried thyme or	Zest and juice of 1 lemon
½ tablespoon chopped fresh	Flaky sea salt, for serving
thyme	(optional)
Sea salt and freshly ground	

1. In a medium bowl, toss together the asparagus, avocado oil, and thyme, and season with sea salt and pepper. 2. Place the asparagus in the air fryer basket in a single layer. Set the air fryer to 400ºF (204ºC) and air fry for 4 to 8 minutes, to your desired doneness. 3. Transfer to a serving platter. Top with the goat cheese, lemon zest, and lemon juice. If desired, season with a pinch of flaky salt.

Crispy Green Beans

Prep time: 5 minutes | Cook time: 8 minutes | Serves 4

2 teaspoons olive oil	¼ teaspoon salt
½ pound (227 g) fresh green	¼ teaspoon ground black
beans, ends trimmed	pepper

1. In a large bowl, drizzle olive oil over green beans and sprinkle with salt and pepper. 2. Place green beans into ungreased air fryer basket. Adjust the temperature to 350ºF (177ºC) and set the timer for 8 minutes, shaking the basket two times during cooking. Green beans will be dark golden and crispy at the edges when done. Serve warm.

Cheesy Cauliflower Tots

Prep time: 15 minutes | Cook time: 12 minutes | Makes 16 tots

1 large head cauliflower	1 large egg
1 cup shredded Mozzarella	¼ teaspoon garlic powder
cheese	¼ teaspoon dried parsley
½ cup grated Parmesan cheese	⅛ teaspoon onion powder

1. On the stovetop, fill a large pot with 2 cups water and place a steamer in the pan. Bring water to a boil. Cut the cauliflower into florets and place on steamer basket. Cover pot with lid. 2. Allow cauliflower to steam 7 minutes until fork tender. Remove from steamer basket and place into cheesecloth or clean kitchen towel and let cool. Squeeze over sink to remove as much excess moisture as possible. The mixture will be too soft to form into tots if not all the moisture is removed. Mash with a fork to a smooth consistency. 3. Put the cauliflower into a large mixing bowl and add Mozzarella, Parmesan, egg, garlic powder, parsley, and onion powder. Stir until fully combined. The mixture should be wet but easy to mold. 4. Take 2 tablespoons of the mixture and roll into tot shape. Repeat with remaining mixture. Place into the air fryer basket. 5. Adjust the temperature to 320ºF (160ºC) and set the timer for 12 minutes. 6. Turn tots halfway through the cooking time. Cauliflower tots should be golden when fully cooked. Serve warm.

Cauliflower Rice Balls

Prep time: 10 minutes | Cook time: 8 minutes | Serves 4

1 (10-ounce / 283-g) steamer	1 large egg
bag cauliflower rice, cooked	2 ounces (57 g) plain pork
according to package	rinds, finely crushed
instructions	¼ teaspoon salt
½ cup shredded Mozzarella	½ teaspoon Italian seasoning
cheese	

1. Place cauliflower into a large bowl and mix with Mozzarella. 2. Whisk egg in a separate medium bowl. Place pork rinds into another large bowl with salt and Italian seasoning. 3. Separate cauliflower mixture into four equal sections and form each into a ball. Carefully dip a ball into whisked egg, then roll in pork rinds. Repeat with remaining balls. 4. Place cauliflower balls into ungreased air fryer basket. Adjust the temperature to 400ºF (204ºC) and air fry for 8 minutes. Rice balls will be golden when done. 5. Use a spatula to carefully move cauliflower balls to a large dish for serving. Serve warm.

Spinach and Cheese Stuffed Tomatoes

Prep time: 20 minutes | Cook time: 15 minutes | Serves 2

4 ripe beefsteak tomatoes	1 (5.2-ounce / 147-g) package
¾ teaspoon black pepper	garlic-and-herb Boursin
½ teaspoon kosher salt	cheese
1 (10-ounce / 283-g) package	3 tablespoons sour cream
frozen chopped spinach,	½ cup finely grated Parmesan
thawed and squeezed dry	cheese

1. Cut the tops off the tomatoes. Using a small spoon, carefully remove and discard the pulp. Season the insides with ½ teaspoon of the black pepper and ¼ teaspoon of the salt. Invert the tomatoes onto paper towels and allow to drain while you make the filling. 2. Meanwhile, in a medium bowl, combine the spinach, Boursin cheese, sour cream, ¼ cup of the Parmesan, and the remaining ¼ teaspoon salt and ¼ teaspoon pepper. Stir until ingredients are well combined. Divide the filling among the tomatoes. Top with the remaining ¼ cup Parmesan. 3. Place the tomatoes in the air fryer basket. Set the air fryer to 350°F (177°C) for 15 minutes, or until the filling is hot.

Burger Bun for One

Prep time: 2 minutes | Cook time: 5 minutes | Serves 1

2 tablespoons salted butter, melted	¼ teaspoon baking powder
	⅛ teaspoon apple cider
¼ cup blanched finely ground almond flour	vinegar
	1 large egg, whisked

1. Pour butter into an ungreased ramekin. Add flour, baking powder, and vinegar to ramekin and stir until combined. Add egg and stir until batter is mostly smooth. 2. Place ramekin into air fryer basket. Adjust the temperature to 350°F (177°C) and bake for 5 minutes. When done, the center will be firm and the top slightly browned. Let cool, about 5 minutes, then remove from ramekin and slice in half. Serve.

Asian Tofu Salad

Prep time: 25 minutes | Cook time: 15 minutes | Serves 2

Tofu:	¼ cup rice vinegar
1 tablespoon soy sauce	1 tablespoon sugar
1 tablespoon vegetable oil	1 teaspoon salt
1 teaspoon minced fresh ginger	1 teaspoon black pepper
1 teaspoon minced garlic	¼ cup sliced scallions
8 ounces (227 g) extra-firm	1 cup julienned cucumber
tofu, drained and cubed	1 cup julienned red onion
Salad:	1 cup julienned carrots
	6 butter lettuce leaves

1. For the tofu: In a small bowl, whisk together the soy sauce, vegetable oil, ginger, and garlic. Add the tofu and mix gently. Let stand at room temperature for 10 minutes. 2. Arrange the tofu in a single layer in the air fryer basket. Set the air fryer to 400°F (204°C) for 15 minutes, shaking halfway through the cooking time. 3. Meanwhile, for the salad: In a large bowl, whisk together the vinegar, sugar, salt,

pepper, and scallions. Add the cucumber, onion, and carrots and toss to combine. Set aside to marinate while the tofu cooks. 4. To serve, arrange three lettuce leaves on each of two plates. Pile the marinated vegetables (and marinade) on the lettuce. Divide the tofu between the plates and serve.

Tofu Bites

Prep time: 15 minutes | Cook time: 30 minutes | Serves 4

1 packaged firm tofu, cubed and pressed to remove excess water	1 teaspoon liquid smoke
	1 teaspoon hot sauce
	2 tablespoons sesame seeds
1 tablespoon soy sauce	1 teaspoon garlic powder
1 tablespoon ketchup	Salt and ground black pepper,
1 tablespoon maple syrup	to taste
½ teaspoon vinegar	Cooking spray

1. Preheat the air fryer to 375°F (191°C). 2. Spritz a baking dish with cooking spray. 3. Combine all the ingredients to coat the tofu completely and allow the marinade to absorb for half an hour. 4. Transfer the tofu to the baking dish, then air fry for 15 minutes. Flip the tofu over and air fry for another 15 minutes on the other side. 5. Serve immediately.

Spinach and Sweet Pepper Poppers

Prep time: 10 minutes | Cook time: 8 minutes | Makes 16 poppers

4 ounces (113 g) cream cheese, softened	½ teaspoon garlic powder
	8 mini sweet bell peppers,
1 cup chopped fresh spinach leaves	tops removed, seeded, and halved lengthwise

1. In a medium bowl, mix cream cheese, spinach, and garlic powder. Place 1 tablespoon mixture into each sweet pepper half and press down to smooth. 2. Place poppers into ungreased air fryer basket. Adjust the temperature to 400°F (204°C) and air fry for 8 minutes. Poppers will be done when cheese is browned on top and peppers are tender-crisp. Serve warm.

Mexican Corn in a Cup

Prep time: 5 minutes | Cook time: 10 minutes | Serves 4

4 cups frozen corn kernels (do not thaw)	fresco)
	2 tablespoons fresh lemon or
Vegetable oil spray	lime juice
2 tablespoons butter	1 teaspoon chili powder
¼ cup sour cream	Chopped fresh green onion
¼ cup mayonnaise	(optional)
¼ cup grated Parmesan cheese (or feta, cotija, or queso	Chopped fresh cilantro (optional)

1. Place the corn in the bottom of the air fryer basket and spray with vegetable oil spray. Set the air fryer to 350°F (177°C) for 10 minutes. 2. Transfer the corn to a serving bowl. Add the butter and stir until melted. Add the sour cream, mayonnaise, cheese, lemon juice, and chili powder; stir until well combined. Serve immediately with green onion and cilantro (if using).

Mole-Braised Cauliflower

Prep time: 10 minutes | Cook time: 15 minutes | Serves 2

8 ounces (227 g) medium cauliflower florets	peanuts
1 tablespoon vegetable oil	1 tablespoon toasted sesame seeds, plus more for garnish
Kosher salt and freshly ground black pepper, to taste	1 tablespoon finely chopped golden raisins
1½ cups vegetable broth	1 teaspoon kosher salt
2 tablespoons New Mexico chile powder (or regular chili powder)	1 teaspoon dark brown sugar
	½ teaspoon dried oregano
	¼ teaspoon cayenne pepper
2 tablespoons salted roasted	⅛ teaspoon ground cinnamon

1. In a large bowl, toss the cauliflower with the oil and season with salt and black pepper. Transfer to a cake pan. Place the pan in the air fryer and roast at 375ºF (191ºC) until the cauliflower is tender and lightly browned at the edges, about 10 minutes, stirring halfway through. 2. Meanwhile, in a small blender, combine the broth, chile powder, peanuts, sesame seeds, raisins, salt, brown sugar, oregano, cayenne, and cinnamon and purée until smooth. Pour into a small saucepan or skillet and bring to a simmer over medium heat, then cook until reduced by half, 3 to 5 minutes. 3. Pour the hot mole sauce over the cauliflower in the pan, stir to coat, then cook until the sauce is thickened and lightly charred on the cauliflower, about 5 minutes more. Sprinkle with more sesame seeds and serve warm.

Mediterranean Zucchini Boats

Prep time: 5 minutes | Cook time: 10 minutes | Serves 4

1 large zucchini, ends removed, halved lengthwise	¼ cup feta cheese
6 grape tomatoes, quartered	1 tablespoon balsamic vinegar
¼ teaspoon salt	1 tablespoon olive oil

1. Use a spoon to scoop out 2 tablespoons from center of each zucchini half, making just enough space to fill with tomatoes and feta. 2. Place tomatoes evenly in centers of zucchini halves and sprinkle with salt. Place into ungreased air fryer basket. Adjust the temperature to 350ºF (177ºC) and roast for 10 minutes. When done, zucchini will be tender. 3. Transfer boats to a serving tray and sprinkle with feta, then drizzle with vinegar and olive oil. Serve warm.

Scalloped Potatoes

Prep time: 5 minutes | Cook time: 20 minutes | Serves 4

2 cup sliced frozen potatoes, thawed	Freshly ground black pepper, to taste
3 cloves garlic, minced	¾ cup heavy cream
Pinch salt	

1. Preheat the air fryer to 380ºF (193ºC). 2. Toss the potatoes with the garlic, salt, and black pepper in a baking pan until evenly coated. Pour the heavy cream over the top. 3. Place the baking pan in the air fryer basket and bake for 15 minutes, or until the potatoes are tender and top is golden brown. Check for doneness and bake for another 5 minutes as needed. 4. Serve hot.

Charred Okra with Peanut-Chile Sauce

Prep time: 10 minutes | Cook time: 16 minutes | Serves 2

¾ pound (340 g) okra pods	minced (seeded if you want a milder sauce)
2 tablespoons vegetable oil	1 tablespoon tomato paste
Kosher salt and freshly ground black pepper, to taste	1 cup vegetable stock or water
1 large shallot, minced	2 tablespoons natural peanut butter
1 garlic clove, minced	Juice of ½ lime
½ Scotch bonnet chile,	

1. In a bowl, toss the okra with 1 tablespoon of the oil and season with salt and pepper. Transfer the okra to the air fryer and air fry at 400ºF (204ºC), shaking the basket halfway through, until the okra is tender and lightly charred at the edges, about 16 minutes. 2. Meanwhile, in a small skillet, heat the remaining 1 tablespoon oil over medium-high heat. Add the shallot, garlic, and chile and cook, stirring, until soft, about 2 minutes. Stir in the tomato paste and cook for 30 seconds, then stir in the vegetable stock and peanut butter. Reduce the heat to maintain a simmer and cook until the sauce is reduced slightly and thickened, 3 to 4 minutes. Remove the sauce from the heat, stir in the lime juice, and season with salt and pepper. 3. Place the peanut sauce on a plate, then pile the okra on top and serve hot.

Garlic and Thyme Tomatoes

Prep time: 10 minutes | Cook time: 15 minutes | Serves 2 to 4

4 Roma tomatoes	pepper, to taste
1 tablespoon olive oil	1 clove garlic, minced
Salt and freshly ground black	½ teaspoon dried thyme

1. Preheat the air fryer to 390ºF (199ºC). 2. Cut the tomatoes in half and scoop out the seeds and any pithy parts with your fingers. Place the tomatoes in a bowl and toss with the olive oil, salt, pepper, garlic and thyme. 3. Transfer the tomatoes to the air fryer, cut side up. Air fry for 15 minutes. The edges should just start to brown. Let the tomatoes cool to an edible temperature for a few minutes and then use in pastas, on top of crostini, or as an accompaniment to any poultry, meat or fish.

Lush Vegetable Salad

Prep time: 15 minutes | Cook time: 10 minutes | Serves 4

6 plum tomatoes, halved	oil
2 large red onions, sliced	1 teaspoon paprika
4 long red pepper, sliced	½ lemon, juiced
2 yellow pepper, sliced	Salt and ground black pepper, to taste
6 cloves garlic, crushed	
1 tablespoon extra-virgin olive	1 tablespoon baby capers

1. Preheat the air fryer to 420ºF (216ºC). 2. Put the tomatoes, onions, peppers, and garlic in a large bowl and cover with the extra-virgin olive oil, paprika, and lemon juice. Sprinkle with salt and pepper as desired. 3. Line the inside of the air fryer basket with aluminum foil. Put the vegetables inside and air fry for 10 minutes, ensuring the edges turn brown. 4. Serve in a salad bowl with the baby capers.

Herbed Shiitake Mushrooms

Prep time: 10 minutes | Cook time: 5 minutes | Serves 4

8 ounces (227 g) shiitake mushrooms, stems removed and caps roughly chopped	1 teaspoon chopped fresh thyme leaves
1 tablespoon olive oil	1 teaspoon chopped fresh oregano
½ teaspoon salt	1 tablespoon chopped fresh parsley
Freshly ground black pepper, to taste	

1. Preheat the air fryer to 400ºF (204ºC). 2. Toss the mushrooms with the olive oil, salt, pepper, thyme and oregano. Air fry for 5 minutes, shaking the basket once or twice during the cooking process. The mushrooms will still be somewhat chewy with a meaty texture. If you'd like them a little more tender, add a couple of minutes to this cooking time. 3. Once cooked, add the parsley to the mushrooms and toss. Season again to taste and serve.

Saltine Wax Beans

Prep time: 10 minutes | Cook time: 7 minutes | Serves 4

½ cup flour	1 teaspoon sea salt flakes
1 teaspoon smoky chipotle powder	2 eggs, beaten
½ teaspoon ground black pepper	½ cup crushed saltines
	10 ounces (283 g) wax beans
	Cooking spray

1. Preheat the air fryer to 360ºF (182ºC). 2. Combine the flour, chipotle powder, black pepper, and salt in a bowl. Put the eggs in a second bowl. Put the crushed saltines in a third bowl. 3. Wash the beans with cold water and discard any tough strings. 4. Coat the beans with the flour mixture, before dipping them into the beaten egg. Cover them with the crushed saltines. 5. Spritz the beans with cooking spray. 6. Air fry for 4 minutes. Give the air fryer basket a good shake and continue to air fry for 3 minutes. Serve hot.

Air-Fried Okra

Prep time: 10 minutes | Cook time: 10 minutes | Serves 4

1 egg	¼ teaspoon freshly ground black pepper
½ cup almond milk	½ pound (227 g) fresh okra, stems removed and chopped into 1-inch slices
½ cup crushed pork rinds	
¼ cup grated Parmesan cheese	
¼ cup almond flour	
1 teaspoon garlic powder	

1. Preheat the air fryer to 400ºF (204ºC). 2. In a shallow bowl, whisk together the egg and milk. 3. In a second shallow bowl, combine the pork rinds, Parmesan, almond flour, garlic powder, and black pepper. 4. Working with a few slices at a time, dip the okra into the egg mixture followed by the crumb mixture. Press lightly to ensure an even coating. 5. Working in batches if necessary, arrange the okra in a single layer in the air fryer basket and spray lightly with olive oil. Pausing halfway through the cooking time to turn the okra, air fry for 10 minutes until tender and golden brown. Serve warm.

Green Peas with Mint

Prep time: 5 minutes | Cook time: 5 minutes | Serves 4

1 cup shredded lettuce	1 tablespoon fresh mint, shredded
1 (10-ounce / 283-g) package frozen green peas, thawed	1 teaspoon melted butter

1. Lay the shredded lettuce in the air fryer basket. 2. Toss together the peas, mint, and melted butter and spoon over the lettuce. 3. Air fry at 360ºF (182ºC) for 5 minutes, until peas are warm and lettuce wilts.

Garlic Roasted Broccoli

Prep time: 8 minutes | Cook time: 10 to 14 minutes | Serves 6

1 head broccoli, cut into bite-size florets	Sea salt and freshly ground black pepper, to taste
1 tablespoon avocado oil	1 tablespoon freshly squeezed lemon juice
2 teaspoons minced garlic	½ teaspoon lemon zest
⅛ teaspoon red pepper flakes	

1. In a large bowl, toss together the broccoli, avocado oil, garlic, red pepper flakes, salt, and pepper. 2. Set the air fryer to 375ºF (191ºC). Arrange the broccoli in a single layer in the air fryer basket, working in batches if necessary. Roast for 10 to 14 minutes, until the broccoli is lightly charred. 3. Place the florets in a medium bowl and toss with the lemon juice and lemon zest. Serve.

Roasted Sweet Potatoes

Prep time: 10 minutes | Cook time: 25 minutes | Serves 4

Cooking oil spray	Freshly ground black pepper, to taste
2 sweet potatoes, peeled and cut into 1-inch cubes	½ teaspoon dried thyme
1 tablespoon extra-virgin olive oil	½ teaspoon dried marjoram
Pinch salt	¼ cup grated Parmesan cheese

1. Insert the crisper plate into the basket and the basket into the unit. Preheat the unit by selecting AIR ROAST, setting the temperature to 330ºF (166ºC), and setting the time to 3 minutes. Select START/STOP to begin. 2. Once the unit is preheated, spray the crisper plate with cooking oil. Put the sweet potato cubes into the basket and drizzle with olive oil. Toss gently to coat. Sprinkle with the salt, pepper, thyme, and marjoram and toss again. 3. Select AIR ROAST, set the temperature to 330ºF (166ºC), and set the time to 25 minutes. Select START/STOP to begin. 4. After 10 minutes, remove the basket and shake the potatoes. Reinsert the basket to resume cooking. After another 10 minutes, remove the basket and shake the potatoes one more time. Sprinkle evenly with the Parmesan cheese. Reinsert the basket to resume cooking. 5. When the cooking is complete, the potatoes should be tender. Serve immediately.

Blackened Zucchini with Kimchi-Herb Sauce

Prep time: 10 minutes | Cook time: 15 minutes | Serves 2

2 medium zucchini, ends trimmed (about 6 ounces / 170 g each)
2 tablespoons olive oil
½ cup kimchi, finely chopped
¼ cup finely chopped fresh cilantro
¼ cup finely chopped fresh

flat-leaf parsley, plus more for garnish
2 tablespoons rice vinegar
2 teaspoons Asian chili-garlic sauce
1 teaspoon grated fresh ginger
Kosher salt and freshly ground black pepper, to taste

1. Brush the zucchini with half of the olive oil, place in the air fryer, and air fry at 400ºF (204ºC), turning halfway through, until lightly charred on the outside and tender, about 15 minutes. 2. Meanwhile, in a small bowl, combine the remaining 1 tablespoon olive oil, the kimchi, cilantro, parsley, vinegar, chili-garlic sauce, and ginger. 3. Once the zucchini is finished cooking, transfer it to a colander and let it cool for 5 minutes. Using your fingers, pinch and break the zucchini into bite-size pieces, letting them fall back into the colander. Season the zucchini with salt and pepper, toss to combine, then let sit a further 5 minutes to allow some of its liquid to drain. Pile the zucchini atop the kimchi sauce on a plate and sprinkle with more parsley to serve.

Ratatouille

Prep time: 15 minutes | Cook time: 20 minutes | Serves 2 to 3

2 cups ¾-inch cubed peeled eggplant
1 small red, yellow, or orange bell pepper, stemmed, seeded, and diced
1 cup cherry tomatoes
6 to 8 cloves garlic, peeled

and halved lengthwise
3 tablespoons olive oil
1 teaspoon dried oregano
½ teaspoon dried thyme
1 teaspoon kosher salt
½ teaspoon black pepper

1. In a medium bowl, combine the eggplant, bell pepper, tomatoes, garlic, oil, oregano, thyme, salt, and pepper. Toss to combine. 2. Place the vegetables in the air fryer basket. Set the air fryer to 400ºF (204ºC) for 20 minutes, or until the vegetables are crisp-tender.

Broccoli Salad

Prep time: 5 minutes | Cook time: 7 minutes | Serves 4

2 cups fresh broccoli florets, chopped
1 tablespoon olive oil
¼ teaspoon salt
⅛ teaspoon ground black

pepper
¼ cup lemon juice, divided
¼ cup shredded Parmesan cheese
¼ cup sliced roasted almonds

1. In a large bowl, toss broccoli and olive oil together. Sprinkle with salt and pepper, then drizzle with 2 tablespoons lemon juice. 2. Place broccoli into ungreased air fryer basket. Adjust the temperature to 350ºF (177ºC) and set the timer for 7 minutes, shaking the basket halfway through cooking. Broccoli will be golden on the edges when done. 3. Place broccoli into a large serving bowl and drizzle with

remaining lemon juice. Sprinkle with Parmesan and almonds. Serve warm.

Baked Jalapeño and Cheese Cauliflower Mash

Prep time: 10 minutes | Cook time: 15 minutes | Serves 6

1 (12-ounce / 340-g) steamer bag cauliflower florets, cooked according to package instructions
2 tablespoons salted butter, softened
2 ounces (57 g) cream cheese,

softened
½ cup shredded sharp Cheddar cheese
¼ cup pickled jalapeños
½ teaspoon salt
¼ teaspoon ground black pepper

1. Place cooked cauliflower into a food processor with remaining ingredients. Pulse twenty times until cauliflower is smooth and all ingredients are combined. 2. Spoon mash into an ungreased round nonstick baking dish. Place dish into air fryer basket. Adjust the temperature to 380ºF (193ºC) and bake for 15 minutes. The top will be golden brown when done. Serve warm.

Sweet-and-Sour Brussels Sprouts

Prep time: 10 minutes | Cook time: 20 minutes | Serves 2

¼ cup Thai sweet chili sauce
2 tablespoons black vinegar or balsamic vinegar
½ teaspoon hot sauce, such as Tabasco
8 ounces (227 g) Brussels sprouts, trimmed (large

sprouts halved)
2 small shallots, cut into ¼-inch-thick slices
Kosher salt and freshly ground black pepper, to taste
2 teaspoons lightly packed fresh cilantro leaves

1. In a large bowl, whisk together the chili sauce, vinegar, and hot sauce. Add the Brussels sprouts and shallots, season with salt and pepper, and toss to combine. Scrape the Brussels sprouts and sauce into a cake pan. 2. Place the pan in the air fryer and roast at 375ºF (191ºC), stirring every 5 minutes, until the Brussels sprouts are tender and the sauce is reduced to a sticky glaze, about 20 minutes. 3. Remove the pan from the air fryer and transfer the Brussels sprouts to plates. Sprinkle with the cilantro and serve warm.

Zucchini Balls

Prep time: 5 minutes | Cook time: 10 minutes | Serves 4

4 zucchinis
1 egg
½ cup grated Parmesan cheese

1 tablespoon Italian herbs
1 cup grated coconut

1. Thinly grate the zucchinis and dry with a cheesecloth, ensuring to remove all the moisture. 2. In a bowl, combine the zucchinis with the egg, Parmesan, Italian herbs, and grated coconut, mixing well to incorporate everything. Using the hands, mold the mixture into balls. 3. Preheat the air fryer to 400ºF (204ºC). 4. Lay the zucchini balls in the air fryer basket and air fry for 10 minutes. 5. Serve hot.

Corn and Cilantro Salad

Prep time: 10 minutes | Cook time: 10 minutes | Serves 2

2 ears of corn, shucked (halved crosswise if too large to fit in your air fryer)
1 tablespoon unsalted butter, at room temperature
1 teaspoon chili powder
¼ teaspoon garlic powder
Kosher salt and freshly ground black pepper, to taste
1 cup lightly packed fresh cilantro leaves

1 tablespoon sour cream
1 tablespoon mayonnaise
1 teaspoon adobo sauce (from a can of chipotle peppers in adobo sauce)
2 tablespoons crumbled queso fresco
Lime wedges, for serving

1. Brush the corn all over with the butter, then sprinkle with the chili powder and garlic powder, and season with salt and pepper. Place the corn in the air fryer and air fry at 400ºF (204ºC), turning over halfway through, until the kernels are lightly charred and tender, about 10 minutes. 2. Transfer the ears to a cutting board, let stand 1 minute, then carefully cut the kernels off the cobs and move them to a bowl. Add the cilantro leaves and toss to combine (the cilantro leaves will wilt slightly). 3. In a small bowl, stir together the sour cream, mayonnaise, and adobo sauce. Divide the corn and cilantro among plates and spoon the adobo dressing over the top. Sprinkle with the queso fresco and serve with lime wedges on the side.

Flatbread

Prep time: 5 minutes | Cook time: 7 minutes | Serves 2

1 cup shredded Mozzarella cheese
¼ cup blanched finely ground almond flour

1 ounce (28 g) full-fat cream cheese, softened

1. In a large microwave-safe bowl, melt Mozzarella in the microwave for 30 seconds. Stir in almond flour until smooth and then add cream cheese. Continue mixing until dough forms, gently kneading it with wet hands if necessary. 2. Divide the dough into two pieces and roll out to ¼-inch thickness between two pieces of parchment. Cut another piece of parchment to fit your air fryer basket. 3. Place a piece of flatbread onto your parchment and into the air fryer, working in two batches if needed. 4. Adjust the temperature to 320ºF (160ºC) and air fry for 7 minutes. 5. Halfway through the cooking time flip the flatbread. Serve warm.

Hawaiian Brown Rice

Prep time: 10 minutes | Cook time: 12 to 16 minutes | Serves 4 to 6

¼ pound (113 g) ground sausage
1 teaspoon butter
¼ cup minced onion

¼ cup minced bell pepper
2 cups cooked brown rice
1 (8-ounce / 227-g) can crushed pineapple, drained

1. Shape sausage into 3 or 4 thin patties. Air fry at 390ºF (199ºC) for 6 to 8 minutes or until well done. Remove from air fryer, drain, and crumble. Set aside. 2. Place butter, onion, and bell pepper in baking pan. Roast at 390ºF (199ºC) for 1 minute and stir. Cook 3 to 4 minutes longer or just until vegetables are tender. 3. Add sausage, rice, and pineapple to vegetables and stir together. 4. Roast for 2 to 3 minutes, until heated through.

Curried Fruit

Prep time: 10 minutes | Cook time: 20 minutes | Serves 6 to 8

1 cup cubed fresh pineapple
1 cup cubed fresh pear (firm, not overly ripe)
8 ounces (227 g) frozen peaches, thawed

1 (15-ounce / 425-g) can dark, sweet, pitted cherries with juice
2 tablespoons brown sugar
1 teaspoon curry powder

1. Combine all ingredients in large bowl. Stir gently to mix in the sugar and curry. 2. Pour into a baking pan and bake at 360ºF (182ºC) for 10 minutes. 3. Stir fruit and cook 10 more minutes. 4. Serve hot.

Chapter 9
Vegetarian Mains

Greek Stuffed Eggplant

Prep time: 15 minutes | Cook time: 20 minutes | Serves 2

1 large eggplant	hearts
2 tablespoons unsalted butter	1 cup fresh spinach
¼ medium yellow onion, diced	2 tablespoons diced red bell pepper
¼ cup chopped artichoke	½ cup crumbled feta

1. Slice eggplant in half lengthwise and scoop out flesh, leaving enough inside for shell to remain intact. Take eggplant that was scooped out, chop it, and set aside. 2. In a medium skillet over medium heat, add butter and onion. Sauté until onions begin to soften, about 3 to 5 minutes. Add chopped eggplant, artichokes, spinach, and bell pepper. Continue cooking 5 minutes until peppers soften and spinach wilts. Remove from the heat and gently fold in the feta. 3. Place filling into each eggplant shell and place into the air fryer basket. 4. Adjust the temperature to 320ºF (160ºC) and air fry for 20 minutes. 5. Eggplant will be tender when done. Serve warm.

Cauliflower, Chickpea, and Avocado Mash

Prep time: 10 minutes | Cook time: 25 minutes | Serves 4

1 medium head cauliflower, cut into florets	2 tablespoons lemon juice
1 can chickpeas, drained and rinsed	Salt and ground black pepper, to taste
1 tablespoon extra-virgin olive oil	4 flatbreads, toasted
	2 ripe avocados, mashed

1. Preheat the air fryer to 425ºF (218ºC). 2. In a bowl, mix the chickpeas, cauliflower, lemon juice and olive oil. Sprinkle salt and pepper as desired. 3. Put inside the air fryer basket and air fry for 25 minutes. 4. Spread on top of the flatbread along with the mashed avocado. Sprinkle with more pepper and salt and serve.

Cayenne Tahini Kale

Prep time: 5 minutes | Cook time: 15 minutes | Serves 2 to 4

Dressing:	Kale:
¼ cup tahini	4 cups packed torn kale leaves
¼ cup fresh lemon juice	(stems and ribs removed and
2 tablespoons olive oil	leaves torn into palm-size
1 teaspoon sesame seeds	pieces)
½ teaspoon garlic powder	Kosher salt and freshly
¼ teaspoon cayenne pepper	ground black pepper, to taste

1. Preheat the air fryer to 350ºF (177ºC). 2. Make the dressing: Whisk together the tahini, lemon juice, olive oil, sesame seeds, garlic powder, and cayenne pepper in a large bowl until well mixed. 3. Add the kale and massage the dressing thoroughly all over the leaves. Sprinkle the salt and pepper to season. 4. Place the kale in the air fryer basket in a single layer and air fry for about 15 minutes, or until the leaves are slightly wilted and crispy. 5. Remove from the basket and serve on a plate.

Roasted Vegetable Mélange with Herbs

Prep time: 10 minutes | Cook time: 14 to 18 minutes | Serves 4

1 (8-ounce / 227-g) package sliced mushrooms	3 cloves garlic, sliced
1 yellow summer squash, sliced	1 tablespoon olive oil
1 red bell pepper, sliced	½ teaspoon dried basil
	½ teaspoon dried thyme
	½ teaspoon dried tarragon

1. Preheat the air fryer to 350ºF (177ºC). 2. Toss the mushrooms, squash, and bell pepper with the garlic and olive oil in a large bowl until well coated. Mix in the basil, thyme, and tarragon and toss again. 3. Spread the vegetables evenly in the air fryer basket and roast for 14 to 18 minutes, or until the vegetables are fork-tender. 4. Cool for 5 minutes before serving.

Mediterranean Pan Pizza

Prep time: 5 minutes | Cook time: 8 minutes | Serves 2

1 cup shredded Mozzarella cheese	leaves
¼ medium red bell pepper, seeded and chopped	2 tablespoons chopped black olives
½ cup chopped fresh spinach	2 tablespoons crumbled feta cheese

1. Sprinkle Mozzarella into an ungreased round nonstick baking dish in an even layer. Add remaining ingredients on top. 2. Place dish into air fryer basket. Adjust the temperature to 350ºF (177ºC) and bake for 8 minutes, checking halfway through to avoid burning. Top of pizza will be golden brown and the cheese melted when done. 3. Remove dish from fryer and let cool 5 minutes before slicing and serving.

Fried Root Vegetable Medley with Thyme

Prep time: 10 minutes | Cook time: 22 minutes | Serves 4

2 carrots, sliced	2 tablespoons olive oil
2 potatoes, cut into chunks	Salt and black pepper, to taste
1 rutabaga, cut into chunks	2 tablespoons tomato pesto
1 turnip, cut into chunks	2 tablespoons water
1 beet, cut into chunks	2 tablespoons chopped fresh thyme
8 shallots, halved	

1. Preheat the air fryer to 400ºF (204ºC). 2. Toss the carrots, potatoes, rutabaga, turnip, beet, shallots, olive oil, salt, and pepper in a large mixing bowl until the root vegetables are evenly coated. 3. Place the root vegetables in the air fryer basket and air fry for 12 minutes. Shake the basket and air fry for another 10 minutes until they are cooked to your preferred doneness. 4. Meanwhile, in a small bowl, whisk together the tomato pesto and water until smooth. 5. When ready, remove the root vegetables from the basket to a platter. Drizzle with the tomato pesto mixture and sprinkle with the thyme. Serve immediately.

Caprese Eggplant Stacks

Prep time: 5 minutes | Cook time: 12 minutes | Serves 4

1 medium eggplant, cut into ¼-inch slices	Mozzarella, cut into ½-ounce / 14-g slices
2 large tomatoes, cut into ¼-inch slices	2 tablespoons olive oil
4 ounces (113 g) fresh	¼ cup fresh basil, sliced

1. In a baking dish, place four slices of eggplant on the bottom. Place a slice of tomato on top of each eggplant round, then Mozzarella, then eggplant. Repeat as necessary. 2. Drizzle with olive oil. Cover dish with foil and place dish into the air fryer basket. 3. Adjust the temperature to 350ºF (177ºC) and bake for 12 minutes. 4. When done, eggplant will be tender. Garnish with fresh basil to serve.

Crispy Tofu

Prep time: 30 minutes | Cook time: 15 to 20 minutes | Serves 4

1 (16-ounce / 454-g) block extra-firm tofu	1 tablespoon olive oil
2 tablespoons coconut aminos	1 tablespoon chili-garlic sauce
1 tablespoon toasted sesame oil	1½ teaspoons black sesame seeds
	1 scallion, thinly sliced

1. Press the tofu for at least 15 minutes by wrapping it in paper towels and setting a heavy pan on top so that the moisture drains. 2. Slice the tofu into bite-size cubes and transfer to a bowl. Drizzle with the coconut aminos, sesame oil, olive oil, and chili-garlic sauce. Cover and refrigerate for 1 hour or up to overnight. 3. Preheat the air fryer to 400ºF (204ºC). 4. Arrange the tofu in a single layer in the air fryer basket. Pausing to shake the pan halfway through the cooking time, air fry for 15 to 20 minutes until crisp. Serve with any juices that accumulate in the bottom of the air fryer, sprinkled with the sesame seeds and sliced scallion.

Super Vegetable Burger

Prep time: 15 minutes | Cook time: 12 minutes | Serves 8

½ pound (227 g) cauliflower, steamed and diced, rinsed and drained	1 tablespoon flaxseeds plus 3 tablespoons water, divided
2 teaspoons coconut oil, melted	1 teaspoon mustard powder
2 teaspoons minced garlic	2 teaspoons thyme
¼ cup desiccated coconut	2 teaspoons parsley
½ cup oats	2 teaspoons chives
3 tablespoons flour	Salt and ground black pepper, to taste
	1 cup bread crumbs

1. Preheat the air fryer to 390ºF (199ºC). 2. Combine the cauliflower with all the ingredients, except for the bread crumbs, incorporating everything well. 3. Using the hands, shape 8 equal-sized amounts of the mixture into burger patties. Coat the patties in bread crumbs before putting them in the air fryer basket in a single layer. 4. Air fry for 12 minutes or until crispy. 5. Serve hot.

Cheesy Cauliflower Pizza Crust

Prep time: 15 minutes | Cook time: 11 minutes | Serves 2

1 (12-ounce / 340-g) steamer bag cauliflower	2 tablespoons blanched finely ground almond flour
½ cup shredded sharp Cheddar cheese	1 teaspoon Italian blend seasoning
1 large egg	

1. Cook cauliflower according to package instructions. Remove from bag and place into cheesecloth or paper towel to remove excess water. Place cauliflower into a large bowl. 2. Add cheese, egg, almond flour, and Italian seasoning to the bowl and mix well. 3. Cut a piece of parchment to fit your air fryer basket. Press cauliflower into 6-inch round circle. Place into the air fryer basket. 4. Adjust the temperature to 360ºF (182ºC) and air fry for 11 minutes. 5. After 7 minutes, flip the pizza crust. 6. Add preferred toppings to pizza. Place back into air fryer basket and cook an additional 4 minutes or until fully cooked and golden. Serve immediately.

Garlicky Sesame Carrots

Prep time: 5 minutes | Cook time: 16 minutes | Serves 4 to 6

1 pound (454 g) baby carrots	Freshly ground black pepper, to taste
1 tablespoon sesame oil	6 cloves garlic, peeled
½ teaspoon dried dill	3 tablespoons sesame seeds
Pinch salt	

1. Preheat the air fryer to 380ºF (193ºC). 2. In a medium bowl, drizzle the baby carrots with the sesame oil. Sprinkle with the dill, salt, and pepper and toss to coat well. 3. Place the baby carrots in the air fryer basket and roast for 8 minutes. 4. Remove the basket and stir in the garlic. Return the basket to the air fryer and roast for another 8 minutes, or until the carrots are lightly browned. 5. Serve sprinkled with the sesame seeds.

Pesto Spinach Flatbread

Prep time: 10 minutes | Cook time: 8 minutes | Serves 4

1 cup blanched finely ground almond flour	cheese
2 ounces (57 g) cream cheese	1 cup chopped fresh spinach leaves
2 cups shredded Mozzarella	2 tablespoons basil pesto

1. Place flour, cream cheese, and Mozzarella in a large microwave-safe bowl and microwave on high 45 seconds, then stir. 2. Fold in spinach and microwave an additional 15 seconds. Stir until a soft dough ball forms. 3. Cut two pieces of parchment paper to fit air fryer basket. Separate dough into two sections and press each out on ungreased parchment to create 6-inch rounds. 4. Spread 1 tablespoon pesto over each flatbread and place rounds on parchment into ungreased air fryer basket. Adjust the temperature to 350ºF (177ºC) and air fry for 8 minutes, turning crusts halfway through cooking. Flatbread will be golden when done. 5. Let cool 5 minutes before slicing and serving.

Black Bean and Tomato Chili

Prep time: 15 minutes | Cook time: 23 minutes | Serves 6

1 tablespoon olive oil	2 cans diced tomatoes
1 medium onion, diced	2 chipotle peppers, chopped
3 garlic cloves, minced	2 teaspoons cumin
1 cup vegetable broth	2 teaspoons chili powder
3 cans black beans, drained	1 teaspoon dried oregano
and rinsed	½ teaspoon salt

1. Over a medium heat, fry the garlic and onions in the olive oil for 3 minutes. 2. Add the remaining ingredients, stirring constantly and scraping the bottom to prevent sticking. 3. Preheat the air fryer to 400°F (204°C). 4. Take a dish and place the mixture inside. Put a sheet of aluminum foil on top. 5. Transfer to the air fryer and bake for 20 minutes. 6. When ready, plate up and serve immediately.

Eggplant and Zucchini Bites

Prep time: 30 minutes | Cook time: 30 minutes | Serves 8

2 teaspoons fresh mint leaves, chopped	1 pound (454 g) eggplant, peeled and cubed
1½ teaspoons red pepper chili flakes	1 pound (454 g) zucchini, peeled and cubed
2 tablespoons melted butter	3 tablespoons olive oil

1. Toss all the above ingredients in a large-sized mixing dish. 2. Roast the eggplant and zucchini bites for 30 minutes at 325°F (163°C) in your air fryer, turning once or twice. 3. Serve with a homemade dipping sauce.

Cheesy Cabbage Wedges

Prep time: 5 minutes | Cook time: 20 minutes | Serves 4

4 tablespoons melted butter	cheese
1 head cabbage, cut into wedges	Salt and black pepper, to taste
1 cup shredded Parmesan	½ cup shredded Mozzarella cheese

1. Preheat the air fryer to 380°F (193°C). 2. Brush the melted butter over the cut sides of cabbage wedges and sprinkle both sides with the Parmesan cheese. Season with salt and pepper to taste. 3. Place the cabbage wedges in the air fryer basket and air fry for 20 minutes, flipping the cabbage halfway through, or until the cabbage wedges are lightly browned. 4. Transfer the cabbage wedges to a plate and serve with the Mozzarella cheese sprinkled on top.

Loaded Cauliflower Steak

Prep time: 5 minutes | Cook time: 7 minutes | Serves 4

1 medium head cauliflower	melted
¼ cup hot sauce	¼ cup blue cheese crumbles
2 tablespoons salted butter,	¼ cup full-fat ranch dressing

1. Remove cauliflower leaves. Slice the head in ½-inch-thick slices. 2.

In a small bowl, mix hot sauce and butter. Brush the mixture over the cauliflower. 3. Place each cauliflower steak into the air fryer, working in batches if necessary. 4. Adjust the temperature to 400°F (204°C) and air fry for 7 minutes. 5. When cooked, edges will begin turning dark and caramelized. 6. To serve, sprinkle steaks with crumbled blue cheese. Drizzle with ranch dressing.

Tangy Asparagus and Broccoli

Prep time: 25 minutes | Cook time: 22 minutes | Serves 4

½ pound (227 g) asparagus, cut into 1½-inch pieces	Salt and white pepper, to taste
½ pound (227 g) broccoli, cut into 1½-inch pieces	½ cup vegetable broth
2 tablespoons olive oil	2 tablespoons apple cider vinegar

1. Place the vegetables in a single layer in the lightly greased air fryer basket. Drizzle the olive oil over the vegetables. 2. Sprinkle with salt and white pepper. 3. Cook at 380°F (193°C) for 15 minutes, shaking the basket halfway through the cooking time. 4. Add ½ cup of vegetable broth to a saucepan; bring to a rapid boil and add the vinegar. Cook for 5 to 7 minutes or until the sauce has reduced by half. 5. Spoon the sauce over the warm vegetables and serve immediately. Bon appétit!

Teriyaki Cauliflower

Prep time: 5 minutes | Cook time: 14 minutes | Serves 4

½ cup soy sauce	2 cloves garlic, chopped
⅓ cup water	½ teaspoon chili powder
1 tablespoon brown sugar	1 big cauliflower head, cut
1 teaspoon sesame oil	into florets
1 teaspoon cornstarch	

1. Preheat the air fryer to 340°F (171°C). 2. Make the teriyaki sauce: In a small bowl, whisk together the soy sauce, water, brown sugar, sesame oil, cornstarch, garlic, and chili powder until well combined. 3. Place the cauliflower florets in a large bowl and drizzle the top with the prepared teriyaki sauce and toss to coat well. 4. Put the cauliflower florets in the air fryer basket and air fry for 14 minutes, shaking the basket halfway through, or until the cauliflower is crisp-tender. 5. Let the cauliflower cool for 5 minutes before serving.

Air Fryer Veggies with Halloumi

Prep time: 5 minutes | Cook time: 14 minutes | Serves 2

2 zucchinis, cut into even chunks	6 ounces (170 g) halloumi cheese, cubed
1 large eggplant, peeled, cut into chunks	2 teaspoons olive oil
1 large carrot, cut into chunks	Salt and black pepper, to taste
	1 teaspoon dried mixed herbs

1. Preheat the air fryer to 340°F (171°C). 2. Combine the zucchinis, eggplant, carrot, cheese, olive oil, salt, and pepper in a large bowl and toss to coat well. 3. Spread the mixture evenly in the air fryer basket and air fry for 14 minutes until crispy and golden, shaking the basket once during cooking. Serve topped with mixed herbs.

Lush Summer Rolls

Prep time: 15 minutes | Cook time: 15 minutes | Serves 4

1 cup shiitake mushroom, sliced thinly
1 celery stalk, chopped
1 medium carrot, shredded
½ teaspoon finely chopped ginger
1 teaspoon sugar

1 tablespoon soy sauce
1 teaspoon nutritional yeast
8 spring roll sheets
1 teaspoon corn starch
2 tablespoons water

1. In a bowl, combine the ginger, soy sauce, nutritional yeast, carrots, celery, mushroom, and sugar. 2. Mix the cornstarch and water to create an adhesive for the spring rolls. 3. Scoop a tablespoonful of the vegetable mixture into the middle of the spring roll sheets. Brush the edges of the sheets with the cornstarch adhesive and enclose around the filling to make spring rolls. 4. Preheat the air fryer to 400°F (204°C). When warm, place the rolls inside and air fry for 15 minutes or until crisp. 5. Serve hot.

Chapter 10
Desserts

Zucchini Bread

Prep time: 10 minutes | Cook time: 40 minutes | Serves 12

2 cups coconut flour	1 teaspoon vanilla extract
2 teaspoons baking powder	3 eggs, beaten
¾ cup erythritol	1 zucchini, grated
½ cup coconut oil, melted	1 teaspoon ground cinnamon
1 teaspoon apple cider vinegar	

1. In the mixing bowl, mix coconut flour with baking powder, erythritol, coconut oil, apple cider vinegar, vanilla extract, eggs, zucchini, and ground cinnamon. 2. Transfer the mixture into the air fryer basket and flatten it in the shape of the bread. 3. Cook the bread at 350ºF (177ºC) for 40 minutes.

Vanilla Pound Cake

Prep time: 10 minutes | Cook time: 25 minutes | Serves 6

1 cup blanched finely ground almond flour	1 teaspoon baking powder
¼ cup salted butter, melted	½ cup full-fat sour cream
½ cup granular erythritol	1 ounce (28 g) full-fat cream cheese, softened
1 teaspoon vanilla extract	2 large eggs

1. In a large bowl, mix almond flour, butter, and erythritol. 2. Add in vanilla, baking powder, sour cream, and cream cheese and mix until well combined. Add eggs and mix. 3. Pour batter into a round baking pan. Place pan into the air fryer basket. 4. Adjust the temperature to 300ºF (149ºC) and bake for 25 minutes. 5. When the cake is done, a toothpick inserted in center will come out clean. The center should not feel wet. Allow it to cool completely, or the cake will crumble when moved.

Pineapple Wontons

Prep time: 15 minutes | Cook time: 15 to 18 minutes per batch | Serves 5

1 (8-ounce / 227-g) package cream cheese	pineapple
1 cup finely chopped fresh	20 wonton wrappers
	Cooking oil spray

1. In a small microwave-safe bowl, heat the cream cheese in the microwave on high power for 20 seconds to soften. 2. In a medium bowl, stir together the cream cheese and pineapple until mixed well. 3. Lay out the wonton wrappers on a work surface. A clean table or large cutting board works well. 4. Spoon 1½ teaspoons of the cream cheese mixture onto each wrapper. Be careful not to overfill. 5. Fold each wrapper diagonally across to form a triangle. Bring the 2 bottom corners up toward each other. Do not close the wrapper yet. Bring up the 2 open sides and push out any air. Squeeze the open edges together to seal. 6. Insert the crisper plate into the basket and the basket into the unit. Preheat the unit by selecting AIR FRY, setting the temperature to 390ºF (199ºC), and setting the time to 3 minutes. Select START/STOP to begin. 7. Once the unit is preheated, spray the crisper plate with cooking oil. Place the wontons into the basket. You can work in batches or stack the wontons. Spray the wontons with the cooking oil. 8. Select AIR FRY, set the temperature to 390ºF (199ºC), and set the time to 18 minutes. Select START/STOP to begin. 9. After 10 minutes, remove the basket, flip each wonton, and spray them with more oil. Reinsert the basket to resume cooking for 5 to 8 minutes more until the wontons are light golden brown and crisp. 10. If cooking in batches, remove the cooked wontons from the basket and repeat steps 7, 8, and 9 for the remaining wontons. 11. When the cooking is complete, cool for 5 minutes before serving.

Glazed Cherry Turnovers

Prep time: 10 minutes | Cook time: 14 minutes per batch | Serves 8

2 sheets frozen puff pastry, thawed	1 egg, beaten
1 (21-ounce / 595-g) can premium cherry pie filling	1 cup sliced almonds
2 teaspoons ground cinnamon	1 cup powdered sugar
	2 tablespoons milk

1. Roll a sheet of puff pastry out into a square that is approximately 10-inches by 10-inches. Cut this large square into quarters. 2. Mix the cherry pie filling and cinnamon together in a bowl. Spoon ¼ cup of the cherry filling into the center of each puff pastry square. Brush the perimeter of the pastry square with the egg wash. Fold one corner of the puff pastry over the cherry pie filling towards the opposite corner, forming a triangle. Seal the two edges of the pastry together with the tip of a fork, making a design with the tines. Brush the top of the turnovers with the egg wash and sprinkle sliced almonds over each one. Repeat these steps with the second sheet of puff pastry. You should have eight turnovers at the end. 3. Preheat the air fryer to 370ºF (188ºC). 4. Air fry two turnovers at a time for 14 minutes, carefully turning them over halfway through the cooking time. 5. While the turnovers are cooking, make the glaze by whisking the powdered sugar and milk together in a small bowl until smooth. Let the glaze sit for a minute so the sugar can absorb the milk. If the consistency is still too thick to drizzle, add a little more milk, a drop at a time, and stir until smooth. 6. Let the cooked cherry turnovers sit for at least 10 minutes. Then drizzle the glaze over each turnover in a zigzag motion. Serve warm or at room temperature.

Lemon Raspberry Muffins

Prep time: 5 minutes | Cook time: 15 minutes | Serves 6

2 cups almond flour	¼ teaspoon salt
¾ cup Swerve	2 eggs
1¼ teaspoons baking powder	1 cup sour cream
⅓ teaspoon ground allspice	½ cup coconut oil
⅓ teaspoon ground anise star	½ cup raspberries
½ teaspoon grated lemon zest	

1. Preheat the air fryer to 345ºF (174ºC). Line a muffin pan with 6 paper liners. 2. In a mixing bowl, mix the almond flour, Swerve, baking powder, allspice, anise, lemon zest, and salt. 3. In another mixing bowl, beat the eggs, sour cream, and coconut oil until well mixed. Add the egg mixture to the flour mixture and stir to combine. Mix in the raspberries. 4. Scrape the batter into the prepared muffin cups, filling each about three-quarters full. 5. Bake for 15 minutes, or until the tops are golden and a toothpick inserted in the middle comes out clean. 6. Allow the muffins to cool for 10 minutes in the muffin pan before removing and serving.

Chickpea Brownies

Prep time: 10 minutes | Cook time: 20 minutes | Serves 6

Vegetable oil
1 (15-ounce / 425-g) can chickpeas, drained and rinsed
4 large eggs
⅓ cup coconut oil, melted
⅓ cup honey
3 tablespoons unsweetened

cocoa powder
1 tablespoon espresso powder (optional)
1 teaspoon baking powder
1 teaspoon baking soda
½ cup chocolate chips

1. Preheat the air fryer to 325ºF (163ºC). 2. Generously grease a baking pan with vegetable oil. 3. In a blender or food processor, combine the chickpeas, eggs, coconut oil, honey, cocoa powder, espresso powder (if using), baking powder, and baking soda. Blend or process until smooth. Transfer to the prepared pan and stir in the chocolate chips by hand. 4. Set the pan in the air fryer basket and bake for 20 minutes, or until a toothpick inserted into the center comes out clean. 5. Let cool in the pan on a wire rack for 30 minutes before cutting into squares. 6. Serve immediately.

Protein Powder Doughnut Holes

Prep time: 25 minutes | Cook time: 6 minutes | Makes 12 holes

½ cup blanched finely ground almond flour
½ cup low-carb vanilla protein powder
½ cup granular erythritol

½ teaspoon baking powder
1 large egg
5 tablespoons unsalted butter, melted
½ teaspoon vanilla extract

1. Mix all ingredients in a large bowl. Place into the freezer for 20 minutes. 2. Wet your hands with water and roll the dough into twelve balls. 3. Cut a piece of parchment to fit your air fryer basket. Working in batches as necessary, place doughnut holes into the air fryer basket on top of parchment. 4. Adjust the temperature to 380ºF (193ºC) and air fry for 6 minutes. 5. Flip doughnut holes halfway through the cooking time. 6. Let cool completely before serving.

Almond-Roasted Pears

Prep time: 10 minutes | Cook time: 15 to 20 minutes | Serves 4

Yogurt Topping:
1 container vanilla Greek yogurt (5 to 6 ounces / 142 to 170 g)
¼ teaspoon almond flavoring

2 whole pears
¼ cup crushed Biscoff cookies (approx. 4 cookies)
1 tablespoon sliced almonds
1 tablespoon butter

1. Stir almond flavoring into yogurt and set aside while preparing pears. 2. Halve each pear and spoon out the core. 3. Place pear halves in air fryer basket. 4. Stir together the cookie crumbs and almonds. Place a quarter of this mixture into the hollow of each pear half. 5. Cut butter into 4 pieces and place one piece on top of crumb mixture in each pear. 6. Roast at 360ºF (182ºC) for 15 to 20 minutes or until pears have cooked through but are still slightly firm. 7. Serve pears warm with a dollop of yogurt topping.

Chocolate Peppermint Cheesecake

Prep time: 5 minutes | Cook time: 18 minutes | Serves 6

Crust:
½ cup butter, melted
½ cup coconut flour
2 tablespoons stevia
Cooking spray
Topping:

4 ounces (113 g) unsweetened baker's chocolate
1 cup mascarpone cheese, at room temperature
1 teaspoon vanilla extract
2 drops peppermint extract

1. Preheat the air fryer to 350ºF (177ºC). Lightly coat a baking pan with cooking spray. 2. In a mixing bowl, whisk together the butter, flour, and stevia until well combined. Transfer the mixture to the prepared baking pan. 3. Place the baking pan in the air fryer and bake for 18 minutes until a toothpick inserted in the center comes out clean. 4. Remove the crust from the air fryer to a wire rack to cool. 5. Once cooled completely, place it in the freezer for 20 minutes. 6. When ready, combine all the ingredients for the topping in a small bowl and stir to incorporate. 7. Spread this topping over the crust and let it sit for another 15 minutes in the freezer. 8. Serve chilled.

Olive Oil Cake

Prep time: 10 minutes | Cook time: 30 minutes | Serves 8

2 cups blanched finely ground almond flour
5 large eggs, whisked
¾ cup extra-virgin olive oil

⅓ cup granular erythritol
1 teaspoon vanilla extract
1 teaspoon baking powder

1. In a large bowl, mix all ingredients. Pour batter into an ungreased round nonstick baking dish. 2. Place dish into air fryer basket. Adjust the temperature to 300ºF (149ºC) and bake for 30 minutes. The cake will be golden on top and firm in the center when done. 3. Let cake cool in dish 30 minutes before slicing and serving.

Mixed Berries with Pecan Streusel Topping

Prep time: 5 minutes | Cook time: 17 minutes | Serves 3

½ cup mixed berries
Cooking spray
Topping:
1 egg, beaten
3 tablespoons almonds, slivered
3 tablespoons chopped pecans

2 tablespoons chopped walnuts
3 tablespoons granulated Swerve
2 tablespoons cold salted butter, cut into pieces
½ teaspoon ground cinnamon

1. Preheat the air fryer to 340ºF (171ºC). Lightly spray a baking dish with cooking spray. 2. Make the topping: In a medium bowl, stir together the beaten egg, nuts, Swerve, butter, and cinnamon until well blended. 3. Put the mixed berries in the bottom of the baking dish and spread the topping over the top. 4. Bake in the preheated air fryer for 17 minutes, or until the fruit is bubbly and topping is golden brown. 5. Allow to cool for 5 to 10 minutes before serving.

Cream-Filled Sandwich Cookies

Prep time: 8 minutes | Cook time: 8 minutes | Makes 8 cookies

Oil, for spraying	8 cream-filled sandwich
1 (8-ounce / 227-g) can	cookies
refrigerated crescent rolls	1 tablespoon confectioners'
¼ cup milk	sugar

1. Line the air fryer basket with parchment and spray lightly with oil. 2. Unroll the crescent dough and separate it into 8 triangles. Lay out the triangles on a work surface. 3. Pour the milk into a shallow bowl. Quickly dip each cookie in the milk, then place in the center of a dough triangle. 4. Wrap the dough around the cookie, cutting off any excess and pinching the ends to seal. You may be able to combine the excess into enough dough to cover additional cookies, if desired. 5. Place the wrapped cookies in the prepared basket, seam-side down, and spray lightly with oil. 6. Bake at 350ºF (177ºC) for 4 minutes, flip, spray with oil, and cook for another 3 to 4 minutes, or until puffed and golden brown. 7. Dust with the confectioners' sugar and serve.

Pecan and Cherry Stuffed Apples

Prep time: 10 minutes | Cook time: 20 minutes | Serves 4

4 apples (about 1¼ pounds / 567 g)	1 tablespoon melted butter
	3 tablespoons brown sugar
¼ cup chopped pecans	¼ teaspoon allspice
⅓ cup dried tart cherries	Pinch salt
Ice cream, for serving	

1. Cut off top ½ inch from each apple; reserve tops. With a melon baller, core through stem ends without breaking through the bottom. (Do not trim bases.) 2. Preheat the air fryer to 350ºF (177ºC). Combine pecans, cherries, butter, brown sugar, allspice, and a pinch of salt. Stuff mixture into the hollow centers of the apples. Cover with apple tops. Put in the air fryer basket, using tongs. Air fry for 20 to 25 minutes, or just until tender. 3. Serve warm with ice cream.

Ricotta Lemon Poppy Seed Cake

Prep time: 10 minutes | Cook time: 55 minutes | Serves 4

Unsalted butter, at room temperature	¼ cup coconut oil, melted
	2 tablespoons poppy seeds
1 cup almond flour	1 teaspoon baking powder
½ cup sugar	1 teaspoon pure lemon extract
3 large eggs	Grated zest and juice of 1
¼ cup heavy cream	lemon, plus more zest for
¼ cup full-fat ricotta cheese	garnish

1. Generously butter a baking pan. Line the bottom of the pan with parchment paper cut to fit. 2. In a large bowl, combine the almond flour, sugar, eggs, cream, ricotta, coconut oil, poppy seeds, baking powder, lemon extract, lemon zest, and lemon juice. Beat with a hand mixer on medium speed until well blended and fluffy. 3. Pour the batter into the prepared pan. Cover the pan tightly with aluminum foil. Set the pan in the air fryer basket. Set the air fryer to 325ºF (163ºC) for 45 minutes. Remove the foil and cook for 10 to 15 minutes more, until a knife (do not use a toothpick) inserted into the center of the cake comes out clean. 4. Let the cake cool in the pan on a wire rack for 10 minutes. Remove the cake from pan and let it cool on the rack for 15 minutes before slicing. 5. Top with additional lemon zest, slice and serve.

Baked Apple

Prep time: 10 minutes | Cook time: 20 minutes | Makes 6 apple halves

3 small Honey Crisp or other baking apples	3 tablespoons chopped pecans
	1 tablespoon firm butter, cut
3 tablespoons maple syrup	into 6 pieces

1. Put ½ cup water in the drawer of the air fryer. 2. Wash apples well and dry them. 3. Split apples in half. Remove core and a little of the flesh to make a cavity for the pecans. 4. Place apple halves in air fryer basket, cut side up. 5. Spoon 1½ teaspoons pecans into each cavity. 6. Spoon ½ tablespoon maple syrup over pecans in each apple. 7. Top each apple with ½ teaspoon butter. 8. Bake at 360ºF (182ºC) for 20 minutes, until apples are tender.

Butter and Chocolate Chip Cookies

Prep time: 20 minutes | Cook time: 11 minutes | Serves 8

1 stick butter, at room temperature	⅓ cup cocoa powder, unsweetened
1¼ cups Swerve	1 ½ teaspoons baking powder
¼ cup chunky peanut butter	¼ teaspoon ground cinnamon
1 teaspoon vanilla paste	¼ teaspoon ginger
1 fine almond flour	½ cup chocolate chips,
⅔ cup coconut flour	unsweetened

1. In a mixing dish, beat the butter and Swerve until creamy and uniform. Stir in the peanut butter and vanilla. 2. In another mixing dish, thoroughly combine the flour, cocoa powder, baking powder, cinnamon, and ginger. 3. Add the flour mixture to the peanut butter mixture; mix to combine well. Afterwards, fold in the chocolate chips. Drop by large spoonfuls onto a parchment-lined air fryer basket. Bake at 365ºF (185ºC) for 11 minutes or until golden brown on the top. Bon appétit!

Simple Apple Turnovers

Prep time: 10 minutes | Cook time: 10 minutes | Serves 4

1 apple, peeled, quartered, and thinly sliced	Juice of ½ lemon
	1 tablespoon granulated sugar
½ teaspoons pumpkin pie spice	Pinch of kosher salt
	6 sheets phyllo dough

1. Preheat the air fryer to 330ºF (166ºC). 2. In a medium bowl, combine the apple, pumpkin pie spice, lemon juice, granulated sugar, and kosher salt. 3. Cut the phyllo dough sheets into 4 equal pieces and place individual tablespoons of apple filling in the center of each piece, then fold in both sides and roll from front to back. 4. Spray the air fryer basket with nonstick cooking spray, then place the turnovers in the basket and bake for 10 minutes or until golden brown. 5. Remove the turnovers from the air fryer and allow to cool on a wire rack for 10 minutes before serving.

Coconut Mixed Berry Crisp

Prep time: 5 minutes | Cook time: 20 minutes | Serves 6

1 tablespoon butter, melted	½ teaspoon ground cinnamon
12 ounces (340 g) mixed berries	¼ teaspoon ground cloves
	¼ teaspoon grated nutmeg
⅓ cup granulated Swerve	½ cup coconut chips, for garnish
1 teaspoon pure vanilla extract	

1. Preheat the air fryer to 330ºF (166ºC). Coat a baking pan with melted butter. 2. Put the remaining ingredients except the coconut chips in the prepared baking pan. 3. Bake in the preheated air fryer for 20 minutes. 4. Serve garnished with the coconut chips.

Brown Sugar Banana Bread

Prep time: 20 minutes | Cook time: 22 to 24 minutes | Serves 4

1 cup packed light brown sugar	1 teaspoon ground cinnamon
	½ teaspoon salt
1 large egg, beaten	1 banana, mashed
2 tablespoons butter, melted	1 to 2 tablespoons oil
½ cup milk, whole or 2%	¼ cup confectioners' sugar (optional)
2 cups all-purpose flour	
1½ teaspoons baking powder	

1. In a large bowl, stir together the brown sugar, egg, melted butter, and milk. 2. In a medium bowl, whisk the flour, baking powder, cinnamon, and salt until blended. Add the flour mixture to the sugar mixture and stir just to blend. 3. Add the mashed banana and stir to combine. 4. Preheat the air fryer to 350ºF (177ºC). Spritz 2 mini loaf pans with oil. 5. Evenly divide the batter between the prepared pans and place them in the air fryer basket. 6. Cook for 22 to 24 minutes, or until a knife inserted into the middle of the loaves comes out clean. 7. Dust the warm loaves with confectioners' sugar (if using).

Strawberry Pastry Rolls

Prep time: 20 minutes | Cook time: 5 to 6 minutes per batch | Serves 4

3 ounces (85 g) low-fat cream cheese	8 ounces (227 g) fresh strawberries
2 tablespoons plain yogurt	8 sheets phyllo dough
2 teaspoons sugar	Butter-flavored cooking spray
¼ teaspoon pure vanilla extract	¼ to ½ cup dark chocolate chips (optional)

1. In a medium bowl, combine the cream cheese, yogurt, sugar, and vanilla. Beat with hand mixer at high speed until smooth, about 1 minute. 2. Wash strawberries and destem. Chop enough of them to measure ½ cup. Stir into cheese mixture. 3. Preheat the air fryer to 330ºF (166ºC). 4. Phyllo dough dries out quickly, so cover your stack of phyllo sheets with waxed paper and then place a damp dish towel on top of that. Remove only one sheet at a time as you work. 5. To create one pastry roll, lay out a single sheet of phyllo. Spray lightly with butter-flavored spray, top with a second sheet of phyllo, and spray the second sheet lightly. 6. Place a quarter of the filling (about 3 tablespoons) about ½ inch from the edge of one short side. Fold the end of the phyllo over the filling and keep rolling a turn or two. Fold

in both the left and right sides so that the edges meet in the middle of your roll. Then roll up completely. Spray outside of pastry roll with butter spray. 7. When you have 4 rolls, place them in the air fryer basket, seam side down, leaving some space in between each. Air fry at 330ºF (166ºC) for 5 to 6 minutes, until they turn a delicate golden brown. 8. Repeat step 7 for remaining rolls. 9. Allow pastries to cool to room temperature. 10. When ready to serve, slice the remaining strawberries. If desired, melt the chocolate chips in microwave or double boiler. Place 1 pastry on each dessert plate, and top with sliced strawberries. Drizzle melted chocolate over strawberries and onto plate.

Pecan Brownies

Prep time: 10 minutes | Cook time: 20 minutes | Serves 6

½ cup blanched finely ground almond flour	¼ cup unsalted butter, softened
½ cup powdered erythritol	1 large egg
2 tablespoons unsweetened cocoa powder	¼ cup chopped pecans
½ teaspoon baking powder	¼ cup low-carb, sugar-free chocolate chips

1. In a large bowl, mix almond flour, erythritol, cocoa powder, and baking powder. Stir in butter and egg. 2. Fold in pecans and chocolate chips. Scoop mixture into a round baking pan. Place pan into the air fryer basket. 3. Adjust the temperature to 300ºF (149ºC) and bake for 20 minutes. 4. When fully cooked a toothpick inserted in center will come out clean. Allow 20 minutes to fully cool and firm up.

Shortcut Spiced Apple Butter

Prep time: 5 minutes | Cook time: 1 hour | Makes 1⁴⁄ cups

Cooking spray	3 tablespoons fresh lemon juice
2 cups store-bought unsweetened applesauce	½ teaspoon kosher salt
⅔ cup packed light brown sugar	¼ teaspoon ground cinnamon
	⅛ teaspoon ground allspice

1. Spray a cake pan with cooking spray. Whisk together all the ingredients in a bowl until smooth, then pour into the greased pan. Set the pan in the air fryer and bake at 340ºF (171ºC) until the apple mixture is caramelized, reduced to a thick purée, and fragrant, about 1 hour. 2. Remove the pan from the air fryer, stir to combine the caramelized bits at the edge with the rest, then let cool completely to thicken. Scrape the apple butter into a jar and store in the refrigerator for up to 2 weeks.

Simple Pineapple Sticks

Prep time: 5 minutes | Cook time: 10 minutes | Serves 4

½ fresh pineapple, cut into sticks	¼ cup desiccated coconut

1. Preheat the air fryer to 400ºF (204ºC). 2. Coat the pineapple sticks in the desiccated coconut and put each one in the air fryer basket. 3. Air fry for 10 minutes. 4. Serve immediately

Vanilla Cookies with Hazelnuts

Prep time: 20 minutes | Cook time: 10 minutes | Serves 6

1 cup almond flour	1 cup Swerve
½ cup coconut flour	2 teaspoons vanilla
1 teaspoon baking soda	2 eggs, at room temperature
1 teaspoon fine sea salt	1 cup hazelnuts, coarsely
1 stick butter	chopped

1. Preheat the air fryer to 350ºF (177ºC). 2. Mix the flour with the baking soda, and sea salt. 3. In the bowl of an electric mixer, beat the butter, Swerve, and vanilla until creamy. Fold in the eggs, one at a time, and mix until well combined. 4. Slowly and gradually, stir in the flour mixture. Finally, fold in the coarsely chopped hazelnuts. 5. Divide the dough into small balls using a large cookie scoop; drop onto the prepared cookie sheets. Bake for 10 minutes or until golden brown, rotating the pan once or twice through the cooking time. 6. Work in batches and cool for a couple of minutes before removing to wire racks. Enjoy!

Hazelnut Butter Cookies

Prep time: 30 minutes | Cook time: 20 minutes | Serves 10

4 tablespoons liquid monk fruit	2 cups almond flour
½ cup hazelnuts, ground	1 cup coconut flour
1 stick butter, room temperature	2 ounces (57 g) granulated Swerve
	2 teaspoons ground cinnamon

1. Firstly, cream liquid monk fruit with butter until the mixture becomes fluffy. Sift in both types of flour. 2. Now, stir in the hazelnuts. Now, knead the mixture to form a dough; place in the refrigerator for about 35 minutes. 3. To finish, shape the prepared dough into the bite-sized balls; arrange them on a baking dish; flatten the balls using the back of a spoon. 4. Mix granulated Swerve with ground cinnamon. Press your cookies in the cinnamon mixture until they are completely covered. 5. Bake the cookies for 20 minutes at 310ºF (154ºC). 6. Leave them to cool for about 10 minutes before transferring them to a wire rack. Bon appétit!

Dark Chocolate Lava Cake

Prep time: 5 minutes | Cook time: 10 minutes | Serves 4

Olive oil cooking spray	½ teaspoon baking powder
¼ cup whole wheat flour	¼ cup raw honey
1 tablespoon unsweetened dark chocolate cocoa powder	1 egg
⅛ teaspoon salt	2 tablespoons olive oil

1. Preheat the air fryer to 380°F(193ºC). Lightly coat the insides of four ramekins with olive oil cooking spray. 2. In a medium bowl, combine the flour, cocoa powder, salt, baking powder, honey, egg, and olive oil. 3. Divide the batter evenly among the ramekins. 4. Place the filled ramekins inside the air fryer and bake for 10 minutes. 5. Remove the lava cakes from the air fryer and slide a knife around the outside edge of each cake. Turn each ramekin upside down on a saucer and serve.

Baked Brazilian Pineapple

Prep time: 10 minutes | Cook time: 10 minutes | Serves 4

½ cup brown sugar	cored, and cut into spears
2 teaspoons ground cinnamon	3 tablespoons unsalted butter,
1 small pineapple, peeled,	melted

1. In a small bowl, mix the brown sugar and cinnamon until thoroughly combined. 2. Brush the pineapple spears with the melted butter. Sprinkle the cinnamon-sugar over the spears, pressing lightly to ensure it adheres well. 3. Place the spears in the air fryer basket in a single layer. (Depending on the size of your air fryer, you may have to do this in batches.) Set the air fryer to 400ºF (204ºC) for 10 minutes for the first batch (6 to 8 minutes for the next batch, as the fryer will be preheated). Halfway through the cooking time, brush the spears with butter. 4. The pineapple spears are done when they are heated through and the sugar is bubbling. Serve hot.

Chocolate Soufflés

Prep time: 5 minutes | Cook time: 14 minutes | Serves 2

Butter and sugar for greasing the ramekins	½ teaspoon pure vanilla extract
3 ounces (85 g) semi-sweet chocolate, chopped	2 tablespoons all-purpose flour
¼ cup unsalted butter	Powdered sugar, for dusting the finished soufflés
2 eggs, yolks and white separated	Heavy cream, for serving
3 tablespoons sugar	

1. Butter and sugar two 6-ounce (170-g) ramekins. (Butter the ramekins and then coat the butter with sugar by shaking it around in the ramekin and dumping out any excess.) 2. Melt the chocolate and butter together, either in the microwave or in a double boiler. In a separate bowl, beat the egg yolks vigorously. Add the sugar and the vanilla extract and beat well again. Drizzle in the chocolate and butter, mixing well. Stir in the flour, combining until there are no lumps. 3. Preheat the air fryer to 330ºF (166ºC). 4. In a separate bowl, whisk the egg whites to soft peak stage (the point at which the whites can almost stand up on the end of your whisk). Fold the whipped egg whites into the chocolate mixture gently and in stages. 5. Transfer the batter carefully to the buttered ramekins, leaving about ½-inch at the top. (You may have a little extra batter, depending on how airy the batter is, so you might be able to squeeze out a third soufflé if you want to.) Place the ramekins into the air fryer basket and air fry for 14 minutes. The soufflés should have risen nicely and be brown on top. (Don't worry if the top gets a little dark, you'll be covering it with powdered sugar in the next step.) 6. Dust with powdered sugar and serve immediately with heavy cream to pour over the top at the table.

Pecan Bars

Prep time: 5 minutes | Cook time: 40 minutes | Serves 12

2 cups coconut flour
5 tablespoons erythritol
4 tablespoons coconut oil, softened

½ cup heavy cream
1 egg, beaten
4 pecans, chopped

1. Mix coconut flour, erythritol, coconut oil, heavy cream, and egg. 2. Pour the batter in the air fryer basket and flatten well. 3. Top the mixture with pecans and cook the meal at 350ºF (177ºC) for 40 minutes. 4. Cut the cooked meal into the bars.

Strawberry Pecan Pie

Prep time: 15 minutes | Cook time: 10 minutes | Serves 6

1½ cups whole shelled pecans
1 tablespoon unsalted butter, softened
1 cup heavy whipping cream

12 medium fresh strawberries, hulled
2 tablespoons sour cream

1. Place pecans and butter into a food processor and pulse ten times until a dough forms. Press dough into the bottom of an ungreased round nonstick baking dish. 2. Place dish into air fryer basket. Adjust the temperature to 320ºF (160ºC) and set the timer for 10 minutes. Crust will be firm and golden when done. Let cool 20 minutes. 3. In a large bowl, whisk cream until fluffy and doubled in size, about 2 minutes. 4. In a separate large bowl, mash strawberries until mostly liquid. Fold strawberries and sour cream into whipped cream. 5. Spoon mixture into cooled crust, cover, and place in refrigerator for at least 30 minutes to set. Serve chilled.

Appendix 1: Air Fryer Cooking Chart

Air Fryer Cooking Chart

Vegetables					
INGREDIENT	AMOUNT	PREPARATION	OIL	TEMP	COOK TIME
Asparagus	2 bunches	Cut in half, trim stems	2 Tbsp	420°F	12-15 mins
Beets	1½ lbs	Peel, cut in ½-inch cubes	1Tbsp	390°F	28-30 mins
Bell peppers (for roasting)	4 peppers	Cut in quarters, remove seeds	1Tbsp	400°F	15-20 mins
Broccoli	1 large head	Cut in 1-2-inch florets	1Tbsp	400°F	15-20 mins
Brussels sprouts	1lb	Cut in half, remove stems	1Tbsp	425°F	15-20 mins
Carrots	1lb	Peel, cut in ¼-inch rounds	1 Tbsp	425°F	10-15 mins
Cauliflower	1 head	Cut in 1-2-inch florets	2 Tbsp	400°F	20-22 mins
Corn on the cob	7 ears	Whole ears, remove husks	1 Tbps	400°F	14-17 mins
Green beans	1 bag (12 oz)	Trim	1 Tbps	420°F	18-20 mins
Kale (for chips)	4 oz	Tear into pieces, remove stems	None	325°F	5-8 mins
Mushrooms	16 oz	Rinse, slice thinly	1 Tbps	390°F	25-30 mins
Potatoes, russet	1½ lbs	Cut in 1-inch wedges	1 Tbps	390°F	25-30 mins
Potatoes, russet	1lb	Hand-cut fries, soak 30 mins in cold water, then pat dry	½ -3 Tbps	400°F	25-28 mins
Potatoes, sweet	1lb	Hand-cut fries, soak 30 mins in cold water, then pat dry	1 Tbps	400°F	25-28 mins
Zucchini	1lb	Cut in eighths lengthwise, then cut in half	1 Tbps	400°F	15-20 mins

MEASUREMENT CONVERSION CHART

VOLUME EQUIVALENTS(DRY)

US STANDARD	METRIC (APPROXIMATE)
1/8 teaspoon	0.5 mL
1/4 teaspoon	1 mL
1/2 teaspoon	2 mL
3/4 teaspoon	4 mL
1 teaspoon	5 mL
1 tablespoon	15 mL
1/4 cup	59 mL
1/2 cup	118 mL
3/4 cup	177 mL
1 cup	235 mL
2 cups	475 mL
3 cups	700 mL
4 cups	1 L

VOLUME EQUIVALENTS(LIQUID)

US STANDARD	US STANDARD (OUNCES)	METRIC (APPROXIMATE)
2 tablespoons	1 fl.oz.	30 mL
1/4 cup	2 fl.oz.	60 mL
1/2 cup	4 fl.oz.	120 mL
1 cup	8 fl.oz.	240 mL
1 1/2 cup	12 fl.oz.	355 mL
2 cups or 1 pint	16 fl.oz.	475 mL
4 cups or 1 quart	32 fl.oz.	1 L
1 gallon	128 fl.oz.	4 L

TEMPERATURES EQUIVALENTS

FAHRENHEIT(F)	CELSIUS(C) (APPROXIMATE)
225 °F	107 °C
250 °F	120 °C
275 °F	135 °C
300 °F	150 °C
325 °F	160 °C
350 °F	180 °C
375 °F	190 °C
400 °F	205 °C
425 °F	220 °C
450 °F	235 °C
475 °F	245 °C
500 °F	260 °C

WEIGHT EQUIVALENTS

US STANDARD	METRIC (APPROXIMATE)
1 ounce	28 g
2 ounces	57 g
5 ounces	142 g
10 ounces	284 g
15 ounces	425 g
16 ounces (1 pound)	455 g
1.5 pounds	680 g
2 pounds	907 g

Appendix 2: Measurement Conversion Chart

Air Fryer Cooking Chart

Beef

Item	Temp (°F)	Time (mins)	Item	Temp (°F)	Time (mins)
Beef Eye Round Roast (4 lbs.)	400 °F	45 to 55	Meatballs (1-inch)	370 °F	7
Burger Patty (4 oz.)	370 °F	16 to 20	Meatballs (3-inch)	380 °F	10
Filet Mignon (8 oz.)	400 °F	18	Ribeye, bone-in (1-inch, 8 oz)	400 °F	10 to 15
Flank Steak (1.5 lbs.)	400 °F	12	Sirloin steaks (1-inch, 12 oz)	400 °F	9 to 14
Flank Steak (2 lbs.)	400 °F	20 to 28			

Chicken

Item	Temp (°F)	Time (mins)	Item	Temp (°F)	Time (mins)
Breasts, bone in (1 ¼ lb.)	370 °F	25	Legs, bone-in (1 ¾ lb.)	380 °F	30
Breasts, boneless (4 oz)	380 °F	12	Thighs, boneless (1 ½ lb.)	380 °F	18 to 20
Drumsticks (2 ½ lb.)	370 °F	20	Wings (2 lb.)	400 °F	12
Game Hen (halved 2 lb.)	390 °F	20	Whole Chicken	360 °F	75
Thighs, bone-in (2 lb.)	380 °F	22	Tenders	360 °F	8 to 10

Pork & Lamb

Item	Temp (°F)	Time (mins)	Item	Temp (°F)	Time (mins)
Bacon (regular)	400 °F	5 to 7	Pork Tenderloin	370 °F	15
Bacon (thick cut)	400 °F	6 to 10	Sausages	380 °F	15
Pork Loin (2 lb.)	360 °F	55	Lamb Loin Chops (1-inch thick)	400 °F	8 to 12
Pork Chops, bone in (1-inch, 6.5 oz)	400 °F	12	Rack of Lamb (1.5 – 2 lb.)	380 °F	22

Fish & Seafood

Item	Temp (°F)	Time (mins)	Item	Temp (°F)	Time (mins)
Calamari (8 oz)	400 °F	4	Tuna Steak	400 °F	7 to 10
Fish Fillet (1-inch, 8 oz)	400 °F	10	Scallops	400 °F	5 to 7
Salmon, fillet (6 oz)	380 °F	12	Shrimp	400 °F	5
Swordfish steak	400 °F	10			

Appendix 3: Recipe Index

Q

R

S

T

V

W

Z

Made in the USA
Las Vegas, NV
10 August 2023

75820744R00057